The Rhetoric
of Lincoln's Letters

The Rhetoric of Lincoln's Letters

MARSHALL MYERS

McFarland & Company, Inc., Publishers
Jefferson, North Carolina

All photographs are from the Library of Congress.

ISBN (print) 978-0-7864-6320-6
ISBN (ebook) 978-1-4766-3115-8

LIBRARY OF CONGRESS CATALOGUING DATA ARE AVAILABLE

BRITISH LIBRARY CATALOGUING DATA ARE AVAILABLE

© 2018 Marshall Myers. All rights reserved

No part of this book may be reproduced or transmitted in any form or by any means, electronic or mechanical, including photocopying or recording, or by any information storage and retrieval system, without permission in writing from the publisher.

Front cover images: Abraham Lincoln (Library of Congress); *background* letter from Lincoln to George McClellan, 1862 (New York Public Library)

Manufactured in the United States of America

*McFarland & Company, Inc., Publishers
Box 611, Jefferson, North Carolina 28640
www.mcfarlandpub.com*

To Linda
who loves me just as I am
and fills my life with joy and meaning

Acknowledgments

Books may have one author or more, but most books are collaborations of not just the author but also several other people. This one was, in part, the result of a sabbatical leave I was granted by Eastern Kentucky University. With time off from my teaching and administrative duties, I was able to gather relevant sources and to write a lengthy chapter.

I owe a debt of gratitude to the Department of English, chaired by Dr. James Keller, for their encouragement.

I am quite thankful, too, for the proofreading skills of Dr. Gil Hunter, whose keen eye and knowledge caught errors that I had overlooked.

I also thank Norma Bowling for her tireless typing.

I am grateful to Mary Muller and her staff at the Taylor Francis Group, representing *Rhetoric Review*, for allowing me to use an article on Lincoln as a writer. Gratitude also goes to Sally Hain, a cousin, who provided me with an important article, and cousins Susy Shinkle and Joanne Reese for their support.

The people who work in the Interlibrary Loan division of the Eastern Kentucky University Library were always helpful and accommodating in finding and ordering arcane sources.

I give my thanks to Dr. John Sellers at the Library of Congress for his cooperation and much motivation for this project. I am grateful, too, for his patience and his kindness toward my grandson, Ryan.

But above all others, I thank my wife Linda for all her patience, concern, and motivation, but most of all for her love. Without her, this project would never have been done.

Table of Contents

Acknowledgments — vi
Preface — 1
Introduction — 5

1. The Need to Study Lincoln's Letters — 9
2. The Letter as Genre — 20
3. Influences on Lincoln's Writing Style — 51
4. Early Letters — 69
5. Letters to His Generals — 86
6. The Logician — 110
7. The Problem of Clemency — 125
8. The Love Letters — 144
9. Letters to His Cabinet — 180

Conclusions — 201
Bibliography — 203
Index — 209

Preface

Rather than examining Lincoln's letters as a way of fleshing out biographical or historical details, this work examines his letters rhetorically. In other words, this work looks not at the "what" and "why" of the letters, but instead examines how Lincoln's letters are effective communicators of his thoughts and ideas.

Thus, the importance of this study is twofold: not only is it a careful study of a Lincoln corpus, his letters in particular; it is also an extended study of the rhetoric of those letters. For example, when Lincoln sought to encourage General George McClellan to take action, the president took various rhetorical stances.

Writing about Lincoln's prose seems to be a topic in almost every biography of Lincoln. Yet while these studies analyze the prose style of Lincoln's writing in his speeches and public papers, such as the Second Inaugural Address and the Emancipation Proclamation, few biographers have carefully looked at Lincoln's rhetoric in depth. In fact, when his biographers do attempt to deal with his prose, the treatment tends to be superficial and limited.

In spite of that, a few studies have focused on his rhetorical acumen. Garry Wills' book *Lincoln at Gettysburg* does an excellent job of looking at the speech and then examines its rich rhetoric; but, of course, Wills deals with just the Gettysburg Address. Similarly, James Tackach's *Lincoln's Moral Vision* looks at Lincoln's language in the Second Inaugural Address, but Tackach himself admits that his "study fits the category of literary criticism." Writing about the same speech, Ronald White says, "Lincoln's rhetoric is Lincoln himself." *Lincoln's Sword* by Douglas Wilson and *Lincoln: The Biography of a Writer* by Fred Kaplan represent extensive treatments of Lincoln's prose style, but they mainly cover the most famous pieces of Lincoln's political career. Nobody, in fact, attempts an extensive treatment of Lincoln's letters.

Through letter writing Lincoln learned to compose exemplary prose, prose he would later so artfully use during his presidency. This present study surveys the development of Lincoln's style and places it within a rhetorical framework. Studying his letters provides, then, the opportunity of seeing Lincoln mature as a writer when he wrote for several types of audiences, acquiring skills he would later use in his most famous speeches.

I came to write about Lincoln's prose over a number of years. While attending a one-room school in a "company town," the other twenty-two students and I had limited space in which to play since we had only a narrow strip of land. When the Ohio River flooded, as it did each year, we had no place to play. On those days, our teacher would read aloud from the classics—*Oliver Twist, Tom Sawyer, Huckleberry Finn,* and *Hoosier Schoolmaster,* just to name a few. The sound of his voice, its rhythms, and its flow taught me to appreciate the written word. From that point on, I have had a lifelong fascination with what words could do to the reader or listener. Later, I studied literature, but, more important to this study, I settled on earning a Ph.D. in rhetoric and composition.

This study covers the development of Lincoln's rhetorical skills as they manifested themselves in his letters. The earlier chapters provide the background of Lincoln the writer, and then Lincoln as a letter writer, including his use of certain rhetorical forms, such as the *philippic* or the letter of consolation. After that, this study looks at Lincoln's early letter writing as he developed and adapted his letter-writing skills to various audiences, including his early letters of friendship, romance, and politics. Next, I deal with Lincoln's letters to his generals and the various rhetorical stances he used to motivate them. Following that, this study treats the exchange of letters between Lincoln and a political friend who was critical of the president's handling of his first term in office. In the exchange, Lincoln displays his ability to use formal logic in an argument. The book concludes with a "public" letter in which he uses a clever organizational structure to explain to his supporters back in Illinois why he issued the Emancipation Proclamation, a very touchy subject to this group of men.

Since over 5,000 letters have been identified as Lincoln's, I do not classify or analyze all of them. Instead I deal with a representative sample from various categories and audiences, using a number of rhetorical strategies for studying his letters. Covering all 5,000 letters and classifying them as to type would be a herculean effort, but I do provide a variety of methodologies for other students to employ to study his letters.

In order to examine his letters, I read various biographies of Lincoln, such as David Donald's *Lincoln*, to get a view of the context of Lincoln's life. Following that, I carefully read works on his prose style. Research into Lincoln's letter writing next led me to examine a letter stored in the Library of Congress to see it in its original form. In addition, I examined copies of Lincoln's letters available online and used various search devices like Boolean descriptors, word searches and the like. In the end, I employed all these sources to conduct a rich rhetorical analysis of his letters, examining such things as rhetorical schemes and tropes and the various canons of rhetoric, including arrangement and style. While I did not use the exact same methodology for all the letters, I developed several methodologies that could be used by others in studying them.

Studying Lincoln's letters carefully helps students of Lincoln understand the man better, but it also opens up a whole new perspective on Lincoln the writer.

Introduction

Yet another book on Lincoln? What can be said about the Great Emancipator that has not already been said?

Every aspect of Lincoln's life seems to have already been examined with careful and perceptive eyes: his early life in Kentucky and Indiana; his life as a nascent, then a successful Illinois lawyer; his struggles with clinical depression; his love life; his marriage; his leadership during the Civil War; his seemingly endless search for a competent general; his memorable speeches; and his tragic death—just to name a few areas of his life that have endured minute scrutiny. Lincoln was a man whose personality and biography continue to fascinate a reading public still wanting to know more about him.

One side of Lincoln that has been the subject of examination lately is his writing. A number of books, including Garry Wills' groundbreaking study of the Gettysburg Address and Fred Kaplan's study of Lincoln as a writer, have focused on the memorable speeches in Lincoln's short life, including the circumstances that provided the historical background, the broad, timeless implications of those speeches, and their enduring effect.

Part of the reason for the scant attention to the effect, or rhetorical power of his works, is that most of the speeches Lincoln gave are treated in the language and through the methodology of historians, who have specific areas of interest but are not trained to comment on the rhetorical schemes and tropes of Lincoln's writings. Historians believe that if readers understand the history behind the speech, they will understand the speech itself better. Myriad examples and extensive studies find historians trying to decipher the meaning of a particular speech by providing almost ethnographic detail about the zeitgeist and the context of the speech. They have

Introduction

in the main rendered expertly to an eager public the *why* and *when* of a speech under careful historical analysis.

But historical analysis is not the only way to study Lincoln's words and create a better understanding of the man and his works. In fact, it almost defies good scholarship to limit examination and interpretation to only historical perspectives to understand Lincoln's writing and all their nuances of meaning.

Lincoln surely was someone who clearly understood that meaning was important, but method was equally important. He didn't write "...that the government of, by, and for the people..."; instead, he wrote "...that the government of the people, by the people, and for the people...." He could have written, "I have been controlled by events," but Lincoln chose this instead: "I claim not to have controlled events, but confess plainly that events have controlled me." Such examples illustrate that again and again, Lincoln chose not only the matter he discussed, but also the manner. He sought not just what he wanted to say, but also how he wanted to say it.

But precious little has been written on Lincoln's ability to play the rhetorician: a writer who was concerned not only about what he wanted to say, but also about how he would express himself. While there have been a few who would applaud Lincoln's writing with phrases like "laudable," "memorable," and "quite effective," and while these complimentary phrases are valuable, they hardly explain why some of Lincoln's words are such effective golden nuggets of nineteenth century American English. At times, the responses to such gems are sometimes ineffable, left on the written page of his biographers to let them speak for themselves.

But just how good a writer was Lincoln? Where did he learn to write so well? How did he use certain rhetorical strategies to guide the thinking of his readers? These and other questions are the subject of this book.

The first part of the book looks at Lincoln the writer and the influences on his struggle to learn to write. Next, it examines how Lincoln himself looked at writing, and how important writing was to his success as a young lawyer in frontier Illinois. What significant factors, in particular, should be considered when examining the most prolific portion of Lincoln's writing: the many letters he composed? Most biographers and critics have mined biographical details about how Lincoln felt about slavery, his many friendships, and his romantic adventures from his letters, for example, but few have studied the letters for their rhetorical power. Viewed closely, Lincoln's early letters show him to have been a student without a

Introduction

teacher who depended on the responses to his addressees to determine if he made himself clear, while often unconsciously following models from ancient Greece and Rome. Lincoln wrote a wide variety of letters: some letters of friendship, some letters to clients, some to fellow political friends and some "public" letters addressed broadly to the nation, not just to one person. From his experience of writing so many letters, Lincoln learned the fundamentals of communication, how to make his ideas clear and concise, and even how to make his words memorable, lessons he would put to work later as president when addressing his recalcitrant generals. A few letters even reveal how Lincoln was lacking in certain rhetorical skills, but curiously was not willing to admit it.

Letters have advantages over other kinds of communication. Granted, Lincoln did spend considerable time at the telegraph office, checking on the latest reports of battles and strategies from his generals. But when he really wanted to speak in a personal voice, when what he was saying was vastly important to the country, when he wanted to cultivate friendships and devotion to the cause, he used letters to his fellow politicians, to his partners in romance, to those who served him in his presidency, and to his cabinet members.

Because he composed so many letters prior to the presidency, Lincoln was keenly aware of his skills as a letter writer. He knew how to praise, but with caution. He knew how to scold and still retain the allegiance of his generals. He even knew how to admit his weakness in knowledge of military strategy; yet his ability to use a variety of techniques from his toolbox of rhetorical strategies redeemed him even in the country's darkest hours. For he also learned how to write his feelings in romance and to communicate with his cabinet in perilous times. In the end, Lincoln had learned much about writing from studying the writing of others and from his own practice of letter writing, skills that served him well in his conduct of the war.

1

The Need to Study Lincoln's Letters

Garry Wills' 1992 Pulitzer Prize–winning work, *Lincoln at Gettysburg: The Words That Remade America,* set in motion a movement that produced a series of books focusing on the major speeches and public documents of the sixteenth president. Certainly, in the past, many studies have looked at Lincoln's rhetoric and the historical circumstances behind his major utterances, while commenting broadly on Lincoln as a rhetorician. What makes this recent crop of books different is that whole books are devoted to just one speech, with most works remarking extensively on the history of the speech, its composition, and to a lesser degree in most cases, its rhetorical power.

In many ways, Wills' book set the standard. Almost ethnographic in its approach, Wills' valuable study not only devotes attention to the history surrounding the Gettysburg Address, but also spends considerable time discussing the intellectual climate that led up to and surrounded the speech, while documenting, too, the theme of sentimentality, and the nineteenth century's fascination with death. He also covers topics such as the authentication of the manuscript, the circumstances surrounding its composition, delivery and reception, and, finally—and uniquely—its stylistic qualities, concentrating particularly on the epideictic speech tradition; that is, a speech that Aristotle describes as "ceremonial" address that "praises or censures somebody" (1992, 32). Following Aristotle's definition of epideictic rhetoric as that done to "praise or attack a man ... proving him worthy of honour or the reverse" (33), Wills spends considerable time showing how the Gettysburg Address fits into the epideictic tradition by praising the living and dead who fought at the Battle of Gettysburg. In addition, Wills explores other matters of rhetorical analysis, including some basic principles of oratorical rhetoric, and catalogs the different figures of speech present in the address. In essence, Wills weaves a rather thorough and complex tapestry, pulling together a number of threads of thought that had not been gathered before, and tying them neatly together in such a way as to make the fabric generally accessible to the layperson and, at the same time, quite acceptable to scholars as well.

Since Wills' book there have been a number of books devoted to Lincoln's other most important writings and speeches, constructed in some ways on the Wills model. For example, William C. Klingaman's 2001 work, *Abraham Lincoln and the Road to Emancipation, 1861–1863*, discusses the intricate history behind the document, this time the Emancipation Proclamation, while he canvasses, to a lesser degree than Wills, the rhetorical circumstances behind the birth of one of America's important legal proclamations. Although its discussion of the rhetorical principles is not nearly as detailed as Wills' study is, perhaps because of the legal language used, there is, however, considerable attention given to the actual composition of the document, bringing to light how Lincoln went about writing the edict.

One year later, two Lincoln scholars attempted extended similar studies of the Emancipator's Second Inaugural Address, perhaps Lincoln's most piercing analysis of the meaning and purpose of the Civil War; the speech remains one of the nation's most cherished and profound documents. The first book, Ronald White's *Lincoln's Greatest Speech*, aptly discusses the great moral and vexing questions raised by the Second Inaugural Address. White also analyzes the language of this relatively short speech. James Tachach's *Lincoln's Moral Vision: The Second Inaugural Address* covers much of the same ground as White, but he gives his analysis an interesting rhetorical turn by positing that the speech arose out of the jeremiad tradition of early New England. In this particular way, Tachach, like Wills, places the speech in a rhetorical tradition that helps to explain some of the interesting nuances of the address that lie hidden to those unaware of just what framework Lincoln was using. But on the whole, besides this revealing quality, the attention, once again, to what might be called strict rhetorical analysis pales compared to Wills' work. In 2004, well-respected and well-known Lincoln scholar Harold Holzer devoted his energies to studying a speech traditionally viewed as historically important to Lincoln's nascent political career and his later ascendency to the presidency, but not among his most creative pieces: well-reasoned, certainly; timely,

1. The Need to Study Lincoln's Letters

yes, but generally less important than his later speeches. In this work, *Lincoln at Cooper's Union: The Speech That Made Abraham Lincoln President,* however, Holzer assembles a wealth of information to argue that the address deserves more than mere political and historical analysis. Although Holzer does not use the word, he sees the speech as a good working example of how important kairos is to understanding the ultimate impact of an address.

Singled out in an article by James Kinneavy as a too often "neglected" concept from classical rhetoric (1996, 211), kairos, a topic treated in more detail later, refers to "right timing and proper measure—directly related to the rhetorical importance of time, place, speaker, and audience" (Sloane 2001, 371). As it applies to Lincoln's speech, Holzer shows, for example, how Lincoln says just the right thing at just the right time in just the right amount to his New York City audience. But Holzer's treatment of the address within a rhetorical framework is obviously sketchy at best, giving little attention to important rhetorical principles evident in the speech, and choosing instead to emphasize how the speech led to Lincoln's nomination for and election to the presidency.

After examining the major speeches one by one in great detail, scholars then turned their attention to a discussion of Lincoln's prose in general, rather than examining the prose within the context of a particular speech.

Three books need mentioning: *The Eloquent President* by Ronald White, Jr. (author of the earlier examination of Lincoln's Second Inaugural Address, *Lincoln's Greatest Speech), Lincoln's Greatest Speeches Reconsidered* by John Channing Briggs, and *Lincoln's Sword* by Douglas Wilson, the first two in 2005, the last in 2006. Each of the three books focuses primarily on what White calls Lincoln's "eloquence" and Wilson calls his "literary" gift. And as did the earlier studies, White, Briggs, and Wilson concentrate on Lincoln's major speeches and public letters, letters later published in newspapers and other venues available to the general public, giving little or no attention to his private correspondence.

White's *The Eloquent President* is, in the main, a thorough rhetorical analysis of Lincoln's most famous pieces. White pays attention to a number of rhetorical issues, including Lincoln's development as a rhetorician from a humble background, his composing habits, his attention to his audiences, his keen understanding of arrangement, his apparent knowledge and use of schemes and tropes, his consideration of the techniques of persuasion, and his seemingly innate understanding of the purpose and power of introductions and perorations. For example, White's discussion of the famous Hodges letter covers all these elements, suggesting that while White may not use the terminology of rhetorical analysis, he does indeed understand how a rhetorical analysis aids him in supporting his basic thesis that Lincoln was one of our most eloquent presidents (2004, 260–276). White's book, although quite comprehensive in its scope, looks at not only Lincoln's major speeches but also some lesser lights to support his thesis that Lincoln was, indeed, an eloquent writer. But unfortunately, in most of the book, White relies on what might be called subjective criticism. The book's intent seems to be to glean particularly striking passages from Lincoln's writing and hold them up as models of eloquent expression so that the reader, too, can then appreciate Lincoln's unusual ability to write memorable prose. While the bare basics of rhetoric provide the backdrop for most of his remarks, and while most of White's audience are lay people with little or no formal training in rhetoric, much of what White says about Lincoln's craft as a writer has been said many other times, unfortunately, in similar ways.

On the other hand, operating from the viewpoint of the sensitive literary critic that he is, Briggs traces the evolution of certain recurring themes in Lincoln's work by looking at documents not usually studied in the Lincoln canon, such as his "Lyceum Address," "Lecture on Discoveries and Inventions," and the "Milwaukee Address," while also analyzing the more familiar pieces, such as the "House Divided" speech, the Cooper Union Address, and the Gettysburg Address, each of which serves a particular purpose in Brigg's overall analysis. To that end, Briggs, using close readings of some of these lesser lights, traces the development, interrelationship, and consistency in Lincoln's thoughts. In many ways, Briggs' book is less like Wills' book than those already mentioned since the historical circumstances of the documents examined, as Briggs sees it, are of limited importance. Instead, Briggs gives readers a clear sense of the workings of Lincoln's mind in a way that a literary scholar might trace a theme in the work of Emily Dickinson or Nathaniel Hawthorne. Briggs' background in literary criticism provides him with tools for this type of analysis, and they serve him well. But, of course, it is literary analysis, not a rhetorical analysis.

Douglas Wilson's *Lincoln's Sword* advances the argument that Lincoln was an effective leader because his "presidential writing proved to be timely, engaging, consistently lucid, compelling in argument, and most important of all, invested with memorable and even inspiring language." In fact, much of the book sets out to detail Lincoln's literary ability" (2006, 3). For instance, the prologue uses the word "literary" or its equivalent, "man of letters," a total of ten times in a mere six pages, indicating clearly that Wilson intends a literary analysis. To his credit, Wilson provides his audience with sufficient historical and biographical background on the occasion of the writing of the document being examined, and Wilson does share many of the recently discovered rough drafts of these documents, but as he indicates early on, his purpose is to show how Lincoln's literary ability helped him govern so effectively. For example, Wilson's analysis of Albert G. Hodges' letter explores the historical background that occasioned the letter, an analysis of the letter's political importance, and speculation about Lincoln's composing strategy, but Wilson uses words like "literary" and "artful" to describe the work. In other words, Wilson does not attempt to characterize the rhetorical strategies used in the letter in any specific way, other than to point out the argument and certain stylistic devices. Questions about the letter as a rhetorical genre and its influence on the Hodges letter, the organization of the argument, the role of ethos in the letter— just to name a few—are not discussed. While Wilson mentions Aristotle in passing in a brief discussion of ethos elsewhere in the book, the allusion is largely unexplained and is applied only briefly to Lincoln's prose (147– 160). At what he attempts to do in the way he proposes to do it, *Lincoln's Sword* does a masterful job. What is important to this present study, however, is what Wilson does not do, and the need to study a body of Lincoln's work from an entirely different perspective, the rhetorical perspective.

Roy Basler's "Abraham Lincoln's Rhetoric," appearing in the journal *American Literature,* needs mentioning also. Basler addresses four main aspects of Lincoln's writing, particularly his speeches: the use of repetition, grammatical parallelism, antithesis, and metaphors, all stylistic devices. Basler includes a discussion of Lincoln's public letter to newspaper editor Horace Greeley, but the overall discussion of the article focuses on the tropes and schemes, not unexpectedly for a literature journal.

This survey of recent books and article devoted to Lincoln's writings leads to several observations. First, Lincoln's stature as a writer remains lofty, and, in some ways, these books help enhance that reputation. Of all our presidents, Lincoln seems to rank highest on a scale of eloquence. His words have been memorized by generations of school children, immortalized in the speeches of politicians, and studied by those seeking to imitate his ability to write with refreshing clarity and clear logic. Second, Lincoln scholars have explored Lincoln's most of his major documents in considerable detail. Scholars now know much more about how these important documents arose, the particular occasions for them, the public's reaction to them, their effect on Lincoln's political life, and their ultimate place in United States history. Third, while scholars know much more about these speeches, the authors cited, while not really measuring up to the Wills model, have covered their topics in enough depth to leave precious little to say more about the documents they studied. Certainly, in places, a more thorough rhetorical analysis of the works would probably add completeness to the study of Lincoln's oeuvre.

Yet reexamining these same Lincoln documents with this more discerning lens would be a truly monumental task, given their number and the extent of scholarship surrounding Lincoln, as would be surveying the often arcane scholarship on Lincoln's major documents written in the past; their number is so vast as to boggle the mind of even the most energetic Lincoln scholar. But rather than plowing the same old ground with a different plow, and filling the small holes in scholarship along the way, there is still another field of Lincoln's writing rich enough to deserve attention it has not gotten in the past. That area is unburdened by the many tangles of scholarship that surround many of Lincoln's better known pieces, while it also provides scholars with the opportunity to study Lincoln the rhetor in another rhetorical genre.

The works in need of careful examination are Lincoln's letters, particularly his personal rather than his public letters, places where most Lincoln scholars have not been. While the ground is not virgin to historians and biographers, it has been largely unexplored for its rhetorical content, an oversight almost unexplainable in view of what scholars know about letters and their importance during the Greco-Roman period, the Middle Ages, the eighteenth century, Lincoln's age, and even today.

To be sure, a small number of scholars have studied a limited number of Lincoln's letters. The famous Bixby letter, for example, is a part of an ongoing discussion in Lincoln lore, not for its rhetorical power but for questions about its authorship. Other letters are important for their historical, political, and biographical information, but seldom do scholars focus on their rhetorical power. The so-called Horace Greeley letter, a public letter in which Lincoln explains to the newspaper reading public early in the Civil War what his chief aims as president were, has been cited countless times by the countless biographers of the Great Emancipator, but with little attention paid to its rhetoric. Lincoln's letter to General Hooker illustrates vividly how Lincoln persisted in his belief in democracy, despite the fact that another form of government during these critical times might be a more efficient way to govern; but, once again, little is said about its power as a rhetorical artifact. His letters to his best friend, Joshua Speed, often help to explain the character of the often inscrutable, inner Lincoln, but, once more, there is little comment on the letters' rhetorical effects. His letter to his ne'er-do-well stepbrother, excoriating him for his laziness, is sometimes cited to reveal a less well-known side of Lincoln's personality, yet the letter's power as a rhetorical document remains unexplored. Most of his letters, then, numbering 5,178 in all, have been largely ignored by scholars of rhetoric and examined, if examined at all, only for their political, biographical and historical significance.

Initially, it is easy to understand why. The letters, at first glance, seem to be of minor importance. Many of them are quickly written notes to an underling, requesting a particular matter be dealt with, or asking questions of the addressee, or for favors from friends and acquaintances, three or four line messages: hardly consequential to most historians, but still, however, of interest to rhetoricians. To historians and political scientists, some letters merely serve to demonstrate the kind of communication necessary for an ambitious politician trying to maintain his important contacts and support another person's political ambitions. While they may be important to understanding how Lincoln's political mind worked, there are so many of them with the same general themes that most biographers dismiss the bulk of them as needless repetition and cite the same apt ones over and over.

But within the limitations of this work, I want to demonstrate that rhetorical analyses of two letters do indeed provide valuable information about how Lincoln worked as a letter writer, information not available, in large part, by using a literary, political, or biographical methodology. Thus, in the first section, I trace the history of the evolution of the "letter of consolation" from its earliest beginnings to Lincoln's time and show how Lincoln follows the many remaining conventions for that type of letter; in another section, I examine the Bixby letter, positing that the letter illustrates the concept of kairos, which in turn leads to a keener understanding of the letter's power and influence; and in the last section, I discuss the second letter written by Lincoln to his stepbrother, seeing it as a kind of crude, epistolary philippic. While other possible methodologies for studying these letters as rhetorical artifacts are available, in the case of these two letters, the rhetorical analyses employed seem particularly well suited to these individual letters.

The corpus of Lincoln's letters can be found in the eight-volume *Collected Works of Abraham Lincoln,* edited by Roy Basler, published in 1953–

Abraham Lincoln—he wrote more than 5,000 letters.

1. The Need to Study Lincoln's Letters

1955 in book form. (For simplicity's sake, citations to the nine volumes of this work will be given in the form of "Basler I," etc.) Fortunately for scholars, the Abraham Lincoln Association created and maintains an online site that contains the collected works and is available to the general public. Hosted by the University of Michigan Digital Library Production Service, the site allows scholars to do one-word searches, use Boolean descriptors, and perform proximity searches within the boundaries of 120 characters, among other things. While there are two supplements to the original collection by Basler, published in 1974 and 1990, those works are not posted online, because scholars at the Abraham Lincoln Association felt that there were nagging questions about the authenticity of some of the letters. Particularly, the association says that while *The Collected Works of Abraham Lincoln* was "the result of a true historical documentary editing project that required the input and review of a team of scholars and researchers ... the two supplemental volumes are the result of one editor's solo effort" (Swartz e-mail). Consequently, because of questions about the letters' authenticity, these Lincoln scholars decided against posting the two supplements online, too. In truth, though, the supplements contain few letters of any length at all; almost all are short, one-sentence notes, so even if these letters were authenticated, their value to this present study would be minimal.

According to Basler's introduction to *The Collected Works of Abraham Lincoln*, the letters reside in 101 places, some in private collections, some in museums, and some in libraries. Presumably, the largest collection of Lincoln's letters is in the Library of Congress in Washington, D.C. The curator of that collection is Dr. John Sellers, who shows the letters at special request and answers questions about them, based on his study of them as curator. In a personal interview, he made several observations about the letters. He noted that sometimes Lincoln's handwriting is difficult to read, especially when distinguishing the letters *d* and *a*, for example. The missives are written in black ink with individual cursive letters from the alphabet ranging from one quarter to one half inch in height. The letters are generally written on white paper, but other colors such as blue do appear. Picking seven letters at random, I found the size of the paper the letters are written on varies greatly, ranging from a height of 8 to 16 inches. The width varies considerably also, measuring from 4¾ or 5 up to 8 inches in width. The White House stationery is the largest and comes in the form of a folio, folded down the middle, making four separate pages. A random sampling of the letters does not indicate that the size or dimensions of the paper in any way influenced the length of the letters that Lincoln wrote. In other words, letters on different sizes of paper did not prompt Lincoln to write longer or shorter letters. The physicality of the letters themselves appears *not* to influence their content or theme. The last public sale of a Lincoln letter, according to Dr. Sellers, netted $800,000, a clear indication of their value to collectors.

On one hand, while historians and biographers may not see the value of these hundreds of letters for their purposes, Lincoln's letters do offer rhetoricians the opportunity to see how a man widely venerated for his rhetorical skills went about the business of producing one of the world's most common rhetorical artifacts, the letter, a genre that stretches its history back to the dawn of Western civilization and remains vastly important to the history of written rhetoric.

In many ways, letters represent the very first time in the history of rhetoric that the focus was exclusively on the production of a written document. Stanley K. Stowers's *Letter Writing in Greco-Roman Antiquity* points out the important role of the letter in these two high civilizations, citing a number of books novices studied in antiquity to learn how to write effective letters by imitating the models written by ancient and important letter writers such as Seneca, Cicero, and Pliny. Letters became the means to transfer news about government policies and inform the few literates about ecclesiastical matters (1986, 175, 177–179).

In addition to the Greco-Roman period, which includes the New Testament epistles, in Western Europe the letter as a rhetorical genre flourished during two different eras. Aron Morgan, writing in the *Encyclopedia of Rhetoric and Composition,* says that during the Middle Ages, letter writing developed into one of the "three rhetorical arts," along with preaching and poetics. Morgan notes that in AD 1087, the monk Alberic was the "first to link rhetoric with letter-writing" (1996, 433), applying the parts of the Ciceronian speech to the structure of the letter, resulting in letter-writing manuals stressing standardized patterns or "formularies" (432–433). The other period when the letter figured prominently in England and Europe was the eighteenth century, when letter writing was revered as a means of both communication and literary expression, while, at the same time, it proved to be an agent in the evolution of the novel as a genre. *The Familiar Letter in the Eighteenth Century,* edited by Howard Anderson et al., and *The Converse of the Pen: Acts of Intimacy in the Eighteenth Century*

1. The Need to Study Lincoln's Letters

Familiar Letter by Bruce Radford, for example, treat the familiar letter during this era, while *Epistolarity: Approaches to a Form* by Janet Gurkin Altman, theorizes in part about the development of the epistolary novel during this same time. Elizabeth Hewitt's *Correspondence in American Literature 1770–1865,* and perhaps more germane for this present study, William Merrill Decker's *Epistolarity Practices: Letter Writing in America before Telecommunications,* also are major works chronicling the letter as both a rhetorical and literary form in the United States and help provide, in part, an adequate background for studying Lincoln's letters in their American setting. Making the job a little easier when examining Lincoln's letters is that, as Decker points out, there is no letter form "unique to American correspondents" (1998, 10). As a nation, we tended to follow the long tradition of letter writing that began in Greece and Rome, moved through the Middle Ages, and re-appeared in the eighteenth century, but did not develop into a genre radically different from that found in the rest of the Western world.

2

The Letter as Genre

To the student of Lincoln's rhetoric, studying Lincoln's letters offers several advantages. First, since most of them have not been viewed through a rhetorical lens, casting light on them could generate interest in Lincoln as the letter writer and add another dimension to our understanding of him as a rhetor. Second, studying Lincoln's letters could help rhetoricians better understand the gradual evolution of Lincoln's talent with a pen. While many of the early Lincoln documents collected in *The Collected Works* are legal tracts, contracts, and agreements, often written in the typical formal "legalese" of the time, the early samples we have of Lincoln the writer are his letters. These letters help us to trace how Lincoln evolved from the somewhat clumsy but largely committed writer to the practiced and admired letter writer he was regarded as in his adulthood. Third, examining Lincoln's letters also demonstrates how closely Lincoln followed the letter-writing conventions of his era and the conventions that go as far back as the ancient Greeks and Romans. A study from this perspective helps to redefine Lincoln as a writer who may be seen by some as a less powerful and a more derivative writer than he is generally regarded as; the common assumption being that Lincoln was always a powerful writer. But in order to assume this lofty place, he had to acquire the conventions of a literate society, one of which encompassed the protocols for letter writing. Decker, for example, notes that the letter "is ever a locus of class markers: masteries of protocol, refinements of taste, levels of cultivation, grades of literacy" (1998, 14). Was Lincoln, anxious to climb the social ladder, a slavish imitator of the letter form as it was practiced in his time?

Letters were very much a part of Lincoln's life, beginning as a young boy growing up on the southern Indiana frontier. Both Carl Sandburg and

2. The Letter as Genre

David Herbert Donald, author of the Pulitzer Prize–winning biography *Lincoln*, mention that as a young lad in frontier Indiana, Lincoln had a reputation as an efficient and effective letter writer (Donald 1996, 30; Sandburg 1993, 9). Neighbors quite frequently called on the young man to compose letters for them, since many were illiterate, or not literate enough to carry on the necessary but limited correspondence of the day. This experience must have assured the young boy that writing letters was something he could do fairly well, building in him the kind of confidence a youthful yet verbally talented writer needed to carry into adulthood. In addition, it is a commonplace in Lincoln scholarship that Lincoln knew his Bible well. He quoted the Bible often and quoted it accurately. H. Jack Lang in *Lincoln's Fireside Reading* points out that the Bible was "[f]or many years ... the only book available to young Abe" (1965, 65). It is easy to understand why the beauty of expression in the King James version of the Bible became very important in the life of the verbally gifted young boy. From his "House Divided" speech to the Second Inaugural Address, Lincoln used biblical quotations frequently. Such frequent citations from the Bible may be, as Lang says, because of the limited amount of reading material available; an eager reader, young Lincoln studied the scriptures carefully with his youthful and impressionable mind, absorbing the rhythms and tones of holy writ. In his careful reading of scripture, Lincoln would have also been exposed to suitable models in the twenty-one letters in the Bible, such as the epistles of Paul and the letters of Hebrews, James, Peter, John, and Jude. Therein, he would have seen sterling examples of the power and grace of these timeless letters, written in the often poetic strains of the Authorized Version. In addition, since these biblical epistles were considered scripture, the budding writer would probably have regarded these examples with great care and deep respect.

According to government sources, Lincoln also had contact with letters when he was postmaster in New Salem, Illinois, an office he assumed as a young man on May 7, 1833 (Dolliver 1956, 165). He would have observed how important letters were to these early settlers on the frontier, whose only contact with friends and family back East was often through letters. Decker notes that letters were ways to bring the voice of a faraway relative on paper to the early Midwest pioneers and to alleviate, for a time at least, the "human isolation" these early settlers felt (1998, 6). For many must have feared, as Decker concludes, that amid the "separation, loneliness, and apprehension that death will intervene before the parties can re-unite"

(22), a common theme in their letters and a reason to hold letters so dear. There are indications that Lincoln understood just how important letters were to his customers, because to shield the letters from the weather, he often transported them by sticking them in his hat and delivering them dry to their rightful and appreciative recipients.

It is quite probable that Lincoln would have read a bit of rhetorical theory about letters, too. While a resident of New Salem, Illinois, Lincoln and Ann Rutledge borrowed a very popular book on rhetoric that includes a discussion of letter writing from another local resident, Henry Rankin. According to Edward P.J. Corbett, in his studies of the history of rhetoric, during the early nineteenth century, Hugh Blair's *Lectures on Rhetoric and Belle Lettres* endured "great popularity" (1971, 5). Lucille M. Schultz confirms that idea in her study of the teaching of writing in nineteenth century America, noting that Blair's book served as a theoretical model for many other books like it at that time (1999, 36). Finally, James Berlin (1984), in his study of how writing was taught in nineteenth century schools, concludes,

> The most popular treatment of rhetoric until after the Civil War was Blair's *Lectures on Rhetoric and Belle Lettres* (25). In fact, Blair's book was so popular in the United States and England that Berlin records that between 1783 and 1911, the book went through an astounding 130 editions (25). Consequently, it seems highly likely that Lincoln did read Blair: M.L. Houser in *Lincoln's Education and Other Essays*, after extensive consultation with other Lincoln scholars, also lists Blair's book as one of the books Lincoln read [318].

In Lecture 37 of *Lectures on Rhetoric and Belle Lettres*, Blair discusses the epistolary form as it is practiced in the public and private letters of late eighteenth century by contemporaries such as Pope and Swift, and by what he calls the "Antients," people such as Cicero, Pliny, and Seneca. Blair cautions readers that public letters by these authors often are burdened by affectation (1829, 419), so he advises his readers instead to view the private letter as "conversation," to be written with "native grace and ease," so they are "natural and simple" (418). Speaking of their range, Blair says, "there is no subject whatever, on which one may not convey his thoughts" (417), advice Lincoln, apparently, took to heart. As we shall see, it is the personal letter's range, informality, and discursive nature that make it particularly relevant to any discussion of Lincoln the letter writer.

According to Wilson's *Lincoln's Sword*, by the time Lincoln was admitted to the bar in the fall of 1836, he would have understood how much of lawyer's day was spent composing letters to clients, witnesses, government officials, and fellow lawyers (2006, 107). As they do now, lawyers had to write many letters to order to transact the business of their profession. Later, as president, Lincoln continued to write hundreds of letters, scratching off quick notes to his staff and cabinet members, answering letters from those seeking political appointments, composing replies to those begging for mercy for their sons serving in the Union army, writing formal letters to foreign dignitaries such as Queen Victoria on her birthday, giving out orders to recalcitrant generals and sometimes even encouraging them, and writing passes for his wife's relatives who wished to cross Union lines; in other words, dealing daily, in the form of letters, with the all the correspondence required in a law office and as part of his duties as president.

In addition, Lincoln had contact with letters in a rather oblique way. Some might argue that Lincoln abused the postal system, at the time the mechanism for carrying letters from one place to another. Wayne E. Fuller in *The American Mail: Enlarger of the Common* concludes that Lincoln and his postmaster general, Montgomery Blair, "proved to be the greatest manipulators of the spoils system the nation had seen." Fuller says that within four years, the two appointed a whopping 21,000 postmasters, at a time when such offices were not covered by strict civil service laws and regulations. Some of Lincoln's critics even accused the Lincoln administration of being more concerned about who was postmaster than about what was going on in the Civil War (1972, 292). Others, however, may counter that Lincoln's attention to the postal service demonstrates that Lincoln keenly understood how important the post office was to a country in crisis, how vital getting letters through to soldiers was to the war effort, thus explaining why he spent so much time giving out appointments in the postal system.

Finally, there is even some evidence that Lincoln used letter writing as a kind of personal and cathartic experience, a way of getting in touch with and venting his emotions. Lincoln sometimes wrote flaming letters, for example, to vent his anger, and then, when he had regained his composure, decided not to send them after all. Doris Kearns Goodwin's *Team of Rivals* records how Lincoln expressed his deep and abiding anger toward General George Meade, who, in Lincoln's mind, should have vigorously pursued Robert E. Lee's Confederate Army after defeating him at Gettysburg. Some years later, in a letter found after Lincoln's death, Lincoln wrote that he was "distressed immeasurably" by Meade's actions. But Lincoln, in spite of all his anger, put the letter to Meade away and never sent it. Writing the letter, then, was Lincoln's way of dealing with his frustration and letting his anger out (2006, 536).

Obviously, letters were important to Lincoln, and since his letters have not been studied carefully for their rhetorical value, they invite an examination.

A number of rhetorical theoretical models could provide suitable and fruitful methodologies with which to look at Lincoln's letters. Using the approach of Kenneth Burke, we could see the letters as attempts on Lincoln's part to establish "consubstantiation" with his readers (David Williams 1996). Or Richard Weaver's view of rhetoric as "sermonic," "as moving the audience toward the right thought and action" (Duffy 1996), may be useful in unlocking the core of Lincoln's rhetoric in his letters. Or Mikhail Bakhtin's thinking could be used to explore how a text "uses discourse to put social values into dialogic relations with each other" (Phelan 1996). These are just three of the many ways to study Lincoln's letters. Unfortunately, using all these models on a large number of sample letters requires a much more extensive treatment of the missives than is possible within the scope of this essay. But more importantly, one might argue that these three approaches do not generate the rich and complex data that the approaches detailed below do.

This study uses a more productive way to understand Lincoln the letter writer, a method not often employed but still quite helpful in this case: exploring how the history of the genre of letter writing itself helped shape the choices Lincoln made as a writer. By the time Lincoln wrote his first letter, the genre had been around over two thousand years and had experienced at least two periods of time in the English language tradition when it was highly venerated. Those two periods, the medieval era and the eighteenth century, detailed in books such as James Murphy's *Three Medieval Arts* and Bruce Redford's *The Converse of the Pen: Acts of Intimacy in the Eighteenth Century Familiar Letter,* help to explain how the letter had acquired the largely formulary nature it had by Lincoln's time. Rather than launch into a detailed history of the letter as a rhetorical genre, it is probably more fruitful to point out only those bits of the letter's history that particularly apply to studying Lincoln as a letter writer. The long and interesting history of the letter is a topic well worth scholarly examination in another context, but that history contains much information that does not directly apply to understanding Lincoln as a letter writer.

2. The Letter as Genre

During much of the development of the letter as a rhetorical genre, the emphasis was on using the appropriate salutation: that is, how was the letter writer to address the letter's addressee? Handbooks of letter writing in the Middle Ages, for example, listed page after page of samples of the correct salutations appropriate for the addressee. How should one address the pope? How does one address a prince? A parent? A relative? James Murphy, one of the leading scholars of *ars dictaminis*, the Latin words for "the art of letter writing" during the Middle Ages, points out that Hugh of Bologna's influential handbook for writing letters, published in the 1100s, lists salutations for everyone from the pope to the emperor, emperor to the pope, bishop to his subordinates, and subordinates to their bishop, as well as many others, including appropriate salutations to teachers, friends, fathers, scholars, brothers and soldiers, just to name a few (1971, 217). Another manual of the period, the anonymous *Rationes dictandi*, concludes that salutations are so important that, according to Murphy, the tome spends "nearly one-third of the book" discussing them (221).

A few examples will suffice to illustrate both their length and complexity. From the anonymous *Principles of Letter Writing*, another of the many letter-writing manuals of the period, come examples such as the suggested lengthy salutation of a teacher to his pupil: "N___, promoter of the scholastic profession, wishes N___, his most dear friend and companion, to acquire the teachings of all literature, to possess fully all the diligence of the philosophical profession, to pursue not folly but the wisdom of Socrates and Plato." The salutation of parents to their son also runs some length: "Peter the father and Mary the mother, to John their most beloved son, send parental blessings with their greetings" (Anonymous 2001, 436). Understandably, as the standard work on medieval society, Mark Bloch's *Feudal Society*, points out, the decisions about the appropriate salutations were quite important in a civilization where proper respect was a requirement in a particularly stratified, class-conscious society (1961, 325). Indeed, the previously mentioned letter-writing handbook emphasizes this same point by defining the salutation as "an expression of greeting conveying a friendly sentiment not inconsistent with the social rank of the person involved" (Anonymous 2001, 432).

Yet the situation in Lincoln's day and place was quite different, the choice of the salutation being much less complicated in the more egalitarian society of the United States. Even today, James Calvert Scott, for example, observes that business communication "is conceived, transacted, and perceived somewhat differently in the United Kingdom than in the United States." In the British Isles, letter writing requires that American and British letter writers be strictly aware of the importance of the various titles in British society (Scott 1998, 50–51). But the differences go even beyond speakers of the same language. Linda Flower and John Ackerman, for instance, point out that modern Japanese letters begin with elaborate salutations such as, "Allow us to open with all reverence to you" (1994, 83). Even now in our culturally conscious world, knowing the appropriate salutation is very much a part of carrying on a cordial relationship with those of other countries. Things were and are different, however, in the United States.

In Lincoln's time, one of the most popular handbooks on letter writing, *Chesterfield's Letter-Writer*, published in the United States in 1857, doesn't even treat the subject of salutations as a specific topic. Instead the author presents model letters that use relatively simple forms of address such as "Sir" or "Gentlemen" for business correspondence (35), greetings such as "My dear Mother" or "My dear Child" (42, 46) for more familiar letters, and greetings such as "My dearest Fanny" and "My dearest, ever-beloved Charles" (56–57) for what it calls "letters of courtship." In nineteenth century American society, salutations apparently were much less of a problem, with the elaborate and deferential salutations used in class-conscious societies reduced to a mere "dear" in American correspondence. Yet it is significant to note that the same letter-writing manual also included a rather extensive treatment of etiquette in American society, tying the two subjects together, and suggesting that proper form in letter writing and proper conduct in social events were still important in polite American society, but that there was less need to show the elaborate deference to class structure present in other parts of the world.

Lincoln's salutations are also very similar in their simplicity and fairly limited in number, much like those suggested by the Chesterfield manual, indicating that Lincoln understood the customs of polite nineteenth century American society and practiced them when necessary. For instance, in dealing with a formal business relationship, he uses "Dear Sir," "My dear Sir," and "Dear Madam" almost always, varying it only in special circumstances. In his collected letters, he uses "Dear Sir" 1,459 times, an apparently popular form of address for him, while he employs "Dear Madam" fifteen times. Probably, in nineteenth century American society, where women were less likely a part of the business and professional world, Lincoln had fewer occasions to address women than would be true today. In contrast, he addresses his best friend, Joshua Speed, as "Dear Speed" twenty-one times and, on at least two occasions, "My dear Speed," much in the spirit of adolescents and even men today in the United States who often address each other in a familiar relationship not by their first names but by their last names. He likewise addresses other friends this way, opening six letters to his friend Orville H. Browning with "Dear Browning," and using the salutation "Dear Johnston" to address a friend named Andrew Johnston. One time, however, Lincoln addresses his stepbrother, John Johnston, whom he sees as sorely lacking in ambition, as "Dear Johnston," a salutation probably expressing his lack of patience with the addressee, rather than being a sign of friendship between men, especially since Lincoln had shared a small log cabin from boyhood to manhood with Johnston and would have more likely addressed him as "John," if the circumstances and Lincoln's attitude were different, a subject discussed in detail later in this study.

Eleven times, Lincoln also used a somewhat curious salutation directed primarily to men: "Friend White," "Friend Butler," "Friend Davis," "Friend Thomas," "Friend Sam," "Friend Walter," "Friend McLean," and "Friend Schooler," using a mixture of "friend" and first *and* last names. Two other times he uses "friend" as a salutation; only this time, interestingly, it is to a woman he was courting, Mary Owens. In the body of those two letters, Lincoln spells out his romantic intentions to some degree, although at one point offering to end the romance, if she cared to, but the curious salutation of "Friend Mary" seems quite out of place. Many biographers have made much of the young Lincoln's apparent awkwardness around women, which may explain the use of a salutation he uses at other times only with men. Years later, when William Herndon, a Lincoln biographer and Lincoln's law partner, asked Mary Owens about her relationship with Lincoln, she quipped, "Lincoln was deficient in those little links which make up the chain of [a] woman's happiness—at least it was so in my case" (1930, 119), an observation that may be, in part, a reference to the rather odd salutation with which he began his letters to her. On the other hand, Lincoln uses the more customary "Dear Mary" and "Dear Wife" when addressing his wife Mary Todd Lincoln, and employs "My dear son" when writing to his son, Robert Todd Lincoln.

While the salutation "friend" seems different from the norm of today, most of Lincoln's greetings are fairly common for the day and circumstances.

In fact, most of the salutations Lincoln uses are quite common even now. The use of fairly typical salutations may indicate that Lincoln was following conventions for several reasons. Of course, the obvious explanation is that he was merely doing what was conventional for the time. If he had used the long and elaborate salutations, say, of St. Paul's letters, which he no doubt had exposure to, he would have begun a letter in a way quite out of keeping with the times. The addressee, then, would have been likely to see Lincoln as more different than Lincoln probably would have wished. Choice of salutations, of course, relates to the ethos Lincoln wanted to project in his letters; that is, the image he would project of himself in the prose itself. As a good rhetorician, consciously or unconsciously, Lincoln would have understood how important ethos was to a rhetor's power. Aristotle, for example, says that a rhetor's "character may almost be called the most effective means of persuasion [he or she] possesses" (*Rhetoric*, 25). In *On Style*, the Greek rhetorician Demetrius also noted that the "letter ... should abound in glimpses of character. It may be said that everybody reveals his own soul in his letters. In every other form of composition, it is possible to discern the writer's character, but in none so clearly as in the epistolary" (1986, Demetrius quoted in Stowers, 38). With Lincoln implicitly or explicitly knowing that, he would have realized that using appropriate salutations introduced his readers from the beginning to the tone of the relationship that he wanted to establish with them.

At times, then, part of the ethos he wanted to establish was that he was a nineteenth century American man who understood the proper place for respectful salutations of a relatively formal nature, so in more formal letters he used "Dear sir" and "Dear madam," but he also realized that when the occasion arose he could employ more affectionate terms like "My dear" and "Friend." The letter-writing manual of the day, *Chesterfield's Letter-Writer*, uses the word "tact" to describe this unconscious ability to distinguish what was suitable for the occasion of the letter: "Tact," the author says, "consists in a clear and ready interpretation of our thoughts and wishes, as well as in a prompt and graceful understanding of those of another" (Chesterfield 1857, 3). Such thinking suggests that in order to display this "tact," the writer had to begin with an appropriate salutation, for this is the first place where the letter writer first meets the reader, the first hint of the ethos the writer intends to impart to the reader.

To acquire this "tact," *Chesterfield's Letter-Writer* suggests, requires a "regular correspondence with those who themselves write well" (4). Lincoln, of course, was a well-practiced letter writer who carried on a rich correspondence with people quite literate for their day. Despite the fact that many of his letters are lost, his collected works alone, which include, as mentioned earlier, 5,178 letters, suggests quite an output for anyone's lifetime and a clear indication that he was a prolific letter writer.

As a young man in nineteenth century Illinois, Lincoln realized that he had to conform to the conventions of that particular Springfield society, which represented, in large part, the social and political values of many parts of the United States. He, for example, had to dress appropriately, choosing not to wear the clothing associated with hard-scrabble farmers, such as homemade linsey-woolsey shirts and trousers. He had to modify his social conduct by acknowledging the appropriate social graces of conversation and mannerisms. In addition, Lincoln had to communicate in letter form, since that was an accepted form of written communication during his time, a practice that included the many conventions of epistolary etiquette Lincoln had to master. Lincoln, of course, was not alone in his quest for acceptance into a more genteel society. One indication of that fact was the popularity of guides to proper behavior. According to John F. Kasson's *Rudeness and Civility,* between 1830 and 1910, "more than 150 'etiquette manuals' were published in the United States" (1990, 48), "which boasted that with proper drive, knowledge, and success, an individual or family might climb the social ladder to new heights" (43). Mastering the appropriate letter-writing conventions, then, was a part of the requirements needed to gain acceptance into this more refined society.

Pierre Bourdieu, sociologist and philosopher, names this pull to conform *habitus,* a term dating back to the ancient Greeks, but a concept that Bourdieu explained in some detail in *The Logic of Practice* as being a part of all societies. Habitus refers to "thoughts, perceptions, expressions, and actions—whose limits are set by the historically and socially situated conditions of its production" (1990, 55). Such dispositions tend "to generate all the 'reasonable,' 'common sense' behaviours and only these which are possible within the regularities, and which are sanctioned because they are objectively adjusted to the logic of a particular field" (55–56). In other words, there is only room for any diversity if it falls in line with the "logic of a particular field ... historically and socially situated" (55). In particular, that means that habitus "structures *new* experiences in accordance with the structures produced by *past* experiences, ... dominated by the earliest experiences statistically common to members of that same class" (italics added) (60). To look at the concept through another set of eyes, in *Analyzing Everyday Text,* Glen Stillar summarizes habitus as "a set of embodied cultural dispositions that social agents would bring to bear in social practices. It is an inclination to carry ourselves in particular ways: to eat certain foods, to take on certain jobs, to seek out certain types of entertainment, *to speak and write in particular ways,* and to feel, hope, and desire with particular inclinations" (italics added) (1998, 95). In relation to linguistic habitus, in particular, in *Language and Symbolic Power,* Bourdieu notes, "These dispositions govern both the subsequent linguistic practices of an agent and the anticipation of the value that linguistic products will receive in other fields or markets" (1991, 17). To say it another way, the reader or listener believes the person displaying such habitus knows and reflects well the field he or she represents, something Lincoln obviously aspired to do.

As Stiller then points out, the person who has successfully acquired such habitus accumulates "symbolic capital" (1998, 102). Or as Bourdieu says it: "[T]he value of an utterance depends on the relation of power that is concretely established between the speaker's linguistic competences, understood both as their capacity for production and as their capacity for *appropriation* and *appreciation*" (italics added) (1991, 67). Bourdieu continued: "Linguistic utterances or expressions are always produced in particular contexts or markets, and the properties of these markets endow linguistic products with a certain 'value.' On a given linguistic market, some products are valued more highly than others; and part of the practical competence of speakers is to know how, and to be able, to produce expressions which are highly valued on the markets concerned" (18). Simply stated, Lincoln as a letter writer, if he had aspirations of acquiring any symbolic capital (which he obviously did), had to follow the conventions inherent in his time and place to acquire the societal respect and acceptance he so earnestly sought. To cite an obvious example, Lincoln follows the normal format of the letter, beginning with the date and salutation, because to begin any other way would have marked him as unwilling to acquire the particular linguistic habitus of the group he sought to become a part of. Following that habitus, then, helps him acquire the symbolic capital necessary to exert influence in that particular segment of society. Bourdieu's explanation of habitus goes well beyond the meaning and mere superficiality of the cliché "When in Rome, do as the Romans do." Bourdieu provides a rich accounting of the parts and processes of habitus, or, in this case, the linguistic habitus, as it relates to Lincoln's letters.

Perhaps the clearest example of Lincoln's participation in this letter-writing habitus is how he opens the body of many of his letters. Literally hundreds of times, Lincoln begins letters with an acknowledgment that he has received a letter from the addressee. Typical openings are examples such as a letter to William Butler that opens thus: "Yours of the 22nd is duly received" (Basler I:138–139). Another letter to William Butler starts: "Your letter enclosing one to Mr. Baker, was received on yesterday evening" (141–142), and a letter to William G. Anderson begins: "Your note of yesterday is received" (211). Openings such as these were customary in nineteenth century letters and are attested to by letters from a variety of people. An Indiana Civil War soldier, John R. McClure, opened his February 8, 1864, letter with this: "I received your letter a few days ago" (McClure 1970, 49). Another Civil War soldier named Henry Matrau opened his letter to his parents as follows: "I received your letter of the 15th last Saturday and was very glad to get it" (Matrau 1993, 6). A former slave just learning to write opens in the familiar: "I received your kind and affectionate letter yesterday" (Myers 2004, 476). But it wasn't just a custom of the Civil War period. In 1856, Margaret Ralston Kennedy writing to her friend Phoebe began: "I just received your letter addressed September 10" (Hubalek 1996, 40). Even literary figures such as Ralph Waldo Emerson and Emily Dickinson opened letters in a similar fashion. Dickinson writes: "...just to tell you that we got your letter last evening ... (1986, Johnson, ed., 261)."Emerson in his 1838 letter to Thomas Carlyle begins with this: "Yesterday I had your letter of March" (1964, Slater, ed. 183). *Chesterfield's Letter-Writer* recommends this same opening and cites many examples, including one that starts thus: "Your mournful letter (brief, though so full of a father's heart) has found me here" (1857, 50). This custom of the time may be simply explained by the fact that the postal system in the United States was not as reliable as it is today, and the writer wished to assure the addressee that the letter did, in fact, arrive. Decker notes, for example, that the postal service in the United States was not "anything resembling an organized, efficient, confidence-inspiring postal system" until well into the nineteenth century (1998, 58). Lincoln's letters beginning in this manner could likewise signal his individual assurance to his addressee that the letters the writer had sent had indeed arrived at their destination. At any rate, the custom of opening his letters this way, as many contemporaries did, further strengthens the argument that Lincoln understood the appropriate habitus for letter writing at the time and, to a great degree, followed the customary practice.

Traditionally, in addition to the acknowledgment of receipt of the letter, many letters began the body of the letter with what was termed in the medieval letter-writing manuals *benevolentia*, the expression of goodwill, a strategy borrowed in large part from ancient epistolary practices. Murphy, for example, lists the *benevolentia* as the second part of the formal structure of the letter as outlined in the previously mentioned popular manual, *Rationes dictami* (1971, 220–221). But the same manual carefully notes that this particular part of the letter is, after all, an extension of the salutation (437); that is, it represents an attempt to further enhance the ethos of the writer, a way of ingratiating the writer to the reader, if you will. Perhaps the most well-known examples of securing goodwill that Lincoln would have been familiar with are those that appear in the Bible, for one biographer, William Lee Miller, notes what others have said: that Lincoln's speeches as president are "suffused with the echoes and flavorings of the King James translation" (2002, 50), so it would seem to be only natural that expressions of goodwill would appear in Lincoln's letters. In the King James Version of the Bible, St. Paul offers words of goodwill in his letter to the Romans: "Grace to you and peace from God our Father, and the Lord Jesus Christ" Rom. 1:7). First Corinthians says something quite similar: "Grace be unto you, and peace, from God our Father, and from the Lord Jesus Christ" (1 Cor. 1:3). Second Corinthians uses the exact same words in verse 2, as do Galatians 1:3 and Ephesians 1:2. Such expressions of goodwill are often termed "apostolic greetings," but they serve a similar purpose as the *benevolentia*.

Nineteenth century American letters also exhibit examples of *benevoluntia*. Margaret Ralston Kennedy's 1855 and 1856 letters include greetings such as these: "I send you greetings from the territory of Kansas," "Season's blessing to you and your family," and "Thank you for your recent letter of birthday wishes" (Hubalek 1996, 20, 27, 79). Civil War soldier Major Henry Livermore Abbott is exuberant at getting a letter from his mother and shows his profound appreciation: "I am very glad to hear from you again; I think I could hear from you much oftener, without getting tired of it" (Abbott 1991, 76). Emily Dickinson builds a type of communion with her addressee, beginning "…'I love to write to you—it gives my heart a holiday and sets the bells ringing. If prayers had any answers to them,

2. The Letter as Genre

you were all here tonight..."' (1986, Johnson, ed. 263). In his letter, Emerson greets Carlyle: "I am glad of the opportunity of Mr. Barnard's visit to say health and peace be with you" (1964, Slater, ed. 119). A year later, in April of 1845, Emerson's letter begins: "It is a pleasure to set your name once more at the head of a sheet" (1964, Slater, ed. 143).

Lincoln, too, frequently begins letters with a *benevolentia* in the form of an apology or a request, but the goodwill is often mixed with the actual purpose of the letter. A May 12, 1853, letter to Joshua R. Stanford begins: "I hope the subject-matter will appear a sufficient apology to you for the liberty I, a total stranger, take in addressing you" (Basler II:194). In a short note to an Elisha Embree on May 25, 1849, Lincoln tries to ingratiate himself to the reader by noting that the request he is making will not require that the addressee pay money: "I am about to ask you a favor, one which, I hope will not cost you much" (51). His letter to John Addison on July 22, 1849, makes known his attempt to please his reader: "On the other half of this sheet is what I hope may be both satisfactory and serviceable to you" (59). Others begin similarly. His May 10, 1858, letter to Josiah M. Lucas both acknowledges receipt of the letter and begins thus: "Your long and kind letter was received today," using *kind* as a way of creating goodwill (Basler I:445). He does the same with John Mathers in a July 20, 1858, letter: "Your kind and interesting letter of the 19th was duly received" (Basler II:522). Lincoln varies the same opening a bit with a letter to Cassius Clay dated May 26, 1860: "Yours of the 21st is received, and for which I sincerely thank you" (Basler IV:53). In at least three letters, Lincoln employs a phrase that acts like a *benevolentia* without acknowledging receipt of a letter. For instance, in a March 18, 1861, letter to Salmon P. Chase, he begins: "I shall be obliged if you will inform me" (Basler IV:292). Likewise, his letter of the same day to Gideon Welles opens: "I shall be obliged if you will inform me" (Basler IV:293) A third letter of the same day, to Edward Bates, begins similarly: "I shall be obliged if you will give me your opinion" (Basler IV: 292).

But Lincoln also begins letters in a more modern manner by quickly stating the business at hand. Of course, some of the communication originates with Lincoln, and in these cases he is not answering a letter from the addressee; but for the most part, when he originates the communication, he makes little attempt to employ *benevolentia* as a way to build ethos in the opening in the letter and immediately gets to the overall purpose at hand. He may do so, one could argue, because he realizes that he can create the ethos he wishes to impart by being quite businesslike in not wasting the reader's time. For instance, a letter of December 25, 1848, to his best friend, Joshua Speed, begins: "While I was at Springfield last fall, Wm. Herndon showed me a couple of letters of yours concerning your note against Judge Browne" (Basler II:17). Another friend, Orville H. Browning, received a letter, dated June 5, 1851, that starts with this: "I reached home from the circuit yesterday, after an absence; hence your letter of May the 8th was not sooner answered" (Basler II:105). Even a letter to the wife of the same friend, Orville Browning, goes straight to the point: "Without appologising (*sic*) for being egotistical, I shall make the history of so much of my life, as has elapsed since I saw you, the subject of this letter" (Basler I:117).

The contemporary *Chesterfield's Letter-Writer* advises its readers to dispense with the niceties and to begin by stating the business: "When you sit down to write a letter, think of your subject—of the circumstances you wish to state" (1857, 9). Thus, while there are contemporaries who do begin their letters with expressions of goodwill, which Lincoln does on occasion, Lincoln, at the same time, also does not appear to be completely out of step with many writing letters in this time by not beginning with an obvious *benevolentia*.

The history of the letter in any period often includes a discussion of a large number of what might be called *types* of letters, some types that surprisingly stretch back as far as antiquity and still remain alive today. In particular, Stanley K. Stowers (1886, 142) tells his readers, "consolation was very important in the Greco-Roman world," so important that writing different genres of consolation was a part of the *progymnasmata* of young students of rhetoric. Progymnasmata are what Sean Patrick O'Rourke calls "a series of graduated rhetorical exercises common to the schools of Western and eastern Europe from the Roman republic through the Renaissance" (1996, 562). One exercise students tackled was expressing consolation in speeches, lyric poetry, and the letter of consolation.

Stowers (1886, 143) tells us letters of consolation were also important to the early Christians. St. Paul's first letter to the Thessalonians, for example, contains words of consolation (145), words, once again, that Lincoln no doubt would have read as a youngster while his reading the Bible so that they became a part of his experience with letters.

Since death is inevitable, it is not surprising that virtually every period in human history has felt the need to express sympathy to those mourning a loss of a loved one. Because of the universality of the grieving experience and the human response to that suffering, it follows that over the course of history, certain recurring patterns and themes would emerge. These patterns, as Stillar and Bourdieu contend, set up certain expectations from readers about what to expect in these types of letters, formats that writers often follow. In the end, the letter of consolation would exhibit particular formularies that readers would expect to see.

For instance, Stowers lists certain themes for the letter of consolation in early Christian writings. Not surprisingly, these common themes are, remarkably germane to any discussion of letters of this type in the past, as well as in Lincoln's time. According to Stowers, these themes include "a call to reason, the hope of the resurrection, exhortation to courage, the incomprehensibility of God's purposes, life as a loan, life as a journey, that all experience death, exhortation to emulate the deceased's virtue" (1986, 149). Of course, all letters of consolation don't necessarily contain all of these same themes, but many do draw from this long tradition. *Chesterfield's Letter-Writer,* for example, advises writers to employ "soothing language," "the hope of our blessed religion," "painful sensations," and attention to "the sufferer" as common themes of the letter of consolation. In fact, it seems that this second list from Chesterfield grows naturally out of the "commonplaces" Stowers mentions. Consequently, the "incomprehensibility of God's purpose," one of the recurrent themes Stowers mentions, appears to naturally correspond to the same theme that *Chesterfield's Letter-Writer* calls "the hope of our blessed religion" (1857, 49).

Obviously, the writer of the letter of consolation must also be quite concerned about the ethos projected in this type of missive. Indeed, this is no time for jokes or light-hearted humor, or giving the reader any chance to misinterpret the serious purpose of the letter. Very quickly, writers, if they are to be effective, have to establish that this is a serious duty. So, from the start, writers must also be acutely aware of the tone of the letter; that is, the seriousness with which the writer is approaching the subject. A letter that treats death in an inappropriate or jocose manner or maligns the deceased, for example, risks hurting the feelings of the reader at a most sensitive time. The letter-writing manuals also warn the writer that expressing sympathy requires the writer to be quite sensitive to the reader's grieving process, amid what is sometimes a very confusing time, filled with questions that often do not receive any satisfactory answers. Consequently, calls for courage amid the bewilderment are also very much a part of providing appropriate consolation to the bereaved, for the reader is often unsure of how to deal with the death of a loved one.

Writers of such letters must also compose shorter messages than are often required by other types of writing. If letters are too long and contain lengthy and tedious arguments, they are likely to try the patience of the reader during this sensitive period. All these warnings in mind, it is not surprising that one modern guide to letter writing, published in 1981, says what is probably true for all time: letters of condolence are "among the most difficult to write" (Watson 1948, 58).

While Lincoln wrote at least one other letter of condolence to Ephraim and Phoebe Ellsworth on May 25, 1861, probably the most famous letter of condolence ever written by any writer was Lincoln's letter of November 21, 1864, to the widow Lydia Bixby (Basler VIII:166–117). Jason Emerson, writing in *American Heritage* magazine, calls the letter "America's most famous letter" (2006, 41), while David Herbert Donald describes the letter as "beautiful" (1996, 567). An early biographer of Lincoln, William E. Barton, assessed the letter as written in a "noble and sympathetic spirit" (1925, 258), and Luther Emerson Robinson's *Abraham Lincoln as a Man of Letters* characterizes the Bixby letter as " this perfect gem of prose literature [which] must become a cherished personal possession to give one its full effect of lyric charm and excellence" (1923, 184). Harold Holzer in *Lincoln the Writer* echoes these same sentiments, calling the Bixby letter "so beautifully written" (2000, 84).

Even though there has been some tenuous controversy over the authorship of the letter, most scholars would agree with *The Abraham Encyclopedia* that while a few argue that Lincoln did not write the letter, "there is not a scrap of reliable evidence to prove it" (28–29). Roy Basler, editor of the *Collected Works*, says, "There is no reason to question the authenticity of the text of the letter which appeared in the [newspaper Boston] *Transcript* and other contemporary sources" (Basler VIII:116–117). The assumption herein is, then, that Lincoln is indeed the author of the letter.

Another controversy swirls around the fact that Mrs. Bixby didn't actually have five sons to die in the war, as Lincoln was told by the source he names in the letter; instead the widow lost just two sons in battle. *The Abraham Lincoln Encyclopedia*, however, quotes one journalist, F. Lauriston Bullard, who says that the "beauty of the letter is not destroyed by the fact that the premises were wrong" (Neely 1982, 29).

2. The Letter as Genre

With this background, it is obvious that the Bixby letter has gathered an extensive amount of attention, and much of the attention is about its aesthetic power as a letter. While such information about the effectiveness of the missive indicates that many readers think highly of its power, none of the writers quoted explain *how* the letter so gracefully accomplishes its mission as a letter of consolation. This generates some central questions: If the letter is as good as many say it is, what does Lincoln do as a writer to make it so good? And the parallel question: In reference to the traditional themes of the letter of consolation, what are some of the techniques Lincoln employs effectively to meet the reader's expectations for the letter of consolation? The history of the letter of consolation provides the foundation for one productive way of examining the Bixby letter by noting how carefully Lincoln follows the "commonplaces" for this type of letter, and another method of analysis helps understand how the letter generates its aesthetic power.

The text of the letter is short enough that the letter can be quoted in its entirety and serve as a reference point for the discussion that follows:

To Lydia Bixby
Executive Mansion
Washington,
November 21, 1864
Dear Madam,

I have been shown in the files of the War Department a statement of the Adjutant General of Massachusetts, that you are the mother of five sons who have died gloriously on the field of battle.

I feel how weak and fruitless must be any words of mine which should attempt to beguile you from the grief of a loss so overwhelming. But I cannot refrain from tendering to you the consolation that may be found in the thanks of the Republic they died to save.

I pray that our Heavenly Father may assuage you the anguish of your bereavement, and leave you only the cherished memory of the loved and lost, and the solemn pride that must be yours, to have laid so costly a sacrifice upon the altar of Freedom.

Yours very sincerely and respectfully, A. LINCOLN

First, how closely does Lincoln follow the formularies for the letter of consolation, and thereby live up to the expectations of his readers, as Stillar and Bourdieu suggest? Or to look at it still another way: Is some of the lavish praise for Lincoln's letter unwarranted because Lincoln was merely slavishly following a tradition for this type of letter, which had been around for more than two thousand years? Was he not the great innovator of the letter of consolation many have made him out to be?

In fact, the letter begins rather mundanely, stating how the president learned of the news that Mrs. Bixby had lost five sons in the war. In order to make sure Mrs. Bixby understands that he is speaking with authority and thereby helping to build an appropriate ethos for himself, Lincoln refers to a source that supposedly is believable in such matters: the adjutant general of Massachusetts. Apparently, Lincoln believes that he has cited an authoritative source and speaks from authority. Next, the clause that follows "that" in the same sentence ends with the first hint that the letter has an emotional edge to it: "died gloriously on the field of battle." The obvious insertion of pathos into the letter in that first sentence, which is also the first paragraph, then opens up the subject of the letter: the attempt at consolation on the writer's part in what could be called a reasonable manner, stating facts, citing authority, and then following that with a measure of taste and an appropriate amount of pathos. To be too emotional in the first sentence would blur the picture Lincoln wishes to paint of himself as speaking from authority and thereby possibly negate the ethos he wishes to transmit to his reader. Except for the pathos, the letter, therefore, begins cogently with one of the "commonplaces" Stowers mentions: a "call to reason," an assurance that Lincoln has "the facts" (1986, 144). In this way, the "call to reason" also effectively establishes the ethos of the writer and establishes the writer as not a blithering idiot. He is someone who regards the widow's loss as a serious matter, a loss well worth the writer's studied response, but, at the same time, he inserts enough pathos into the same sentence to allow the widow to see the writer as not necessarily a slave to reason, either.

The next sentence inserts the idea of the "incomprehensibility of God's purpose," another "commonplace." Since one of the characteristics of God is his omnipotence and omniscience, concepts perhaps beyond the understanding of mortals, unused to the exercise of such power and insight, the writer's words, as a mortal, are, then, by comparison, in Lincoln's words, "weak and fruitless." Human beings are weak and limited in their understanding; while God is all powerful and all knowing. Consequently, God would have the words, but Lincoln as a human being admits that he does not. Lincoln's use of the phrase "Heavenly Father" later in the letter helps to tie together the reference to theology at this point in the letter, a reminder of God's inscrutable ways. Not fully understanding the ways of God, Lincoln thus tells the reader that his words would fail and be unsuccessful at freeing her from her "overwhelming" "grief," even if he tried, curiously, to "beguile" her.

Using the online word search options available through the University of Michigan corpus indicates that this is the only time the word "beguile" appears in *The Collected Works*, including all genres, from speeches to lectures, in any written forms. It seems to be a curious choice of words, to say the least. Webster's 1828 dictionary, published in Lincoln's lifetime, says the word's first definition is "to delude; to deceive; to impose on by artifice or craft" and uses a response Eve makes in the book of Genesis to illustrate the definition of the word in use: "The serpent beguiled me and I did eat," seemingly packing the word with pejorative connotations and associating the word with the incarnation of evil itself. At this point, the choice of the word in Lincoln's letter seems unusual indeed, especially in a letter of consolation. The same dictionary, however, cites a second definition: "To elude any thing disagreeable by amusement, or other means." The word "beguile" in all its definitions except this one seems to be a poor choice, for he certainly does not want Mrs. Bixby to see him as some sort of trickster who will "trick" her out of her grief.

In other words, then, Lincoln appears to be saying that he realizes that even a letter from the president of the United States, the commander-in-chief of the armed forces, with all his human power, cannot relieve Mrs. Bixby's all-consuming "grief," acting, again, as a kind of reaffirmation of the theme of mortal weakness expressed just a few words before. Lincoln seems therefore to reassure her of the genuine intent in the letter, and reinforces the idea that he is not trying to "deceive her" in any way.

That meaning seems to fit with the idea in the next sentence. In this sentence, Lincoln uses another "commonplace" from the letter of consolation, offering Mrs. Bixby a way to acquire "courage," by assuring her that her sons have died for a worthy cause: "the Republic they tried to save." In other words, she can gain a measure of courage to go on, and at the same time, a degree of consolation, knowing her sons died for an acceptable and good reason: in defense of their country. Dying for a worthy cause therefore consoles her and provides her with the bravery and assurance to go on with her life.

The next paragraph illustrates still another of the "commonplaces": "the hope of the resurrection." In the letter, Lincoln tells Mrs. Bixby that God will indeed help relieve her sorrow, or as he says, "assuage the anguish of [her] bereavement"; but besides those ways that Lincoln has already cited, he prays that God will lessen Mrs. Bixby's grief in still another way:

by the knowledge that her sons have been transformed into a new life in the form of a "cherished memory of the loved and lost."

Lincoln then says that he hopes that God's incomprehensibility and grace, once again, will include leaving her with still another kind of life after death. Her sons, then, have obtained both an afterlife in "Heaven" and an afterlife in her "cherished memory of the loved and lost," aided and deepened by her "solemn pride."

In a very effective metaphor, the letter closes with the "commonplace" that "life is a loan." In Lincoln's mind, her sons have taken that "loan" and converted it into "a sacrifice" placed then on an altar, particularly, "the altar of Freedom"; thus, in the last words of the body of the letter, subtly tying her sacrifice to other sacrifices, presumably those familiar sacrifices described in the Bible, and perhaps including what Christians see as the ultimate sacrifice: Christ's being offered as a sacrifice for the redemption of humankind.

In *Rhetoric in the Middle Ages,* James Murphy notes that the conclusion of any medieval letter should bring "together in a small space [the matters discussed in the letter] and are thus impressed on the recipient's memory" (2001, 223). In other words, the matters discussed in the letter should be summarized to some degree. But the letter writer should also do so in such a way as to make the matters memorable. One way of making the ending of the letter memorable is to use a kind of rhetorical flourish to act as a climax to the letter. At the end of the Bixby letter, Lincoln follows in the same track by using an apt metaphor with strong theological implications, by fulfilling the purpose of the conclusion that Murphy describes, not only highlighting the major themes of the letter, but by also bringing it to an end in a pleasing and unforgettable way: laying "a sacrifice upon the altar of Freedom." The metaphor that ends Lincoln's letter seems particularly effective because it not only encapsulates the sense of the letter but does so in a memorable way.

The all-important ethos Demetrius talks about in the letter is virtually complete. Lincoln comes away from the letter as being reasonable, God-fearing, kind, sympathetic, caring, in language memorable and appropriate to the situation, language some may describe as "elegaic."

All that is left in completing the letter is the complimentary closing, but Lincoln is careful about what he uses, because it has to reinforce the ethos he has sought to build throughout the letter. If his complimentary closing is too friendly, it could damage the important power of the ethos he has built so far in the letter.

Lincoln uses a variety of closings in his letters. For example, in his collected letters, he uses "Most sincerely, your friend" as a complimentary close one time in a letter to William Seward, his secretary of state, but such a closing seems hardly appropriate in this letter of consolation, since Lincoln is not in reality Mrs. Bixby's friend; he is her president. Lincoln also uses "Very truly" 982 times in his letters, by far his most used complimentary closing, but the careful writer that he is, that closing doesn't seem to be quite formal enough for the letter to Mrs. Bixby. A popular complimentary closing of the day was "Your obedient servant," a closing that Lincoln actually uses 31 times, but once again, that closing doesn't have the ring of dignity to it necessary for the Bixby letter. In other letters, he uses other closings, but a minimum number of times: "Yours sincerely," three times, "Very sincerely yours," two times, "Very sincerely yours, your obedient servant," just once. In fact, most of his memoranda issued while he was president have no complimentary closings at all, just "A. Lincoln." Yet none of these closings have the formality and dignity of the complimentary closing he uses only once in his letters, and that in fact in the Bixby letter: "Very sincerely and respectfully," a closing that shows both reverence and sincerity, themes built upon in the rest of the letter. At the same time, it also exudes an appropriate consideration for the addressee and her loss.

By contrast, another letter of consolation Lincoln wrote to Ephraim and Phoebe Ellsworth presented an entirely different situation, since Lincoln actually knew the Ellsworths' son, Elmer Ellsworth, a soldier in the Union army killed in battle. So it was more appropriate for Lincoln to close that letter with "Sincerely, your friend with common affliction," a closing that reflects obviously more familiarity with the addressees; but since, of course, he did not know Mrs. Bixby nor any of her sons, "Very sincerely and respectfully" seems, in Lincoln's later words, "fitting and proper" (Basler IV:385–386).

While all this minutiae about complimentary closings may seem pedantic, it serves a real purpose: it underscores the idea that Lincoln was aware of his audience and the conventions of the letter of consolation, and he chose his closings accordingly. It also shows his refined sense of taste and appropriateness, a theme that runs through Hugh Blair's treatise on rhetoric. By all indications, Lincoln apparently understood that complimentary closings were the last words, besides his signature, that the reader would see. Such closings, then, would be an integral part of the ethos he created in the body of letter.

Thus far, this analysis demonstrates that Lincoln has rather carefully followed the long tradition of "commonplaces" for the letter of consolation. In the Bixby letter, Lincoln projects the ethos of being reasonable, invokes God's mercy, offers reasons for courage and hope, alludes to life after death for Mrs. Bixby's sons, and acknowledges their sacrifice. In almost every way, Lincoln has met society's expectations for this type of letter. In those ways, as far as Stiller and Bourdieu are concerned, the letter has been a success in giving the reader what society expects the letter of consolation to be. But, of course, and surely Stiller and Bourdieu would agree, merely following an established form does not make a letter especially memorable, or at least as memorable as this letter is said to be. Surely, there are other ways to get at what makes this letter so different from the thousands of maudlin expressions of consolation that also follow the "commonplaces" that readers expect, but that are not particularly memorable and lack the status given the Bixby letter.

One other item must be factored into the equation in order to fully understand the context of the letter. Any discussion of the Bixby letter must also include a reference to the role of *kairos* in the presentation of the letter, because Lincoln's acute political sensitivities told him that other people at that time of the United States' greatest crisis, the Civil War, needed to understand what was said in the missive. To reiterate a definition of the difficult concept, James Kinneavy points out that kairos refers to "the appropriateness of the discourse to the particular circumstances of the time, place, speaker, and audience involved" (Kinneavy 1996, 213), and Lincoln appeared to understand the concept at least unconsciously, perhaps, at first, as a matter of good politics, for the personal letter to the widow was not just disseminated to Mrs. Bixby. Indeed, the text of the letter was sent to two newspapers, *The Transcript* and the *Advertiser*, in her own Boston, and it was published one day (a matter of hours) after Mrs. Bixby herself received her copy of the letter. Subsequently, the letter was distributed to the *Army and Navy Journal* in New York City, a few days later on December 3, 1864, and it was later published elsewhere (Barton 1926, 44).

But it would be a mistake to see this tactic as merely a case where a shrewd politician used a letter to a bereaving widow for political gain. Roger Thompson has aptly pointed out that in the United States, the concept of kairos acquired, in addition to its accepted meaning, an uniquely spiritual flavor to it, something beyond what it had meant to Athens or

Rome. The American essayist, poet, and philosopher Ralph Waldo Emerson, in particular, as Thompson notes, "calls upon America's sense of kairos, its cultural mission to be the new *spiritual* leader of the world" (italics added) (Thompson 2002, 187). Thompson continues: "In terms of American literature, kairos involves a sense of fulfillment of divine promise and the mission to enact that prophesied promise" (189). In other words, in the United States, kairos was a concept inextricably linked to what Thompson calls "a sense of divine urgency and right" (192). But as Thompson sees it, this new definition of kairos, as articulated by Emerson in "The Divinity School Address" and "The American Scholar" speech, was not limited to just Emerson. Lincoln also exhibited in the case of the Emancipation Proclamation, for instance, a sense of "proper timing and propriety and moves the American state toward transcendental principles" (194). Although Lincoln did not use the term kairos, he seemed to understand the concept, observing that the Emancipation Proclamation, for example, was indeed an extraordinary event. He said to his best friend, Joshua Speed, who related it to others, at the issuance of the edict that he wanted "to connect his name with the events transpiring in his day and generation and so impress himself upon them." Lincoln then said to Speed, "I believe that in this measure [the Emancipation Proclamation] my fondest hopes will be realized" (Klingaman 2001, 239).

Consequently, Thompson summarizes, "the American kairos is a moment not just when the eternal breaks into the temporal, but when the temporal individual invokes the eternal in order to transcend his [or her] realm" (2002, 195), a "kairotic tradition that sees America on the cusp of fulfillment of divine promise" (196), or as Lincoln so aptly called it in his address to Congress, "the last best hope of earth." Lincoln seemed to acutely understand that in writing his letter of consolation to Mrs. Bixby and distributing it to the press he was at what might be called an important kairotic moment. To him, this was a unique opportunity, one he had best not let pass by, and one he wisely chose to share with the American people. By relating this moment to the American people by sending copies of the letter to newspapers, he deftly demonstrated how important he understood that crucial moment to be.

Feeling that divine sense, it is not surprising that Lincoln links the loss of Mrs. Bixby's five sons not just to the throes of a civil war and the idea of the ultimate sacrifice for one's country, a concept employed by most governments to honor their fallen soldiers; he also gave the "sacrifice" an added level of spiritual meaning, one encoded into a very appropriate religious metaphor: an "altar," what Lincoln, in particular, calls the "altar of freedom." In that way, Lincoln gives the "sacrifice" an added transcendental meaning, one, as Thompson explains it, in keeping with a unique American interpretation of the concept of kairos. In this sense, the letter is not just a well-written letter of consolation, a crafty piece of prose employing lively verbs and filled with catchy alliteration and solemn rhythms on a somber theme, written during a crucial time in American history. It is most certainly all those things. But it also suggests how Lincoln took the American sense of kairos and employed it expertly in one of the world's greatest letters.

Another productive way of looking at the Bixby letter is to look at certain "facts" about the letter that provide some insight into the nature of the letter. These are simple statistics that illustrate that there are broad differences between the Bixby letter of consolation and the Ellsworth letter of consolation. For example, the Bixby letter has 48.8 percent of the number of words as the Ellsworth letter. In other words, the Bixby letter is less than half as long as the Ellsworth letter. Part of that discrepancy could be because Lincoln knew Ephraim and Phoebe Ellsworth and their son, the subject of the letter. Lincoln, according to this reasoning, would have more to say to the family. On another note, the Bixby letter averages 32 words per sentence, while the Ellsworth figure is a mere 20 words per sentence. I found that modern sales promotion letters average 16.7 words per sentence (Myers 1999, 407), suggesting that the Ellsworth letter comes closer to the modern figure, and that the Bixby letter has nearly twice that figure. One can only speculate that the formal tone of the Bixby letter contributed to this discrepancy between the sentence lengths, since formal writing tends to have longer sentences than more informal writing. Because Lincoln did not know Mrs. Bixby, and the occasion called for solemnity, he assumed a more formal tone. While it is nearly impossible to tie writing quality to any of these figures, the figures do suggest that there were large differences in certain categories between the Bixby letter and the Ellsworth letter.

Two qualities stand out about the Bixby letter. First is its careful obedience to the "commonplaces" of the letter of condolence tradition, so that the reader of the letter well understands that Lincoln is, indeed, following the customary form of such a letter, and the reader gets what she expects. Second, in writing the letter, apparently aware of kairos, Lincoln is extremely careful to project an appropriate ethos, for if the personality of the writer that seeps through his prose is not in consonance with an appropriate tone, the letter loses much of its effectiveness.

Other qualities of the Bixby letter that make it particularly effective could include the short length of the letter, a fact that relates to its nature as a genre. Private letters, generally, are relatively short rhetorical artifacts, usually only a few hundred words long. At a mere 134 words in length, the Bixby letter does not require the reader to spend an inordinate amount of time actually reading the letter and feeling its effect, nothing like what a short story, novel, play, or even an essay would require of the reader.

In literary terms, the Bixby resembles an elegy, what *The Bedford Glossary of Literary Terms* defines as "reflective poems that lament the loss of something or someone (or loss or death more generally)" (Murfin 1997, 102). While some elegies have slightly more words than the Bixby letter—"Lycidas" and "Elegy Written in a Country Churchyard," for example—the language of the Bixby letter and its treatment of death as a theme often soars to the level of poetry. James Channing Briggs in *Lincoln's Speeches Reconsidered* underlines this same idea, noting, "The internal arrangement and sequence of the Bixby letter flawlessly convey an unaffected sublimity" (2005, 332).

One more element, of a minor nature, perhaps, needs noting. Besides the customary capitalization given to the first words in the sentences and to "Heavenly Father," Lincoln also capitalizes two other words: "Republic" and "Freedom." Lincoln's intent seems to be to emphasize the two words by simply writing them in the upper case, an obvious clue to the reader that the two words are important, for they are not ordinarily capitalized in such positions in the sentence. Their position at or near the end of the sentence also adds to their emphases. Lincoln appears, then, to be using capitalization and word positioning as tools in his overall rhetorical strategy in the letter.

A rhetorical analysis of this important letter thus helps readers to understand the complex nature of one the world's most admired letters by focusing closely on the rhetorical elements that give the letter the power it had and still has today.

Evidence also suggests that Lincoln displayed the ability to effectively compose something in letter form similar to another kind of rhetorical genre: the *philippic*. Unfortunately, though, many dictionaries fail to provide a detailed description of this type of speech and use only one-word synonyms and short phrases like "a tirade" and "a harsh, often insulting verbal denunciation" (*American Heritage Dictionary*). Another echoes the first: "A discursive or declamation full of bitter condemnation; a tirade" (*Webster's Ninth New Collegiate Dictionary*). A third dictionary reads: "Any speech or discourse of bitter denunciation" (*Webster's New Universal Unabridged Dictionary*). In addition, all three dictionaries correctly tie the philippic to orations delivered by the Greek orator Demosthenes against Philip of Macedon; or the speeches of the Roman orator, Cicero, against Mark Antony, but these same sources go no farther than just to note the relationship between the two classic orators to the term.

But while these definitions are somewhat helpful in arriving at a rudimentary understanding of the philippic as a rhetorical genre, they are just a bare-bones outline of this unique type of speech. Curiously, even handbooks and encyclopedias of rhetoric offer little assistance in further delineating the definition. The *Encyclopedia of Rhetoric*, the *Encyclopedia of Rhetoric and Composition, Sourcebook on Rhetoric*, and Richard Lanham's *A Handlist of Rhetorical Terms* leave the researcher with the only alternative of devising his own definition by carefully studying the philippics of Demosthenes and Cicero in order to reach a fuller understanding of this particular type of speech.

What strikes the reader first after studying the philippics of these two classical orators is that unlike the uncontrolled tirade of Pap in *The Adventures of Huckleberry Finn* (Twain 1965, 26–27), for example, and while quite impassioned, the philippics of these famous orators are not quite so bombastic that readers could readily imagine the two consummate orators flailing their arms, shouting at the top of their lungs, and gesturing in a broad and fiery fashion—an emotional appeal that Richard Lanham lists as *bdelygma* (1991, 86). In fact, most of these two orators' philippics begin by methodically creating the appropriate ethos for the speakers by ingratiating themselves to the audience, and then often follow that with the presentation of a rather careful and often well-reasoned argument to explain why they feel the way they do toward their political enemies, Philip of Macedon and Mark Antony, respectively.

That is not to say, that the typical philippic doesn't also contain some harsh and vigorous rhetoric not usually present in other types of oratory. For example, characteristically, philippics do employ name calling, as Demosthenes does in his "Third Philippic" when he characterizes Philip as a "barbarian" (1970, 251), or when Cicero in his "Philippic VII" calls

Antony "a worthless man" and "unscrupulous" (1938, 239), a kind of *argumentum ad hominem* (Lanham1991, 191). Similar tactics are also employed. Cicero, for instance, uses biting sarcasm, what Lanham labels as *sarcasmus* (187), to accuse Antony of wanting to control more territory, a notion that Cicero bitterly characterizes as "Very fine! so that from it he may attempt to march to the city, not merely legions, but even nation" (239).

Yet much more common to the philippic than name calling and sarcasm are frequent attempts to use certain stylistic features that in themselves create much of the philippic's rhetorical power. One of such tactics is the effective use of the rhetorical question. Demosthenes in the "Third Philippic" asks (233), "But, in heaven's name, is there any intelligent man who would let words rather than deeds decide the question who is at peace and who is at war with him?" Cicero makes use of this same device in "Philippic I" when he asks about the tactics of the conniving Antony (51), "On what day was the Senate more joyful? on what day was the Roman people which was never at any public assembly gathered in greater numbers?"

Demosthenes and Cicero use still other persuasive strategies in their philippics. One employed frequently is to point out how the enemy is using an accepted aphorism to justify a particular course of action, followed by the orators showing the audience how disingenuous the enemy really is in his use of that aphorism, a tactic usually labeled *argumentum ad verecundiam* (Lanham 1991, 192). In his "First Philippic," for example, Demosthenes announces that "Philip saw clearly that *all these outposts were but the prizes of war, that by natural right of property of the absent belongs to those who are on the spot*" (italics added) and Demosthenes, then, craftily points out how diabolically clever Philip is when he turns the aphorism on its head for his oratorical purposes (71).

Also present in the philippics of both men are passages that prove highly emphatic by repeating an important word and hammering away at an important idea, commonly called *palilogia* (Lanham 1991, 191). Demosthenes, for example, in his "Third Philippic" repeats "something" to drive home a point: "There is *something*, men of Athens, *something* which animated the mass of Greeks, but is lacking now, *something* which triumphed the wealth of Persia…, *something* the decay of which has ruined everything and brought our affairs to a state of chaos" (1970, 245) (italics added). Cicero's "Philippic VII" adds an interesting twist on this tactic by combining a rhetorical question and repetition. Speaking of Antony, he says: "If he did do that for sport, what do you think he will do for the sake of loot? *Will he not* again place rascals on the jury panels? *Will he not* gain canvass those hungry for land? *Will he not* bewail those evicted?" (1938, 351) (italics added).

One last prominent characteristic of the philippic in Demosthenes and Cicero is syntactic repetition, employed when the authors repeat a short clause with the same syntactical patterns, which Lanham (1991, 191) lists as *isocolon*. In some cases, the two orators also repeat the same word. Demosthenes, for instance, in his "First Philippic" (1970, 73), says, "God willing, *you will recover your own, you will restore what has been frittered away, and you will turn the tables on Philip*" (italics added). Likewise, Cicero's "Philippic VI" (1938, 321) contains, "*I know his violence, I know his impudence, I know his audacity*," and then finishes the sentence with an emphatic use of name calling: "In truth we ought not to think of him as a human being, but as a most outrageous *beast*" (italics added).

These characteristics of the philippic, then, attempt to go beyond just defining the term with a synonym or a short phrase and hopefully suggest a more adequate and detailed foundation for examining, surprisingly, one of Lincoln's letters as a kind of crude philippic.

The letter is addressed to Lincoln's stepbrother, John D. Johnston (Basler II:15–17), an apparent ne'er-do-well who has plans on leaving his Illinois home and heading out to Missouri, evidently for a "better life." The content of the letter has a "Dutch uncle talk" aspect, as Lincoln severely chastises Johnston with, at times, bitter recriminations not unlike the qualities outlined above for the philippic. In fact, most of the tactics used by Demosthenes and Cicero appear in Lincoln's letter.

For example, Lincoln resorts to very harsh accusations about Johnston's character. Lincoln calls Johnston's plan to move to Missouri "utterly foolish," and then repeats the word in another form, calling the "notion" "a piece of foolery," ultimately advising him to "face the truth—which truth is, you are destitute because you have idled away all your time." Lincoln goes on: "Your thousand pretenses for not getting along better, are all nonsense [sic]."

Lincoln uses other elements similar to those present in philippics. For example, Lincoln employs a generous portion of sarcasm in dealing with Johnston. He tells Johnston that he will "never ... own a spot big enough to bury you in." Earlier in the letter, he reminds Johnston that "if you intend to go to work, there is no better place than right where you are," charging Johnston with "squirming & crawling about from place...." Lincoln also employs a number of rhetorical questions one right after another, heightening their rhetorical power by their repetition and at the same time lacing them with an additional measure of sarcasm: "What can you do in Missouri, better than here? Is the land any richer? Can you there, any more than here, raise corn, & wheat & oats, without work? Will any body there, any more than here, do your work for you?" In addition, Lincoln, like his classical counterparts, employs the repetition of certain key words and syntactic constructions to reinforce the message he imparts to Johnston. For example, as already noted, he uses a second form of the word "fool" but also couples it with a repetition of the word "feel" to produce: "Now I *feel* it is my duty to have no hand in such a piece of *foolery* [Johnston's plan to move to Missouri]. I *feel* that it is so even on your own account" (italics added). Later, he repeats the phrase "will rent" in reference to supporting Johnston's mother and Lincoln's beloved stepmother: "It *will rent* for enough to support her—at least it *will rent* for something" (italics added). Toward the end of the letter, Lincoln repeats the phrase "write it": "I do not *write it* [the letter] in any unkindness. I *write it*, in order, if possible, to get you to face the truth..." (italics added). Earlier in the letter, Lincoln repeats a whole sentence pattern, using two complex clauses in a row, both beginning with "if": "*If* you intend to go to work, there is no better place than right where you are; *if* you do not intend to go to work, you *can not* get along anywhere" (italics added). Surely Lincoln leaves little doubt about how he feels about Johnston's character.

When examining this letter closely, it is sometimes difficult to imagine that the Lincoln ethos most Americans associate with "The Rail-Splitter" is contained in lines like those of his Second Inaugural Address, "With malice toward none, with charity for all" (Basler VIII:332–333), lines offering tender treatment even of the country's enemies. But the expert rhetor that he was also reminds us that good rhetoricians, should the situation demand it—and apparently Lincoln felt it did—can make full use of all the tools of persuasion in their toolbox, even sarcasm and what appears to be the obvious manifestations of his own anger and frustration with his aimless stepbrother. Not surprisingly then, not seeing the benefit of such a strategy that coddles his stepbrother, Lincoln closes the letter with no tender and honeyed words of encouragement, telling Johnston: "Go to work is the only cure for your case." Like Demosthenes and Cicero, Lincoln leaves little doubt about how he feels about the person who is the object of his derision, and like his Greek and Roman counterparts, his letter convinces readers even now of what Lincoln sees as the absolute necessity of detailing the character flaws of his indolent stepbrother.

Obviously, there are many other Lincoln letters, and, in fact, Lincoln writes many other types of letters that could be examined using the present methodology. There are love letters to Mary Owens and Mary Todd, letters of admonition to General Joseph Hooker, letters of friendship to Joshua Speed, letters with traces of satire, and letters with a subtle edge of frustration to them, just to name a few, that could benefit from careful examination using the above strategies. But the methodology displayed in this brief examination of two of Lincoln's letters should make clear the great need to look at more of Lincoln's letters to understand better his rhetorical power in this often forgotten type of artifact. With the extensive treatment of Lincoln's major speeches by a number of scholars, the letters, then, remain a part of Lincoln's rhetorical canon that demand attention, for even read after more than 170 years, the letters Lincoln wrote still have an impressive immediacy about them that provides unrealized opportunities to study one person communicating with others. For letters in general, no matter their age, and no matter the person, a distinct voice even yet rises silently from the page.

But there are still other ways to use the power of rhetoric to characterize Lincoln's letters. Some of those ways will be the subjects of the chapters that follow.

3

Influences on Lincoln's Writing Style[1]

That Abraham Lincoln was, among other things, a master prose stylist is a commonplace in almost all circles of American life.[2] Millions of young people in every generation since the Gettysburg Address have learned that short speech by heart and made those stirring words a part of their national memories. Scholars today agree about Lincoln's literary skills. Garry Wills (1992, 20) in his Pulitzer Prize–winning book on the same speech concludes that the "power of words has rarely been given a more compelling demonstration," calling the famous address "a revolution in style" (148). One of America's most highly respected early twentieth century social and literary critics, Edmund Wilson, says of Lincoln's writing: "[It] is certain that very few American writers or speakers wield their native language with [such] directness, precision, and force" (1962, 641). Current Civil War historian Charles Roland concludes in his classic *The American Iliad* that "through his masterful use of the English language [Lincoln] communicate[d] his goals and methods to the people" (1991, xi). Another Civil War contemporary historian, Mark Neely, observes that Lincoln "carefully shaped his words in public letters, papers, and proclamations meant to explain the purpose of the war and to inspire devotion to it" (1993, 153). Similarly, highly respected critic Jacques Barzun concludes that one "does not need to be a literary man to see that Lincoln was a born writer" (1971, 60). Kenneth Cmiel, in his study of nineteenth century rhetoric, *Democratic Eloquence*, uses words like powerful, dignity, and sincerity to describe Lincoln's writing (1990, 120). Contemporary historian James McPherson in *Abraham Lincoln and the Second American Revolution* even goes as far as to say that "Lincoln won the war with metaphors" and that Lincoln's "ability to communicate the meaning and purpose"

The Rhetoric of Lincoln's Letters

of the war "in an intelligible, inspiring manner [...] helped energize and mobilize [...] people to make the sacrifices necessary for victory," in direct contrast to the platitude-spouting of his rival Jefferson Davis (1991, 93–94). Thus these sources all indicate that Lincoln was a masterful stylist.

But how did a man who admits to having less than one year's schooling acquire such rhetorical power and grace? Surely we are dealing with a great and keen mind, a mind able to read and study on his own and master everything from Euclidian geometry, to surveying, and to law, and to develop a keen fascination with Shakespeare's tragedies along the way. But that hardly explains the remarkable ability Lincoln possessed to blend sound and sense in such a way as to bring such majesty to American prose—even today.

Unfortunately, when scholars examine Lincoln's manuscripts themselves for clues to understand his composing processes, they are likely to be frustrated because, as Webb Garrison notes, "no one knows with certainty what Lincoln [...] meant when he underlined a word or phrase" (1993, xii). Garrison goes on to say that the original manuscripts of Lincoln's speeches "consist of brief phrases, punctuated with abbreviations that are meaningless to the modern reader" (54). David Herbert Donald, two-time winner of the Pulitzer Prize for biography, does discuss the written suggestions that Secretary of State William Seward made for the First Inaugural Address and Lincoln's subsequent use of them, but an extended written record of Lincoln's revision strategies is seemingly not available (1996, 283–84). As we shall see later, what we do know about his writing habits we gather not from his written records but from clues from those who observed him in the actual process of writing.

While most scholars and biographers are quick to note Lincoln's reading as the greatest influence on his writing—certainly an influence that cannot be discounted—there has been an incomplete discussion of a whole series of considerations that directly influenced Lincoln's writing. These considerations include a lack of the sentimentality so common to his contemporaries, the changing linguistic environment that led to the acceptance of the "plain style," his utter fascination with language, his self-education that included learning protocols much like those of ancient Greek and Roman rhetors, a bevy of important stylistic influences both from his wide reading and from rhetorician Hugh Blair, a leaner prose that showed the influence of the telegraph, and efficient composing habits that emphasized the acquisition of an appropriate voice for speaking and writing. Thus by drawing on a number of sources on Lincoln's acquisition of composing skills, by understanding the historical stylistic views at work at the time, and by offering new insights into Lincoln's quest to be an effective writer and speaker, we can go beyond the mere mention of the usual one or two most-cited influences and offer a comprehensive survey based on a synthesis of the thinking of other theorists in the field of Lincoln's writing and my own careful examination of the evidence. Such a study can more fully explore how Lincoln became the writer he was and tell a richer story than has been told until now, a more accurate and more complete story that would help us better understand Lincoln the writer and offer insights into a creative mind that could serve as a model for others learning to write and speak.

Part of the reason Lincoln's words seem so modern to today's readers is that Lincoln did not express himself in as sentimental a style as that of his age. Edwin Black in *Rhetorical Questions* notes that in the sentimental style of the nineteenth century "[n]o scintilla of reaction is left for the auditor's [that is, listener's or reader's] own reaction; every nuance of effect is regulated by the speech" (1992, 101). While popular orators such as Daniel Webster might pile on heartrending images with generous amounts of figures that "tear passion to tatters," Lincoln understood that effective emotional appeal suggests "ambiguity, but it is ambiguity of a special kind. [...] Lincoln gives the auditor the boundaries of experience, but requires the auditor's own invention of it" (Black 101, 103). In other words, Black says, "One of the reasons that Webster's style now seems archaic to us while we can continue to admire Lincoln's is that Lincoln's discourses are less overtly manipulative" (102). In the end, because Lincoln's prose

Lincoln in his younger days. He quickly realized that writing letters was a way to learn the craft of writing.

lacks the gooey sentimentalism of his age, his writing takes on a modern, less offensive approach to sentimentalism that strikes the modern ear as more palatable.

Another important reason that Lincoln's words ring so eloquently is that his writing style sits in the beginning of a great movement in literary style commonly called the "plain style," a stylistic movement that began in this country in Puritan seventeenth century New England and, according to Richard Bridgman in *The Colloquial Style in America*, reached its apex in Ernest Hemingway in the early twentieth century (1966, 62). A relatively rapid and far-reaching movement in the evolution of American prose style, the "plain style," as Bridgman notes, represented a change in attitudes toward written language that came as a result of a number of different factors, circumstances that surely affected how Lincoln and some of his contemporaries wrote and how Lincoln approached language in written form.

Bridgman says, for example, that the mid-nineteenth century saw some profound changes in speech and writing style because of such factors as strong nationalism, individualism, and what Bridgman calls "practical necessity" (1966, 41). Americans believed in the union that formed the United States: its mission, in other words, its manifest destiny, and, of course, its variety of speakers. They also held sacred the rights of individuals to assert themselves as individuals because the trends in immigration produced a great variety of people who spoke variants of English in an American setting that, in turn, generated new words and expressions and fostered a tolerance of differences in speech. As Bridgman makes obvious, these various strands of dialect interwove British English with all its fineries of speech with the many (and oftentimes substandard) forms into what became very much like the "plain style" (62). Interestingly, Bridgman notes, "The New England Yankees moved to the Northwest, bringing their dialects with them, and Southerners went to the old Southwest. The two met and fused in the middle grounds of Tennessee, Kentucky, Illinois, Indiana, and Missouri" to form what Bridgman calls "this great synthetic central dialect" (61). Lincoln, of course, was born in Kentucky, grew up in Indiana, and then established himself as an adult in central Illinois, a resident, then, of three of the four states mentioned. Plus, at this time, as Kenneth Winkle notes in *The Young Eagle*, Illinois represented a cosmopolitan mixture of settlers from the upper South, lower South, the Midlands, and those called Yankees (2001, 25). It was in this rich mix of varieties of speech that Lincoln came into his intellectual own. Consequently, it would seem that Lincoln's dialect would represent this "compromise speech," the result of a melding of various speech forms, or this "plain style."

Even though Lincoln occasionally exhibits a rhetorical flourish as he so expertly does in both the Gettysburg Address and his Second Inaugural Address, his writing mirrors the plain style, which does, in part, account for the popularity of his writing. Ronald White in *Lincoln's Greatest Speech* notes, for example, that the tone and flavor of Lincoln's Second Inaugural Address has much of the "Puritans of New England" about it (2002, 151). In other words, one of the reasons that Lincoln's writing sounds so good to us is that he writes in a style that we are familiar with. Though Lincoln wrote two hundred years later, Perry Miller's description of the seventeenth century New England "plain style," which became the basis for the later movement, aptly describes those characteristics common to Lincoln's writing:

> [T]he guiding principle was the assurance that content is more important than form, that the essence of any composition was the doctrinal handling of the text, and that style was a secondary concern, a dress or an ornament, that could be varied to suit times and places, that could be furnished with more or less rhetoric, that could be ornamented with many or with a few tropes, the only universal requirement being that the eloquence must not interfere with the major purpose [1954, 354].

Yet Lincoln's propensity to write in the plain style, for which he received ample amounts of criticism from the press, according to Ronald White (2002, 50), only explains the tradition out of which his writing came. And while it accounts for a stylistic zeitgeist, it does not completely answer our original query: How did Lincoln learn to write so well? Were there other considerations that affected how he spoke and wrote?

The young Lincoln realized that he would have to make the most of his limited classroom experience. If he wanted to acquire more knowledge and skills, he had to do so by reading and teaching himself, whether it be mathematics or history or writing, or anything else. To him reading was the key; without that skill he would be just another young man in search of a way to make it in the world. As a result, he could use reading as a method of satisfying his seemingly unquenchable thirst for learning even more about his world. For he knew that he would be strapped to a dismal life clinging to the land and what it grudgingly would yield. And he knew he didn't want that. Neighbor Nat Grisby is reported to have said about young Lincoln's rural way of life: "His father taught him to work, but he never learned to love it" (Winkle 2001, 75).

Consequently, at apparently an early age, he acquired an important attitude: an early and abiding understanding of the nature and purpose of language. He once told his law partner William Herndon that when he was a child, he would listen carefully to the conversations of adults to see if he could pick up any new words. He said, then,

> [A]mong my earliest recollections I remember how, when a mere child, I used to get irritated when anybody talked to me in a way I couldn't understand. I do not think I ever got angry at anything else in my life; but that always disturbed my temper; and has ever since.
>
> I can remember going up to my little bedroom after hearing the neighbors talk of an evening with my father, and spending no small part of the night walking up and down trying to make out what was the exact meaning of some of their, to me, dark sayings.
>
> I could not sleep when I got on such a hunt for an idea until I caught it[;] I was not satisfied until I repeated it over and over until I had put it in the language plain enough, as I thought, for any boy I knew to comprehend.
>
> This was a kind of passion for me, and it stuck by me; for I am never easy now when I am handling a thought till I have bounded it east, and bounded it west [Lang 1965, 11].

In *Simple and Direct: A Rhetoric for Writers*, Jacques Barzun speaks about this fundamental need to be fascinated with words to become an effective writer:

> [T]he price of learning to use words is the development of an acute self-consciousness. Nor is it enough to pay attention to words only when you face the task of writing—that is like playing the violin only on the night of the concert. You must attend to words when you speak, when other speak. Words must become ever present in your waking life, an incessant concern [1975, 3].

This curiosity about language, this love for words in books, stayed with Lincoln his entire life. In fact, in 1859 he gave a lecture in Springfield, Illinois, around February 22, in which he spelled out in more detail just how he thought about language, writing, and reading in particular. The premise of his address was that we, as a nation, would not and could not make "progress" without language, because language in any form allowed human beings to reflect, measure, and cogitate. Lincoln said:

> Writing, the art of communicating thoughts to the mind through the eye, is the great invention of the world. Great is the astonishing range of analysis and combination which necessarily underlies the most crude and general conception of

it—great, very great, in enabling us to converse with the dead, the absent, and the unborn, at all distances of time and space; and great, not only in its direct benefits, but greatest help to all other inventions [1946, Basler, III, 260].

According to White, Lincoln connected writing and printing, focusing particularly on newspapers (2002, 188). Printing is, he said, in reality the "better half of writing; and both together are but the assistants of speech in the communication of thoughts between man and man" (110). Lincoln goes on to say, "[T]o emancipate the mind from this false estimate of itself is the great task which printing came into this world to perform" (11). "It's [sic] utility," Lincoln continues, "may be conceived by the reflection that to it we owe everything which distinguishes us from savages. Take it from us, and the Bible, all history, all science, all government, all commerce, and nearly all social intercourse go[es] with it" (109). Thus Lincoln keenly understood the interconnections of language: how reading and writing reinforced one another, something he learned early in life and used to his distinct advantage. In speaking of what he called his "store of education," "gathered under the pressure of necessity," Lincoln concluded, as quoted by William Lee Miller, "[S]till somehow I could read" (2002, 45). What is so amazing about his self-education is his very early understanding of the larger picture, this keen awareness of different language skills: how to employ them and how they affected each other, a consciousness that would later manifest itself most brilliantly in his own writing.

In his self-education as a writer, interestingly, Lincoln followed at least two steps that parallel the education of young writers in ancient Greece and Rome. There young students went through a series of exercises to train themselves in prose composition. The training, called *progymnasmata*, included as its first step what the *Encyclopedia of Rhetoric and Composition* describes as the "retelling of folk tales in simple, direct style. Sometimes students were asked to expand or abbreviate the fable to identify the moral" (O'Rourke 1996, 562). In *A History of Education in Antiquity*, H.I. Marrou reports that these fables were "attributed to some famous person like Aesop" (1956, 174). Curiously, according to Gerald McMurtry's book on the Lincoln family's migration, we know that among the few books the Thomas Lincoln family owned was a copy of *Aesop's Fables*, a tome believed to have been given to young Abraham by his mother and carried with him, along with the other belongings of the Lincoln family, when they moved from Kentucky to Indiana in 1816 (1999, 11).

In fact, *Aesop's Fables* was the only book, according to M.L. Houser in *Lincoln's Education*, "that Mr. Lincoln said he had read repeatedly, and with such care that he could rewrite it from memory without the loss of a single word" (1951, 115). Although we do not know for certain when he first read the book, we know that because he took it with him on the move to Indiana, he probably read it when he was as young as seven (115). Houser observes that because storytelling was a characteristic of the Lincoln family, *Aesop's Fables* aided in developing what Houser calls Lincoln's "proneness to clarify a thought or enforce an argument with an apt illustration." According to Jack Lang in *Lincoln's Fireside Reading*, a relative of Lincoln, Dennis Hanks, is reported to have said to the young Lincoln, "Abe, them yarns is all lies." Lincoln's reply was, "Mighty darn good lies, Dennis" and continued his readings (1965, 29–30). From *Aesop's Fables* young Lincoln could acquire the rudiments of prose style, taught then and now, through the study of simple narratives, lessons that in many ways form the backbone of training in writing.

Another way that Lincoln followed the format of *progymnastmata* was to copy passages from model writers in much the same manner, Marrou records, that the ancient Romans learned writing skills (1956, 154–55). According to Lincoln biographer Douglas Wilson, Lincoln's stepmother, Sarah Bush Lincoln, described Lincoln's learning process this way:

> Abe read all the books he could lay his hands on—and when he came across a passage that struck him he would write it down on boards if he had no paper and keep it there till he did get paper—then he would rewrite it—look at it—repeat it—He had a copy book—a kind of scrap book in which he put down all things and preserved them [1998, 56].

Biographer Carl Sandburg says that Lincoln "scrawled words with charcoal; he shaped them in the dust, in sand, in snow. Writing had a fascination for him"; he would read a book and take "a piece of charcoal to write on a fire shovel, shaving off what he wrote, and then [write] more" (1993, 9, 14), a painstaking process that combined both reading and writing and implanted into Lincoln's absorbent mind the sound and sense of highly effective prose, a process the ancients called "imitation," and a technique even used today in certain classrooms to teach beginning and even advanced writers.

Word soon spread that young Abe could do what many of the neighbors could not do: write letters. Biographers David Herbert Donald in *Lincoln* (1996, 30) and Carl Sandburg in *Abraham Lincoln: The Prairie and War Years* (1993, 15) aver that Lincoln would compose letters for those illiterate neighbors; Sandburg notes: "[Lincoln] asked questions, 'What do you want to say in the letter? How do you want to say it? Are you sure that is the best way to say it? Or do you think we can fix up a better way to say it?' This was a kind of training in grammar and composition" (15).

But the young Lincoln keenly realized that if he were to perfect those language skills, he needed to know English grammar. Just as did the teachers of rhetoric in ancient Greece and Rome, he concluded he needed to understand how the language was put together in order to perfect the art of crafting sentences for their most masterful effect. He realized, as Douglas Wilson points out, that "the inability to speak and write standard English served to limit the opportunities of those with higher aspirations, and Lincoln's decision to tackle English grammar is strong evidence that the young store clerk [Lincoln] considered himself one of those" who had higher goals (1998, 63). According to Donald, Lincoln's first acquaintance with grammar came from *Dilworth's Spelling Book*, which he used in Kentucky (1996, 29). But he set about more seriously studying grammar when he acquired a copy of Samuel Kirkham's *English Grammar* during his young adult days in New Salem, Illinois. Sandburg records that Mentor Graham, the local schoolmaster, told him about John C. Vance, who had a copy of Kirkham's book, so Lincoln then walked six miles to get the book and then "burned pine shavings at night" in order to study it (1993, 26). Donald concludes that apparently Lincoln "took pride in his mastery of Kirkham, and he thought it sufficiently important to mention in his 1860 autobiographical sketch that he had 'studied English grammar, imperfectly, of course, but so as to speak and write as well'" in Lincoln's words, "'as [I do] now'" (48). According to Wilson, Lincoln also studied Lindley Murray's *Grammar*, described by M. H. Houser in *Lincoln's Education* as having "over 300 pages of fine print, and was comprehensive to a fault" (1951, 60). Lincoln said of studying Murray's work "that it was very dry reading," but Lincoln felt ultimately that he learned more grammar from reading and writing than from studying a grammar book (D. Wilson 1998, 65). What is significant about Lincoln's study of grammar, however, is that once again he set about acquiring writing and speaking skills on his own by reading. As a contemporary remarked, Lincoln "had no teachers, few books and no learned and intellectual companions" (65). He possessed only his tested ability to learn on his own through reading.

Most Lincoln scholars have also duly noted that, in part, Lincoln's writing and speaking ability grew out of his intense and wide reading.[3] Young Lincoln was remembered as saying, "The things I want to know are in books" (Lang 1965, 8). His cousin, Dennis Hanks, described young Lincoln's reading habits this way:

> I never seen Abe after he was twelve 'at he didn't have a book som'ers 'round. He'd put a book inside his shirt an' fill his pants pockets with corn dodgers, an' go off to plow or hoe. When noon come he'd set down under a tree, an' read an' eat. In house at night, he'd tilt a cheer by the chimbly, an' set on his backbone and read. [...] Aunt Sairy never let the children pester him. She always said Abe was goin' to be a great man someday. An' she wasn't goin' to have him hindered [Sandburg 1993, 13].

And Lincoln read almost anything he could find, but a number of books need mentioning. Besides *Aesop's Fables*, he read the plain but enduring prose style of *Pilgrim's Progress*. William Scott's *Lessons in Elocution* was also an influential book in his political life later, while Parson Mason Weems's *Life of George Washington* and William Grimshaw's *History of the United States* taught him the American story (W.L. Miller 2002, 49–57). In studying Lincoln's speeches and writing, Kenneth Cmiel notes that Lincoln read and liked using the Bible as a reference, especially the Psalms and the Gospels. "Three score and ten" from Psalms became "Four score and seven years ago" (1990, 116). Indeed, he often used the Bible in his speeches and writing. In "Lincoln's Development as a Writer," Roy P. Basler observes that the King James Version of the Bible "probably provided the literary examples which Lincoln knew best; and from his fondness for biblical phraseology he may have derived his mastery of the technique," of "poetical cadence" (*ibid.*, 45). One early biographer claimed Lincoln "knew the Bible by heart. There was not a clergyman to be so familiar with it as he" (1885, Arnold, 45). Rufus Rockwell Wilson, an expert on Lincoln's reading, notes that Lincoln's use of the Bible was profound:

> He read and reread the book from first page to last, committing memorable verses and longer passages, which in after years were sure to leap into his thought when the particular need of the moment called for their use. He quoted from the Bible in his letters, his talks to juries and his political speeches, and now and again made it the servant of a sense of humor that could be ironic as well as whimsical [1932, 13].

He also read voraciously from a few novels such as *Robinson Crusoe* and *Sinbad the Sailor*, and the highly influential Murray's *Reader*, a collection of notable sections of the English poets (R. Wilson 1932, 55). In this particular work, he could study how the masters put prose together artistically, learning important lessons in constructing sentences, balancing clauses, and creating a good metaphor.

William H. Townsend in *Lincoln and the Bluegrass* says that a similar book to Murray's *Reader* was a Lincoln favorite: *Elegant Extracts, or Useful and Entertaining Passages from the Best English Authors and Translations*. Townsend notes that "he marked or underscored heavily with a lead pencil such of the poems, or extracts from them, as particularly struck his fancy" (1955, 136). Exercises like those would vividly imprint notable passages on an impressionable mind like Lincoln's. He kept up his wide reading all his life, for he surely understood its value.[4]

While often merely mentioned in Lincoln scholarship, one other book important to understanding just how Lincoln used reading to develop his writing and speaking skills was Hugh Blair's *Lectures on Belles Lettres and Rhetoric*, originally published in 1819 in England. Blair's work was, as Lucille M. Schultz (1999, 82) says in her book on composition instruction in nineteenth century America, quite popular in the United States. James A. Berlin's *Writing Instruction in Nineteenth-Century American Colleges* calls Blair's work "the most popular treatment of rhetoric until after the Civil War" (1984, 25). Cmiel agrees, concluding that Blair's book was "very influential in the middle of the nineteenth century," about the time when Lincoln was honing his composition and speaking skills (1990, 118). S. Michael Halloran in *A Short History of Writing Instruction* notes, too, that trend-setting Yale University adopted Blair's book shortly after its publication in 1783 (1990, 162). Evidence suggests Lincoln knew about Blair's book. For example, M.L. Houser cites Henry B. Ranking, a fellow resident with Lincoln in New Salem, Illinois, who said, "Young Lincoln collaborated with Ann Rutledge in a study, or review of Blair while they were living at New Salem" (1951, 62). What makes this book particularly important in Lincoln's case, and what others have failed to note, is that Blair emphasized the matter of developing "taste" in speaking and writing, something commonly called *belles lettres* in rhetorical theory. In the preface to *Lectures on Rhetoric and Belles Lettres*, Blair tells the reader that the lectures "were originally designed for the initiation of Youth into the study of Belles Lettres and Composition" (1965, 3). Such a purpose would fit well into Lincoln's introduction to the world of speaking and writing. Blair then notes that his series of lectures was designed for those "studying to cultivate their Taste, to form their Style, or to prepare themselves for Public Speaking or Composition" (3). We may speculate that Lincoln must have found that sentence particularly important, for Blair seemed to be connecting, in Lincoln's mind, all those prose models from the literary greats Lincoln so much admired, copied, and memorized in order to develop his own writing and speaking skills. What he had read, then, and many times memorized, neatly fit into what Blair called the development of "taste" in writing and speaking. According to Berlin, Blair taught "that effective writing is learned through studying examples of effective writing," something, again, that Lincoln practiced (1984, 25). Reading Blair's book, Lincoln could find a firm practical and theoretical foundation for what would later blossom into masterful prose. In fact, a whole spate of textbooks on rhetoric during this period emphasized this development of taste in speaking and writing, works such as John Witherspoon's *Lectures on Eloquence* in 1810, Alexander Jamieson's *A Grammar of Rhetoric and Polite Literature* in 1818, and Samuel P. Newman's *A Practical System of Rhetoric* in 1827. It would seem entirely likely that amid all this emphasis on "taste" in speaking and writing, Lincoln could not escape the influence of the belletristic rhetoric so popular nineteenth century America. In fact, Roy P. Basler even goes so far as to conclude that Lincoln "probably had a more thorough training in formal rhetoric than the average college graduate" of the day (1939a, 170–71).

How certain can we be that Blair and the other influences mentioned definitely affected how Lincoln learned to write and speak? Obviously not to a certainty. In *The Creative Mind*, Margaret A. Boden speaks to the issue of influences upon a writer: "Usually, the scholar must present the case to the civil, not the criminal courts: the origin of a particular line or image can sometimes be established beyond a reasonable doubt, but more often we have to do with the balance of probabilities" (1991, 114). So what we are dealing with here with Lincoln's writing and speaking are probabilities, displays of passages and words that suggest that Lincoln was influenced or swayed by a particular rhetorical stance, an image, a trope, a figure of speech.

There is considerable evidence, however, that Lincoln worked on improving his own style even after he was elected and was serving as president. Harold Holzer observes that Lincoln became more careful about the means of communication after he ascended to the presidency. Particularly, he relied more and more on the written text that he would read out loud, a sign of growing affinity to writing. Several contemporaries noted that when Lincoln spoke extemporaneously he "was little better than dreadful" (Holzer 1995, 22). Holzer even records that a pro–Lincoln reporter summed up his speaking ability fairly succinctly: "He sometimes stopped for repairs before finishing a sentence" (107). One of Lincoln's ways of dealing with this problem was to revise and edit his statements before they were published. Holzer notes that one of his secretaries, for example, had a collection of papers labeled: "The following are the speeches delivered by Mr. Lincoln [...] as revised by himself for the *Indianapolis Journal*" (108). There are noticeable differences, for example, between the famous farewell speech he gave at the train station in Springfield, Illinois, and the edited version that Lincoln himself polished (109–10). As was the custom then, Lincoln also did not deliver his messages to Congress; he relied instead on someone to read them aloud to the governing body. Obviously, one of the reasons Lincoln did not speak "off the cuff" had to do with his understanding that what a president said was likely to be taken seriously by his newspaper-reading public. He noted, for example, "In my position, it is somewhat important that I should not say any foolish things" (115). But his relying more on the written text indicates the inherent faith he had in the written word. He knew that writing would probably express more clearly and eloquently just what he wanted and needed to say. In the words of the Renaissance essayist and rhetorician, Francis Bacon, "[R]eading maketh a full man [...] writing an exact man," a thought that Lincoln keenly understood, appreciated, and demonstrated in his own education as a writer (1937, 144).

In *Lincoln at Gettysburg*, Garry Wills points out another way Lincoln's writing changed about the time he assumed the presidency. The Civil War was the first American war to rely so heavily on the telegraph as a way of communicating important information and orders to various generals in the field and back to the commander-in-chief. Consequently, anxious about the fate of his soldiers, Lincoln spent a considerable amount of time in the telegraph office at the War Department waiting for news from the front and relaying messages to his various generals across the wires (1992, 169–70). Homer Bates, who was a military telegrapher in that telegraph office at the War Department, remarks, "From his early contact with the telegraph in March of 1857 [...] until the day of his death, eight years afterward, Lincoln's connection with the telegraph was very close" (1995, 4–6). Bates continues: "There were many times Lincoln remained in the telegraph office till late at night, and occasionally all night long" (118). As

Bates points out, there is also ample evidence that Lincoln didn't just *receive* messages but rather that he composed them in that choppy telegraph style: "During the entire war, the files of the War Department telegraph office were punctuated with short, pithy dispatches from Lincoln. For instance, on May 24, 1862, he sent ten or twelve to various generals; on May 25, as many more and from one to a dozen on nearly every succeeding day for months" (128). As Wills says, Lincoln quickly realized the spare language used in telegraph dispatches "took on new and nervous rhythms," to become, then, new ways of expressing oneself that were quite in contrast to the popular effusive prose used in long letters and reports of the day. Lincoln seemed to understand that the language of telegraphy heralded a very new way of communicating in American English, a way quite different from nineteenth century American prose (1992, 169–70). Accordingly, Lincoln adjusted his writing style to reflect the influence of this no-nonsense language of telegraphy, a language that looked ahead to the writing style of the twentieth century and the apex of the plain style.

Paul M. Angle in "Lincoln's Power with Words" sums up Lincoln's compositional ability by noting, "Measured by many standards, Abraham Lincoln was a master of words. In his writings fuse sincerity and sympathy, logical directness, a severity of style almost classic, and homely plainness" (1981, 27). Lincoln truly was a powerful writer, but equally interesting was how Lincoln was able to teach himself the fundamentals of writing. Jacques Barzun concludes, "All good writing is self-taught…. The truth remains that the would-be writer, using a book or critic, must teach himself. He must learn to spot his own errors and work out his own ways of removing them" (1975, 3).

But how did Lincoln manifest these notions he had about writing? What do we know about how he composed, revised, and thought about the writing act? Answering these questions helps us understand how Lincoln the writer worked his craft.

While we do not possess much knowledge about Lincoln's writing habits, we do know enough to venture some generalizations. One of his three secretaries, William Stoddard, noted that the "greater part of his writing was done alone by himself in his room. He composed somewhat slowly and with care, making few erasures or corrections" (Burlingame 2008, 172). Ronald White records Lincoln as writing his speeches "first with pencil on stiff sheets of white paste board or boxboard." White also cites contemporary Noah Brooks who "tells of observing Lincoln writing in his armchair, his favorite position, with his legs crossed. He laid the sheets, which were five to six inches wide, on his knee. He crossed out words and edited until the text was ready to copy as the final version" (2002, 49).

More particularly, William Klingaman chronicles in some detail how Lincoln wrote the Emancipation Proclamation. He says, for example, that Lincoln composed the document in the telegraph room of the War Department, noting that Lincoln found this location "a congenial place to work, a sanctuary from the constant press of visitors of the White House" (2001, 139). Toward the end of June 1862, Lincoln appeared one morning in the telegraph room and requested a piece of paper "to write something special," he said. The officer there, Captain Thomas T. Eckert, "observed that Lincoln would write a few lines and then look out the window at Pennsylvania Avenue. He didn't write much between these periods of rest." After writing about one page, Lincoln passed the page to Eckert to lock away in a desk. Subsequently, Lincoln returned another day and began writing again, revising and adding more text, putting "question marks in the margins" (139–40). The document seemed to physically evolve the way a person might knit a sweater: correcting what had already been done and adding to it what was appropriate until the document was complete.

Lincoln exhibited signs that to him, a document was only satisfactory if it displayed a clear voice, a practice that Lincoln scholars have not yet noted. Rhetorician Toby Fulwiler defines voice as "some identifying tone or timbre that makes us conscious of the author's presence, that lets us *hear* the person behind the sentences" (1990, 214). According to the *Encyclopedia of Rhetoric and Composition* (Enos 1996, 749), some writers feel that voice comes to a document when "writers listen to the voice that resides within them and allow it to be liberated by tuning out external constraints that tend to its natural expression." Thus some "writers discover what they want to say when they allow writing to flow as naturally as when they speak [...], a kind of self-discovery, for honest expression reveals who a writer really is." The advantage of this approach to writing is that "[p]honological aspects of speech such as pitch, rhythm, intonation, and so on inhere in writing," thereby detailing writers' unique personalities (Jacobs 1996, 749).

Ample evidence suggests that Lincoln keenly understood how important the concept of voice was to writing and delivering a good speech. Basler, for example, cites law partner William Herndon who said that Lincoln once told him that when he read out loud, "I hear what is read and I see it; and hence [in] two senses get it" (1946, 47). White observed, "Lincoln wrote primarily to be heard. He crafted his speeches as much for the ear as for the eye" (2002, 50). Klingaman, for instance, notes that Lincoln asked his son Robert "to read him [the First Inaugural Address] aloud so he could hear it one last time" (12). Lincoln also read the Emancipation Proclamation to his cabinet officers. He noted: "[W]hat I want is an audience. Nothing sounds the same when there isn't anybody to hear it and find fault with it" (Burlingame 2000, 129–30). White even goes so far as to say, "Lincoln's writing resembled poetry in part because he was writing for the ear" (2002, 50).

One of Lincoln's three secretaries, William Stoddard, records one rich moment when Lincoln asked the young man to listen while Lincoln read one of his speeches. Stoddard describes one particular instance this way:

> If you are indeed an audience, you believe [Lincoln] has forgotten you are there for a moment, but that is only while he is beginning. He is more an orator than a writer, and he is quickly warmed up to the place where his voice rises and his long right arm goes out, and he speaks to you somewhat as if you were a hundred thousand people of an audience, and as if he believes that something like fifty thousand of you do not at all agree with him. He will convince that half of you, if he can, before he has done with it [Burlingame 2000, 130].

Stoddard concludes by observing, "Lincoln knows now just how that thing will sound in the ears of millions on millions all over the country, and he doesn't care a corn-husk for the literary critics here or in Europe" (Burlingame 2000, 131).

It seems logical, therefore, that if Lincoln read his speeches aloud for his ear and tested them for good voice, he then would apply that same knowledge about voice and its importance to the writing act. Thus his need to hear his speeches being read aloud carried over to those times when he put pen to paper not just to write a speech but also to compose a written document, which, in Lincoln's mind, still required the strong presence of voice. Consequently, trying to hear voice was probably what Lincoln was after when he insisted on reading the Emancipation Proclamation aloud to his cabinet, as Burlingame reports (2000, 129–30).

Finally, we know that Lincoln many times sought out advice on his writing from those whose opinions he valued. Klingaman, for example, records that Lincoln asked for advice from "a handful of experienced Republican Party leaders," some of whom suggested changes in the First

Inaugural Address (2001, 11). Klingaman also notes that Lincoln sought the opinion of Hannibal Hamlin on the Emancipation Proclamation (140). One person whom Lincoln most consulted, as noted earlier in Lincoln's revision of the First Inaugural Address, was the articulate secretary of state, William Seward, who suggested changes in the Emancipation Proclamation, too (190). Sometimes, though, Lincoln trusted his own judgment and, as Stoddard notes, left "a first draft lying [...] in one of the drawers of [his] writing desk" (86). Stoddard observes one time that another "great state paper has been waiting in one of the pigeon holes of the President's desk. He has taken it out from time to time to ponder over it and to correct it here and there" (95).

Whatever we can say about Lincoln's writing habits, we must surely note that the Great Emancipator went about the business of writing deliberately, struggling to say what he wanted to say, studying it lovingly to see if it said what he sought to say, asking the advice of various people who surrounded him, and ultimately trusting his own judgment of what constituted good writing.

In speaking of Lincoln's literary art, Jacques Barzun makes an interesting observation:

> Lincoln's example, plainly, helped break the monopoly of the dealers in literary plush. After Lincoln comes Mark Twain, and out of Mark Twain comes contemporaries of ours as diverse as Sherwood Anderson, H.L. Mencken, and Ernest Hemingway. Lincoln's use of his style for the intimate genre and for the sublime was his alone; but his workaday style is the American style par excellence [1971, 81].

Surely, Lincoln learned to write from a number of different influences besides his wide reading. And a plethora of historical factors in the history of American prose style also affected how Lincoln learned to compose. But these considerations in total help to tell a complex, previously untold story of a man whose greatness as a president stemmed in large part from his ability to communicate well. Understanding these same considerations and understanding his composing habits, observations not heretofore noted by scholars studying Lincoln's prose, help us better understand in toto Lincoln as a man and Lincoln as a writer. Such knowledge not only aids readers to appreciate his consummate skill with language, but it also provides an approach to better understand just what The Great Emancipator had to say and how his words speak to students learning to write and speak in his time and in our time.

Notes

1. An earlier version of this chapter appeared in *Rhetoric Review* 23.4: 350–367.

2. The authoritative source for Lincoln's writing is Roy P. Basler's *The Collected Works of Abraham Lincoln,* in eleven volumes. Much of Lincoln's writing is scattered about the world in many different hands, private and public, but the largest single collection of original manuscripts is on microfilm in the Library of Congress. According to the preface of vol. 1 in the first nine volumes of Basler's *The Collected Works,* the collection of Lincoln's writing took "more than five years" to gather (vii). The collection included those manuscripts in the "great depositories" of Lincoln papers, such as the Hay and Nicolay Collection, "the Library of Congress, Illinois State Historical Library, The Henry E. Huntington Library, Brown University Library, and the National Archives" (xiv), as well as those that resulted from the "cooperation of hundreds of individuals, distributed throughout the majority of states and even foreign countries" (xiii). Basler describes the editing of the individual manuscripts as being done to "reproduce the original in so far as reasonably possible. [...] [where] [e]ditorial emendations, whether of punctuation, spelling or diction, [are] bracketed" (x).

3. The most thorough treatment of books as an influence on Lincoln's writing and speaking are Roy P. Basler's "Lincoln's Development as a Writer" in *Abraham Lincoln: His Speeches and Writing,* 1–49; and Daniel Dodge's *Abraham Lincoln: The Evolution of His Literary Style.* Of the more than four thousand books on Lincoln, most biographies treat his reading only as a major source of influence on his writing.

4. According to Rufus Rockwell Wilson, after Lincoln's death, his library was scattered over several places, including the Library of Congress (1932, 63). Many of the works Lincoln read were from borrowed sources and thus not preserved in his library and must be gleaned from biographical accounts. The best source on Lincoln's library, however, is *What Lincoln Read* by Rufus Rockwell Wilson. See also Jack Lang's *Lincoln's Fireside Reading.*

4
Early Letters

Abraham Lincoln was a prolific letter writer, with over 5,000 letters contained in his *Collected Works*, and the very real possibility that many others may still be accepted as his, such as those included in the supplements to his work (1974; 1990). Yes, Lincoln wrote letters because other means of communication, like the telephone and e-mail, were not available to him. Yet he also understood the subtle qualities of letters that enabled them to effectively communicate his sundry thoughts and feelings. Lincoln also understood the habitus of the time, which dictated that letter writing was very much a part of his work as an attorney. During the Civil War, his extensive use of the telegraph, for instance, provided him with the information he needed to relay to his commanders (Bates 1995, 5), and there is little doubt that the telegraph was a powerful weapon in the commander-in-chief's arsenal, but Lincoln oftentimes needed to address various generals with more than mere information. Letters provided him that opportunity to express those thoughts and feelings that the telegraph did not.

The ancient rhetorician known as Demetrius said that the letter "reproduces an extemporary utterance" and likens a letter to "a conversation with a friend" ... which provides "glimpses of character" (2006, 6). He concluded that "in every other form of composition it is possible to discern the writer's character, but in none so clearly as in the epistolary" (6). The most popular rhetorician of Lincoln's day, Hugh Blair, author of *Lectures on Rhetoric and Belle Lettres*, maintained that the letter was a "conversation carried on upon paper," advising his readers that letters should have a "natural grace and ease ... [but] they still may be entertaining; more especially if there [is] any thing to interest us, [it is] in the character of those who write them" (2005, 418). A contemporary guide to letter writing, *Chesterfield's Letter Writing Simplified*, noted that letters "speak on paper" (1857, 3), concluding that letters imparted to the reader "gentler feelings of home associations" (4). Lincoln could then use letters—if he were a good letter writer—to form close bonds and cultivate relationships with his readers.

Prior to his ascent to the presidency, Lincoln wrote many types of letters, and while he did, he grew as a writer to become the impressive letter writer that he was. In essence, Lincoln wrote letters of friendship, letters to build political allegiances, letters to his clients, letters to fellow lawyers, letters of endorsement of contemporaries for various positions in government, a limited number of "public" letters, and miscellaneous letters to various audiences. After he was elected president he used his considerable letter-writing skills to try to persuade various generals to follow particular courses of action, the topic of the last chapter.

While it is not possible to examine every letter Lincoln wrote, it is possible to study representative samples of letters in each of those categories to see not only how they fit the classification they represent, but also how Lincoln grew in his ability to express himself in the letter form. It was the habitus of the society Lincoln lived in that helped guide how the letter was organized and what it was to contain. Consequently, the letters Lincoln wrote to friends were like many other letters of the same type produced in his society. In other words, whether Lincoln knew it or not, he was writing letters of friendship based on models that trace at least back to the ancient Greeks. As noted earlier, Demetrius said that letters should "abound with glimpses of character" (2006, 6). That is to say that the letter of friendship provided many situations in which Lincoln had the opportunities to express the idiosyncrasies of his personality, rather than hiding them behind "business at hand" or the exhortation of an idea or concept that was argued in other types of missives. Because of its freedom from the restraints Lincoln might have felt in expressing a particular political position, the letter of friendship was not bound by the restrictions of structure that other types of letters must contain.

Yet the letter of friendship does contain some commonalities that define it. Students of rhetoric call these "commonplaces," subjects, themes, or elements that generally describe letters of friendship. These commonplaces, listed in part by Stowers in reference to Greek letters, are indeed minimal, reflecting and reinforcing the freedom of expression that the letter of friendship exhibits: first "delight at receiving the letter, [second], friends need not verbally express thanks (or praise), and [third] ... the letter writer expresses his desire to have the person to whom the letter is written reciprocate ... [with another letter]" (1986, 61).

In addition, looking at Lincoln's letters of friendship provides the opportunity for examining Lincoln the writer to analyze vestiges of his growth as a writer, although these signs of growth in his letter-writing skills must be taken within the context of the letter of friendship, where the rigid structure of other forms of expression does not exist.

Most of the letters of friendship that Lincoln wrote were to his closest friend Joshua Speed with whom Lincoln had lived when Lincoln first arrived at Springfield. Speed's store became a place where many young men gathered to discuss ideas, politics, and other matters that might concern a young man. But after several years, Speed left Illinois and returned to his native Kentucky, and shortly thereafter married his young bride.

Following the commonplaces, Lincoln does not feel the need to introduce himself to Speed or to apologize to him for writing him a letter, as he might if this were, say, a business letter.

Lincoln began a representative letter to Speed by acknowledging the receipt of Speed's recent letter: "Your letter of the 25th Jany. came to hand to-day" (Basler I:267). As noted earlier, during this period of time it was customary to acknowledge when the letter from the addressee was received. Lincoln's return letter was dated February 3, 1842, indicating that Lincoln felt some compunction to answer the letter a short time after receiving his letter from Speed. While Lincoln did not "delight" at receiving a letter from Speed, Lincoln probably was quite pleased that his friend had written him, especially considering the sympathetic tone of the letter, and the nature of their friendship.

What Lincoln said explained why he was concerned about his friend: "You know I do not feel my own sorrows much more keenly than I do yours, when I know of them; and yet I assure you I was much hurt by what you wrote me of your excessively bad feelings at the time you wrote." Lincoln then explained, "Not that I am less capable of sympathizing with you now than ever; not that I am less your friend than ever." Here, to emphasize his point, Lincoln used a neat balancing of clauses beginning with the same words: "not that I...." Lincoln felt Speed's distress, and he explained: "I hope and believe, that your present anxiety and distress about [your wife Fanny's] health and her life, must and will forever banish those horrid doubts, which I know you sometimes felt, as to the truth of your affection for her" (Basler I:267).

The freedom of expression that Lincoln felt in order to broach this topic also reinforced the idea that the two men had shared such thoughts, perhaps only between themselves. Lincoln appeared to be a good enough and close enough friend that Speed had felt comfortable expressing his doubts to his friend Lincoln.

Lincoln even said that he thought that "the Almighty has sent your present affliction expressly for that object" (Basler I:267). Later in the letter, Lincoln again uses repetition to reinforce this same theme: "But I hope your melancholly [sic] bodings as to her early death, are not well founded. I even hope, that ere this reaches you, she will have returned with improved and still improving health," repeating the word "hope" for rhetorical effect. Later Lincoln used a variation on the same technique, this time using the word "say": "I would say more if I could, but it seems I have *said* enough" (268).

Lincoln then assured Speed that Lincoln, too, had suffered from these same doubts: "You know the Hell I have suffered on that point. You know I do not mean wrong," perhaps repeating the phrase "you know" for special effect to assure Speed that Lincoln too had suffered. The remainder of the letter contained news that Speed might have been interested in, such as Lincoln's law partner's father's death, and then concluded: "I believe this is all the news." Lincoln then used the third commonplace, asking Speed to write him back: "Write me immediately on the receipt of this" (268).

In his letter to Speed, Lincoln used all three of the commonplaces, while also revealing his sympathy to Speed's problem. At the same time, Lincoln's repetition of key phrases ("I hope..., I am less..., I would say more but I have said enough..., and you know...") showed Lincoln the writer using such rhetorical schemes.

Another letter of friendship is quite interesting rhetorically and thematically, because Lincoln was writing to an older friend's wife, indirectly asking her for advice about how to deal with a relationship with a particular female and using an interesting appeal. The situation concerned a relationship he had with Mary Owens, a young woman of marital age that Lincoln had dated three years earlier. Later, Mary Owens' sister let Lincoln know that Mary was coming again for a visit and asked young Lincoln if, when she came, would he marry her? Lincoln quickly told the sister he would. The long letter written to Mrs. Orville Browning, a trusted confidant, explained how Lincoln extracted himself from his promise to marry

Miss Owens since when he saw her again three years later, Lincoln found her most unattractive.

So that Mrs. Browning really understood Lincoln's dilemma thoroughly, Lincoln began: "Without apollogizing [sic] for being egotistical, I shall make the history of so much of my life, as has elapsed since I saw you, [and] the subject of this letter." By explaining that it would take some care to explain Lincoln's problem, Lincoln thereby justified the unusual length of the letter. Lincoln then noted that, through her sister, Lincoln had promised to marry Mary Owens "with all convenient dispatch" (Basler I:117).

Relying on his memory of the attractiveness of Miss Owens three years earlier, Lincoln "saw no objection to plodding through life hand in hand with her." Earlier, Lincoln found her "intelligent" and "agreeable," but three years later Lincoln grew suspicious, because she appeared to be "too willing" to marry—even before Lincoln had seen her again. It occurred to Lincoln that perhaps Miss Owens had come back to Springfield with no thought of marrying Lincoln himself in particular, concluding quickly: "I would consent to this" (Basler I:117).

Then Lincoln saw her face to face three years later, and "she did not look as my immagination [sic] had pictured her.... But what could I do? I had told her sister that I would take her for better or worse; and I made a point of honor and conscience in all things, to stick to my word...." Lincoln went on: "...for I was convinced, that no man on earth would have her, and hence the conclusion that [her sister and Mary] were bent on holding me to my bargain." Lincoln then tried to convince himself that she was "handsome, [except for] her unfortunate corpulency" (Basler I:218).

"But I desired to be free...," he said, "[o]ut clear in every sense of the word; no violation of word, honor or conscience." Yet convinced that he had to keep his word that he would marry her, Lincoln twice asked Miss Owens to marry him, but she both times left him "with the same want of success.... I was mortified ... in a hundred different ways. My vanity was deeply wounded" (Basler I:218).

Lincoln then began to "suspect that I was really a little in love with her.... Others have been made fools by the girls; but this can never be said of me. I most emphatically, in this instance made a fool of myself." Lincoln then surmised, "I can never be satisfied with anyone who would be blockheaded enough to have me" (Basler I:119).

But the letter was more than a mere "pouring out of his heart" about Lincoln's troubles in romance. First, some background. Although practices varied from one location to another, the ancient Greeks taught students to write by following a set course of instruction, something they called *progymnasmata*. One of the students' first tasks was to write something in a narrative format, since the Greeks not only recognized the elementary nature of the narrative, but also understood how necessary it was to be able to tell a good story (O'Rourke 1996, 562–563). While the letter Lincoln wrote Mrs. Browning does not exhibit many rhetorical schemes or tropes, it is an effective narrative, climaxing near the end with Lincoln saying that he had "made a fool of himself" and only a "blockheaded" partner would marry him.

Like other letters of friendship, the letter also revealed the character of the writer, a side of Lincoln that he felt free to show to Mrs. Browning. In fact, in places, Lincoln made himself the butt of his own joke, although such a revelation was perhaps less than flattering to himself. In sum, the letter of friendship revealed a side of his character, almost comedic in places, a side Lincoln was probably less than eager to reveal to another person.

Lincoln's letter to Mrs. Browning also employed one of the "appeals" of ancient Greek rhetoric. The Greeks thought that all rhetoric was concerned with persuasion. While it is difficult to see Lincoln's letter as a persuasive document, it does have as its purpose convincing Mrs. Browning that Lincoln had faced a kind of emotional dilemma and sought her help in helping him see that what he had done was correct. Indirectly, he was also trying to convince Mrs. Browning that he needed further guidance to eliminate his feelings of insecurity, expressed most vividly in his calling himself a "blockhead." It is no surprise then that he closed the letter with: "When you receive this [letter], write me a long yarn about something to amuse me" (Basler I:119). To persuade her, then, Lincoln used a narrative structure, telling her in great detail what had happened, and used that structure to appeal to her emotions. Consequently, he used what the ancient Greeks called "pathos," an appeal to an audience "based upon the rhetor's ability to arouse certain types of emotions in the audience" (Colavito 1996, 493).

Another type of letter that Lincoln wrote was the letter of political allegiance. In these letters, Lincoln was asking for support for a political office or was explaining the political realities as he saw them at a particular time. While these letters could have persuasive natures in that they attempted to persuade the reader of a particular political stance, they also could be letters filled with facts relevant to a political environment. Consequently, some letters could have a highly persuasive nature, employing all sorts of persuasive strategies, while others were mere reports of information relevant to local, state or national politics.

One commonality of the letters of political allegiance and letters of friendship was their emphasis on ethos, persuasion by the force of the personality of the writer, or what Nan Johnson calls "the character of the speaker [or writer]" (1991, 243). Johnson distinguishes two conceptions of ethos: that of Plato and that of Aristotle. In practical terms, Aristotle saw ethos as one type of persuasion that brought about "decisions in matters of civil life" (1932, 243). So the letters of friendship, while long on character revelation, lack the emphasis of persuasion, as letters of political allegiance, by their very nature have. For example, Lincoln could clarify his position on the role of the United States senator who represented all the people in his state and be said to be using his ethos as a persuasive technique. People could then vote for him because he mirrored the kind of belief popular among his supposed constituency who shared Lincoln's belief. Or Lincoln could call upon the friendship with a successful businessman for whom Lincoln had successfully done some legal work, and Lincoln could use the ethos he had acquired because of his legal work for the businessman as a strategy to ask for the businessman's support for Lincoln's senatorial race. Stowers aptly observed, "Friendship was the basis for politics" (1986, 30). Consequently, Lincoln more than likely used ethos throughout his political campaigns. Even politics today involves candidates trying to build an appropriate amount of ethos, because it is such a successful persuasive strategy.

The first letter, dated December 19, 1854, addressed to Elihu B. Washburne, opened with acknowledgment of Washburne's letter. The ancient Greeks would call Lincoln's letter "deliberative" in purpose because it was "concerned with counseling the audience about future course of action in a political forum" (Benjamin 1996b, 171). Lincoln's purpose here was to convince his audience, Washburne, that Lincoln would represent the entire state of Illinois if elected to a statewide office, despite what Washburne had heard from (possibly) Thomas G. Turner. Probably, Lincoln saw as his task in the letter as to persuade Washburne that the insinuation that Lincoln would not represent the entire state of Illinois was false by asserting facts that would dispel that notion.

To do just that, Lincoln began with his major assertion: A senator needed "to be the impartial representative of his whole State," something Lincoln called "so plain a duty, that I pledge myself to the observance of it without hesitation; but not without some mortification that any one should suspect me of an inclination to the contrary." But assertion without support is mere assertion. So Lincoln then assembled narrative facts that supported his assertion. For example, while he served Sangamon in the legislature, "yet it is not without my recollection that the Northern members ever wanted my vote for any interest of theirs, without getting it. My distinct recollection is, that the Northern members and Sangamon members were always on good terms." Later, Lincoln noted that as a member of Congress Mr. Thomas Turner had Lincoln's "service for the asking." Lincoln concluded by saying, "As a Senator, I should claim no right, as I feel no inclination, to give the central portion of the state any preference over the North, or any other portion of [the state]" (Basler II:205).

Lincoln then used narrative examples again, but this time he used the narrative to support his assertion that he would not show any partiality for any portion of the state if he were elected senator, something the Greeks called "anaskeue," or the use of easily understood examples (O'Rourke 1996, 562), a rather simple, elementary rhetorical structure, useful in many instances, and well suited for Lincoln's argument in this letter. In addition, Lincoln used the ethos he wanted to acquire by clarifying his position on the issue of representing all the people from all regions of the state as another persuasive strategy. Perhaps Washburne was convinced that the force of Lincoln's support for his assertion and the ethos Lincoln sought would in tandem be successful persuasive strategies.

Another letter of political allegiance was quite short but representative of this type of letter and very obviously reliant on ethos as a persuasive device. The letter was addressed to a former client of Lincoln, a business man from Clinton, Illinois, who with Lincoln's help was successful in "an important lawsuit involving a patent on a water wheel." Thoughtfully, Lincoln opened the letter by reminding Charles Hoyt of just who Lincoln was: "You used to express a good deal of partiality for me"; Lincoln seemed clearly to point out the ethos Lincoln had with Hoyt. Then Lincoln asked Hoyt to put his feelings of "partiality" to work: "if you are still so, now is the time." Lincoln next was more particular about how he wanted Hoyt to respond: "Some friends here are really for me for the U.S. Senate," implying that Hoyt ought to get on the bandwagon, too. "I should be very grateful if you could make a mark for me among your members. Please write me at all events, giving me the names, post office, and *'political position'* of members round you. Direct to Springfield." Perhaps to make Hoyt feel special, Lincoln closes with "Let this be confidential" and signs the letter with "Yours truly" (Basler II:286).

The argument in this letter seems to be: If you think highly of me, then show those feeling by giving me political information that will be valuable to me in my bid for the U.S. Senate. Lincoln offered no particular political positions, no job for Hoyt if his Senate bid was successful. Instead, Lincoln appeared to be asking Hoyt for support because Lincoln felt that Hoyt had "a great partiality" for him. In other words, because Lincoln had displayed the appropriate ethos, he wanted Hoyt to help him win in his race for the Senate. If Stowers is correct that friendship is the basis for politics (1986, 30), Lincoln displayed in this letter how he sought to convert friendship into votes through a carefully crafted ethos.

The next type of letter Lincoln frequently wrote was the letter to a client. While these letters, too, were demonstrative in purpose, they tended to have the clear purpose of trying to move the reader to a course of action by providing Lincoln with bits of information that Lincoln needed to best serve his client. Lincoln generally did not discuss legal matters to any degree, since he probably broached such matters in face-to-face conversations with his clients. For the most part, Lincoln used such letters to strengthen the ethos he possessed by appearing to be knowledgeable about the law, and well prepared. By doing so, Lincoln engendered faith in his abilities to be the lawyer his clients wanted.

Dated June 23, 1853, the first example of a letter written to his client was addressed to Adam Adams, a farmer in Ogle County, requesting a particular document needed by Lincoln in order to have all the materials Lincoln needed to try Mr. Adams' case. Lincoln requested the document "to be prepared before-hand to get the case in the best shape." Particularly, Lincoln asked Adams to "procure & bring ... the *Register*'s certificate, showing *who* entered the land, and the *date* of the entry. Mind, the *Register*'s certificate—*not* the Receiver's receipt. The *Patent*, which I have, shows *who* entered the land, but does not show the *date* of the entry" (Basler II:199). Significant is the care that Lincoln showed in underlining the documents he needed and didn't need, reflecting the thoughtful preparation with which he prepared his cases, and thus building the kind of ethos he was well known for.

Another example of Lincoln writing to his clients was a letter addressed to John H. Manny and Company, composed on September 1, 1855, about the Reaper case. In the letter, Lincoln wondered why he had not heard from Peter Watson, since Lincoln had sent a letter to him, "requesting him to forward ... the evidence, from time to time, as it should be taken"; but in spite of repeated requests, Lincoln had not heard from Watson (Basler II:325).

Lincoln then asked: "Is it still the understanding that the case is to be heard at Cincinnati on the 20th...?" The question then reminded Manny and Company that Lincoln was concerned about not hearing from Watson, implying that Manning and Company might be able to assist Lincoln in securing the evidence. To reinforce Lincoln's consternation, he asked Manny and Company to reply "on the receipt" of Lincoln's letter.

The letter then reflects Lincoln's concern that he had not received the evidence he needed in the case. The missive thus reflected Lincoln's concern about his client's case without having the evidence that Watson would supply. Lincoln seemed to have given up on receiving the evidence from Watson, while letting his clients know so that Manny and Company might be able to secure the evidence that Lincoln was unable to. The letter also indicated that because Lincoln thought the evidence was crucial to the case, he wanted Manning to know that Lincoln himself had tried to secure the evidence, and he was working to prepare for the case.

Lincoln built his ethos as a careful and thoroughly prepared barrister. If the case rested on the evidence Watson had not sent, then Lincoln was himself not at fault. Albert A. Woldman, in his book *Lawyer Lincoln,* quoted Lincoln as saying: "A lawyer who becomes by admission to the bar of any of our courts part of the judicial establishment of the land, should have integrity beyond question" (1936, 198). His quest for the evidence in this case showed Lincoln as trying to have the integrity necessary to be well prepared. By this point in his career, his reputation as an effective lawyer who was ready for the case and worked for his clients was quite important to his success as a barrister.

Lincoln's letters to fellow lawyers were less likely to engage in ethos building to any extent as a persuasive device, because Lincoln carried a reputation that made ethos building unnecessary. The ethos Lincoln possessed was already known to the addressee. Consequently, the first letter of November 2, 1842, reflects the kind of prose that fellow lawyers would write to each other, sometimes even using Latin phrases that fellow lawyers would understand. This particular letter emphasizes James S. Irwin and Lincoln's willingness to accept certain cases, the question of the fees that Lincoln and James S. Irwin would charge for their services, and the payment of those fees. While the message is clear, it is in the style and language of those in the same community of writers, clearly stating how Lincoln and Logan felt about the matters discussed in their letter of reply, and explaining how much they charge clients and how and when they expected to collect their fees. The letter, then, is lawyer to lawyer, a letter to inform, not a letter of persuasion.

Ever aware that he must be courteous to fellow lawyers in those matters discussed in the letter, Lincoln answered the letter, feeling he must elucidate why there was a delay in reply, part of the habitus of the profession. Thus, Lincoln opened with an explanation for not answering Irwin's letter earlier: "Owing to my absence, yours of [October] 22 was not received til this moment." The next sentence indicated that he and fellow lawyer Judge Logan were willing to "attend to any business in the Supreme Court [of Illinois] you may send us." Lincoln next discussed the matter of fees that Judge Logan and Lincoln would charge: "As to fees, it is impossible to establish a rule that would apply to all, or even a great many cases." Next Lincoln asserted, "We believe we are never accused of being very unreasonable in this particular," assuring Irwin that Lincoln and Logan were not going to charge too much, and adding, "and we would always be satisfied" (with an agreeable fee), with the qualification: "provided we could see the money—but whatever fees we earn at a distance, if not paid *before*, we have noticed we never hear of after the work is done. We are, therefore, growing a little sensitive on that point" (Basler I:304). In the letter, Lincoln had explained Judge Logan and his willingness to accept cases referred to them from Irwin, and their fee policy. There is no attempt to persuade Irwin that he should employ Logan and Lincoln to try cases, but there was a clear explanation of how the charges would be agreed upon and how they were to be collected. The language of the letter is clear and concise, the kind of letter that lawyers would write to one another.

Another example of this type of letter was one in which Lincoln revealed to the addressee what it took to be a lawyer. Lawyers even into the twentieth century often did not attend law school. Instead they read essential works under the guidance of a seasoned lawyer. Dated November 5, 1855, the letter is addressed to Isham Reavis, who after his father's death decided to become a lawyer (Basler I:327). Apparently, Reavis had written to Lincoln, a lawyer fitted by reputation to give advice on how to become a lawyer, for as Woldman says, "Generally speaking, lawyers were then educated by the apprentice method.... The prospective lawyer would make arrangements with an established, successful lawyer to enter his office and read law under his direction for three to four years" (1936, 17). In this letter, Reavis is asking Lincoln to allow Reavis to study law under him.

After acknowledgment of receipt of his letter, Lincoln told Reavis, "I am away from home too much of the time, for a young man to read law with me advantageously." Next the letter became persuasive, telling Reavis, "If you are resolutely determined to make a lawyer of yourself, the thing is more than half done already." Lincoln offered no proof for that assertion other than his ethos as a lawyer who had apparently garnered a respected reputation. Lincoln then dealt with practicalities; that is, the other "half" of the goal of becoming a lawyer: "It is a small matter whether you read *with* any body or not. I did not read with anyone." Instead, Lincoln saw the next step to be to "[g]et the books, and read and study them till, you understand them in their principal features; and that is the main thing." Lincoln then advised Reavis, "It is no consequence to be in a large town while you are reading, I read at New Salem, which never had three hundred people living in it. The *books* and your *capacity* for understanding them, are the same in all places" (Woldman 1936, 17).

Lincoln then turned his attention to Reavis's studying under fellow lawyer Mr. Drummer, arguing that Mr. Drummer "is a very clever man, and excellent lawyer (much better than I, in law-learning); and I have no doubt he will cheerfully tell you what books to read, and also loan you the books." Lincoln's argument that Drummer would be a good lawyer to read with banked also on Drummer's reputation, and thus his ethos, as proof for the argument that Reavis should study with Drummer. Then Lincoln closed the letter to the lawyer-to-be with a repetition of an earlier idea: "Always bear in mind that your resolution to succeed, is more important than any one thing" (Woldman 1936, 17), an assertion that again relied upon Lincoln's ethos as proof.

Lincoln's letters to fellow lawyers were written generally with few persuasive techniques other than ethos, simply because most of the time these correspondences relayed, in the main, information that did not require a substantial amount of proof.

The last type of letter that Lincoln wrote was the letter of endorsement of one kind or other. The intent of this type was to use the ethos that Lincoln possessed (that is, his political, persuasive power) to recommend individuals for certain positions, or to introduce them to various people, or, perhaps, both. Generally these letters were relatively short, since their persuasive qualities lie in the power of the personality of Lincoln, who was intimately involved in politics most of his adulthood. Limiting these letters to those that don't involve politics is nearly impossible, since in most instances, Lincoln was recommending an individual for a political appointment of some sort. The short letters below have a sprinkling of politics about them, but they are not filled with elaborate descriptions of how these people were, say, good Whigs and deserved political appointments. At the same time, like longer letters of endorsement, they contain Lincoln's typical ethical appeals.

The first example is a letter of introduction and a recommendation for Benjamin Bond, written on March 26, 1849, to the Honorable J. M. Clayton, secretary of state in the Zachary Taylor administration.

The letter began with a short introduction of Benjamin Bond: "I take great pleasure in introducing to your acquaintance my good personal and political friend Benjamin Bond, Esq." Then Lincoln included the necessary information: "He is an applicant for the office of Marshall [sic] for Illinois." Next, Lincoln added information Clayton needed to know: "[P]revious to leaving Washington, I filed his recommendations, with my indorsement [sic] upon them to which I refer you. What I there say in his favor, I take great pleasure in repeating" (Basler II:38).

Lincoln's appeal for Clayton's hiring Bond has two parts: first, the information Lincoln had included in his previous recommendation. Presumably, that first recommendation contained information about Bond's application. Perhaps Lincoln included information about the qualifications Bond had, such as his experience in law endorsement. Second, besides the first appeal, Lincoln appealed to Clayton by the force of Lincoln's ethos. Lincoln had earned that power of persuasion by being a member of a political party and his service in Washington as a member of congress. In other words, Clayton should hire Bond because of Lincoln's recommendation about the character of Bond, which Lincoln was attesting to, in these days before non-political civil service government employment.

Another letter of endorsement was a letter to Secretary of the Interior Thomas Ewing, dated June 19, 1849, when N.G. Wilcox was applying for the position of Receiver of the Land Office at Stillwater, Minnesota. After alerting Ewing to the position Wilcox was applying for, Lincoln spoke rather loftily of Wilcox's character: "I hope he may succeed. He is [in] every way worthy of this office. I have once seen his devotion to principle put to the severest test, and come out unshaken. My confidence in him [is] unlimited" (Basler II:37). Lincoln did not speak about Wilcox's experience or training for this job. Instead Lincoln based his recommendation totally on Wilcox's character (his ethos, in other words) and Lincoln's observation of his character, along with Lincoln's ethos, too.

Other types of letters, like so-called public letters, gave opportunities for Lincoln to lay out his political goals to a vast number of people: His letter to Horace Greeley at the New York *Tribune* on August 22, 1862, in which Lincoln explained that his principal aim was to "save the Union" (Basler V:388), and his letter to Albert G. Hodges on April 4, 1864, published in the Frankfort, Kentucky *Sentinel* (Basler VII:281–284), which explained Lincoln's views on slavery, are examples. Unlike the personal letters Lincoln wrote to friends, political allies, or cabinet members to secure a position for a friend or acquaintance, these letters were opportunities to explain his position or aims to a large number of people, since for the most part, these appeared in newspapers such as those above. In other words, these public letters were analogous to today's presidential news conferences or public addresses, opportunities to explain to those who read his policies and thoughts on a given matter. As discussed in Chapter 5, these letters were written with wider audiences in mind than were his personal letters.

As far as growth in writing skills is concerned, the examination of Lincoln's early letters up until his tenure as commander-in-chief of the armed forces provides a number of insights. If, as Aristotle and a myriad of other important rhetoricians contend, an awareness of an audience is key to any communication, Lincoln obviously tried to make himself understood in his letters. At times, for example, he underlined key words or phrases to make sure that the reader of the letter would understand just what he meant. He rarely misspelled words ("melancholy" and "imagination" are among the few) but such misspellings did not cause any misinterpretation. Far from often, Lincoln left out grammatically necessary words in his haste to communicate with a reader, words such as "was," but such omissions do not cause any problems in interpretation.

Interestingly, many of his letters ended with sentences such as these: "I shall be happy to receive a letter from you at any time" (Basler III:515), and "I shall be glad to receive a letter from you at any time you can find

4. Early Letters

leisure to write one" (518). Lincoln, who wrote over 5,000 letters, liked to receive letters also. Perhaps he longed for the personal contact that receiving letters gave him. Perhaps he used letters to further his political goals. Composing over 5,000 letters surely meant that he *received* many letters, too. At any rate, Lincoln seemed to like the letter as a means of communication with real people on a personal basis. Finally, like his idol, Henry Clay, very seldom did Lincoln sign his letters with anything but "A. Lincoln."

Lincoln wrote a variety of other types of letters than those examined thus far. Some were letters to relatives of his; a few were letters to his father and stepbrother. Some were to his wife; some, because of the nature of his position as a congressman, were to dignitaries in congress or even to the president. Finally, and somewhat more complex in their structure, some were to his generals.

Lincoln's writing is impressive, especially that exhibited in treasured documents such as the Second Inaugural Address, the Gettysburg Address, and the Cooper Union speech; flashes of genius from a man who knew during the country's great storm to use language not only to communicate but also to heal, not only to praise but also to chastise; who knew how to remind the country of its mission, and to state clearly where the country should be going—all in some of the finest prose in the English language. These representative samples of his letter writing do not reflect his most well-crafted prose, but they do show a man learning the fundamentals of writing in a laborious but dedicated effort through practice and more practice. Examining Lincoln's letters for their rhetorical effectiveness, students of Lincoln see a man at work, developing his skill through dogged and incessant effort. Writing letters, then, was the classroom Lincoln never had, the tutor he missed.

He wrote poetry, legal tracts, political prose and works in other genres that were generally clear and concise, even more than 150 years after their composition. Many of his contemporaries lapsed into a prose overburdened with excessive and elaborate verbiage. Readers today often level the simplistic charge that writing style of the day emphasized manner over sense, that meaning was made in elaborate figures of speech and classical schemes. The pervasive belief is that language like the common request for surrender given by a general in the Civil War "to prevent the unnecessary effusion of blood" today sounds quite euphuistic. All too often, such prose is seen as an all-encompassing identifying characteristic of the writing of that earlier era.

Nan Johnson in her *Nineteenth-Century Rhetoric in North America* sees the influences on the writing of Lincoln's day as a rich "synthesis" of "classical, belletristic, and epistemological assumptions" (1991, 15). The growing influence of science stressed the "science" of rhetoric through "mental and moral science" (68). Certainly, writers in academia in the day were well aware of classical models as a result of their exposure to the ancients, an integral part of their classical education. It would be foolhardy, too, to dismiss Hugh Blair's *Lectures on Rhetoric and Belle Lettres* as unimportant, given its enormous popularity in academic America. Blair's book proposed the development of taste through the imitation of essentially literary models for writing instruction.

However, these influences on Abraham Lincoln's letter writing should be considered very indirect in any discussion of his development of his writing skills, for Lincoln was not a student in an American university that taught him from Blair's book, for example. Truly, Lincoln had studied models of literary prose in his youth, and while it is true that Lincoln probably learned to write, in the main, as a result of his imitation of the models he read in his wide-ranging perusal of many sorts of models, it still remains unlikely that classical models except in rare imitation played a significant part in the development of his writing style. Lincoln's prose bears the marks of the influence of science and scientific writing with its emphasis on a leaner and less ornate kind of prose, but there is scant scholarship to indicate that Lincoln studied such tracts. His letters seem to reflect the practiced development of his acute sensitivity to the language and its effect on his readers, and a firm, almost obsessive desire to teach himself how to write memorable prose. William Herndon, Lincoln's last law partner, described Lincoln's writing as possessing a "rugged grandeur," a style mostly free from the classical, belletristic, and mental and moral science, and closer to twentieth century "plain style" than the often elaborate attempts at embellished prose of his contemporaries. It is more like twentieth century Willa Cather than nineteenth century contemporary Nathaniel Hawthorne. And most of Lincoln's grappling with the written word began with his letters as the struggling man of the Illinois prairie, one untutored in the classics and from rough but humble beginnings, who expressed himself in language as plain as linsey-woolsey. In the end, Lincoln used language that moved common men's minds like few of his contemporaries. In discussing the common themes popular in Lincoln's age, Nan Johnson notes, "The study of an exemplary canon confers greater mastery over technique and deepens intellectual and moral acumen" (1991, 174). But Lincoln wanted to express himself in his own voice, based in part on the unadorned language of his unlettered countrymen. Lincoln's reading as a youth and into adulthood of a variety of models included works such as William Scott's *Lessons in Elocution*, which "despite its title was a substantial anthology of literary gems, a veritable treasure house of literature, with a large and representative selection from some of the now obscure and many of the still most famous poets of English literature" (Kaplan 2008, 29). Other readings included Lindley Murray's *The English Reader, or Pieces in Prose and Verse*, and Thomas Fitzgerald's *On Grace in Writing (ibid.)*. But Lincoln had his own voice, one that captured the essence of his rugged beginnings.

So how was Lincoln to put into practice those principles of writing he had garnered from his readings? Lincoln seemed to demonstrate those skills in writing in the letters that he wrote. While the principles of writing were the catalyst that fired the engine, his lifelong practice of letter writing was to become vastly important when he had to deal with the conduct of war. His self-taught skills in letter writing acquired through his deep reading and the imitation of models proved to be one of Lincoln's most effective means of governing.

5

Letters to His Generals

Perhaps more than any president, Abraham Lincoln was commander-in-chief of the military. While other presidents also served in time of war, Lincoln is the only president whose total presidency was bounded by the beginning and the end by war. McPherson says, "During those four years military matters required more of Lincoln's time and energy than anything else" (2008, xv).

Other presidents had been in war—notably, Andrew Jackson and Zachary Taylor also served as generals—but Lincoln entered the presidency with virtually no military experience (except a self-styled raging "battle with mosquitos") or training. Virtually everything he knew about military tactic he learned on his own by reading the classical military treatises like those of Carl von Clausewitz, as McPherson's *Tried by War* (2008) makes plain.

Other biographers have also commented on Lincoln's efforts to educate himself about military matters. Geoffrey Perret's *Lincoln's War* notes, "Incredible as it may seem ... when Lincoln became president, there was still a question as to whether the president, even acting as commander in chief, had the power to determine military policy. It fell to Lincoln to create the role of commander in chief" (2004, xiii). Surprisingly, "there was no reference to any such [war powers] in the Constitution" (xii). T. Harry Williams' classic *Lincoln and His Generals* concludes that Lincoln "stands out as a great war president, perhaps the greatest in our history" (1952, v). And Brett Woods' study of Lincoln's letters to his generals says, "Lincoln harbored an aggressive, pragmatic perception of conflict. With no knowledge of the principles of war, and no technical training, he nonetheless became a viable tactician. One in which his pursuit of presidential leadership necessitated a very different image of the chief executive as a military leader" (2013, 277).

5. Letters to His Generals

Given that Lincoln was effective as commander-in-chief, and given that he was virtually self-taught as a military strategist, why would the Great Emanicipator need to be the "great war president" he was? The answer to that question would occupy a full-length book, but the question does tease at the edges of Lincoln's problems as leader of a nation engaged in a civil war. Quite simply, Lincoln had to be an effective military leader because he could not find, till the last, generals capable of carrying out—or at least proving willing to fulfill—what he saw as an effective military campaign, until he finally found General U.S. Grant late in the war. He had tried Irving McDowell, George McClellan, Ambrose Burnside, Joe Hooker, Don Carlos Buell, and George Meade, but they all seemed unwilling to fight, complained of a lack of men and materiel, and suffered from the unwillingness to move and to engage the enemy.

In other words, Lincoln had to be an effective war president because if he were not, the Union would likely have lost the war. A string of defeats at both Battles of Bull Run, at Fredericksburg, at Chancellorsville, and in the Shenandoah Valley, and a marginal victory at Antietam, to cite just a few, indicated that Lincoln had to have control of the federal forces or defeat was imminent. His hands-on approach was an absolute necessity, given the military leaders he had to choose from.

That approach demanded what Lincoln was best at: communication. He needed to encourage, prod, question, advise, and direct his military leaders in order to achieve the minimal success his generals accomplished during the first three years of the war. It is quite significant that after some initial conferences with the president, Grant concluded, "He did not want to know what I proposed to do" (quoted in McPherson 2008, 11). Grant kept the president informed about what he was going to do, but Lincoln had found in Grant a general who didn't need the kind of oversight previous generals had needed.

Consequently, a study of Lincoln's letters to his various generals reveals some interesting insights about Lincoln as a letter writer, this time in time of war. The letters reveal not only *what* Lincoln had to say, but also *how* he said it.

Of all his generals, General George McClellan frustrated Lincoln the most. McClellan, the commander of the Army of the Potomac and General in Chief, at the beginning of the war almost continuously wanted more men, more materiel, and more horses to engage the enemy in battle. In fact, McClellan frequently exaggerated the size of the opposition in order

The Rhetoric of Lincoln's Letters

to justify his call for more of almost everything an army would need, even though in practicality McClellan had all that he needed to wage war. Exasperated, Lincoln accused "Little Mac" of having "the slows," but effected, at the same time, what Perrett describes as "infinite patience with McClellan" (2004, 111).

While Lincoln sent McClellan numerous telegrams, the letters that Lincoln wrote him are more private a record, and more personal than telegrams. Telegrams may be good for orders, spelled out in the fewest number of words, but letters provided Lincoln an opportunity to speak in a personal voice that was seared into the page. For Lincoln was a consummate letter writer who could frame his words so that there was no doubt about his meaning and the voice behind the words on the page. It is that "speaking voice" that letters have and telegrams normally lack.

Arranging the letters to McClellan chronologically provides revealing insight into the evolution of Lincoln's frustration and his "infinite patience" with McClellan, and shows his use of various rhetorical strategies that failed to motivate the general until Lincoln exhausted his patience and ultimately relieved McClellan of his command.

General George McClellan. In his letters to McClellan, Lincoln tried several rhetorical strategies.

The first letter to General McClellan was written November 1, 1861. It was a simple notification that McClellan had "command [of] the whole Army. You will, therefore, assume this enlarged duty at once," but the letter contained a phrase that was quite important to the president's and McClellan's relationship: "conferring with me so far as necessary" (Basler V:9–10). That one phrase was important, because it established Lincoln as the commander-in-chief of the armed forces, making McClellan (whether he liked it or not) subservient to the wishes of the president.

Lincoln followed that first letter with a carefully worded memorandum to McClellan on

5. Letters to His Generals

Lincoln confers with McClellan.

December 1, 1861, in which he made plain to McClellan that he was ready for McClellan to move as soon as possible. It is significant then that the memo began without the niceties of a greeting, but rather with a carefully worded series of three questions that Lincoln wanted answered, reinforcing the idea that Lincoln wanted specific answers to his questions so that the Potomac Campaign could begin:

> If it were determined to make a forward movement of the Army of the Potomac, without awaiting further increase of numbers, or better drill and discipline, how *long* would it require to actually get in motion? After leaving all that would be necessary, how many troops could join the movement from South-West of the river? How many from North-East of it? [italics Lincoln] [Basler V:34]

Lincoln then outlined a detailed strategy for the use of the troops, including their movement, placement, alternative plans, and their locations, even specifying in a closing statement, "Armed vessels and transportation should remain at the Potomac landing to cover a possible retreat" (Basler V:34).

More than anything else, the memo was significant in that Lincoln, who had no training in military tactics, seemed quite comfortable explaining a seemingly detailed strategy to a West Point graduate, a man the president only a month before had made commander of the army. In essence, the memo was quite bold, but it reinforced in McClellan's mind, Lincoln probably hoped, that this was a president who was going to be very involved in the conduct of his forces as commander-in-chief. The nature of the questions, that is, their specificity, gave to the rhetoric a particular tone showing that Lincoln would be a "hands on" commander-in-chief. Also interesting is that Lincoln closed the memo not with a complimentary closing, or a statement of his support for McClellan's actions, but instead a statement of a strategy if there was a need for retreat. The tone of the memo, then, is a no-nonsense description of just what the president expected.

His letter to General McClellan, dated February 3, 1862, expressed a disagreement Lincoln had with McClellan over plans to take Richmond: Lincoln preferred a plan to "move directly to a point on the railroad southwest of Manassas," while McClellan's more elaborate plan involved moving troops by way of the "Chesapeake, up the Rappahannock to Urbana, and across land to the terminus of the railroad on the York River" (Basler V:118–119). Annotations to the letter by Brett Woods in *Abraham Lincoln: Letters to His Generals* indicate that Lincoln, while skeptical, eventually "gave the desired consent" (2013, 63). Respectfully, then, rather than rejecting McClellan's plan outright and outlining a different plan, Lincoln cautiously veiled his criticism in the form of questions, asking instead for answers to his objections:

> First. Does your plan involve a greatly larger expenditure of time and money than mine?
> Second. Wherein is a victory more certain by your plan than mine?
> Third. Wherein is a victory more valuable by your plan than mine?
> Fourth. In fact, would it not be less valuable in this, that it would break no great line of the enemy's communication, but not ours.
> Fifth. In case of disaster, would not a retreat be more difficult by your plan than mine? [Basler V:119].

These are all good questions that McClellan was asked to consider, and should have considered thoughtfully. Significant, too, was that Lincoln, for the most part, had formed the questions in parallel structure, all beginning with a number; the second and third are strictly parallel in grammatical structure, and two others also end with the phrase "than mine," adding clarity that makes Lincoln's questions easy to understand.

Parallel structure or parallelism as a rhetorical device is a scheme Edward Corbett and Robert Connor comment on at some length in *Style and Statement*: "Parallelism is one of the basic principles of grammar and rhetoric. The principle demands that equivalent things be set forth in coordinate grammatical structures.... When this principle is ignored, not only is the grammar of coordination violated, but the rhetoric of coherence is wrenched.... [Writers] must be made to realize that violations of parallelism are serious, not only because they impair communication but because they reflect disorderly thinking" (1999, 45). Lincoln seemed to realize that forming questions in parallel structure would have greatly aided the power of the communication he was sending McClellan, and parallelism was a sign that Lincoln was a careful writer.

Just five days later, on February 8, 1862, Lincoln again used questions to keep McClellan aware that the president was very much interested in just what McClellan was doing:

> Have you farther news from the West?
> Have you heard from the Canal-boats?
> Have you determined, as yet, upon the contemplated movement we last talked of? [Basler V:130]

Lincoln wanted to know the answers to these questions so that he could advise McClellan about just what course of action he wanted the general to pursue. Once again, Lincoln chose parallel structure in the form of questions to be clear and to be direct.

On March 31, 1862, Lincoln wrote a short letter to McClellan "to order [General] Louis Blenker's division to [General John C.] Fremont"; Lincoln wrote, "I write this to assure you I did so with great pain, understanding that you would wish it otherwise" (Basler V:175).

At this point Lincoln wanted McClellan to know that Lincoln had taken such action. But curiously, the last part of the letter starkly reminds McClellan that Lincoln was in charge:

> If you could know the full pressure of the case, I am confident that you would justify it, even beyond a mere acknowledgement that the commander-in-chief may order what he pleases [Basler V:175].

Significant was that Lincoln did not remind McClellan of his commander-in-chief position buried within the middle of a long sentence. Rather, he pushes that idea to the most emphatic position in the letter; that is, Lincoln pushed the thought all the way to the latter part of the last sentence of the letter with a note of stark sarcasm: "the commander-in-chief may order what he pleases."

Just a few days later, on April 6, 1862, the next letter Lincoln wrote to McClellan hinted at the impatience that Lincoln felt:

> You now have over one hundred thousand troops with you, independent of Gen. [John] Wool's command. I think you better break the enemies' line from Yorktown to Warwick Rive at once. They will probably use *time* [emphasis Lincoln's], as advantageously as you can [Basler V:182].

Lincoln thus reminded McClellan of the large army he commanded, and that the enemy would make use of any delay, and strongly suggested that McClellan move his army to meet the enemy. Lincoln did so by italicizing the word *time* and by strongly suggesting that McClellan use his troops "as advantageously as you can," once again saving the full emphasis to the last part of the sentence. Lincoln had not given a direct order, but he made quite plain just what he wanted done.

His April 9, 1862, letter, considerably longer than previous ones, was more forceful, engaging in several rhetorical strategies to get the noncompliant McClellan to take some action. Lincoln began the letter on a personal note: "Your despatches [sic] complaining that you are not properly sustained, while they do not offend me, do pain me very much" (Basler V:184).

Lincoln seemed to be saying that his person had received a painful message from McClellan, a wound, perhaps. In other words, McClellan's message was not just a simple request, but rather a personal affront to Lincoln's role as leader. The strategy seemed to be accusing McClellan of going far beyond a simple transaction with his superior. Instead, McClellan's request had been quite hurtful to Lincoln. The strategy seemed to be aimed at coaxing McClellan into action by asserting that his lack of action had injured the president not simply on an administrative level, but on a personal level, too.

His complaints about McClellan were many. First, he chastised McClellan for leaving Washington, D.C., largely open to enemy attack. To Lincoln, "My explicit order that Washington should, by the judgment of *all* the commanders of Army corps, be left entirely secure, had been neglected. It was precisely this that drove me to detain McDowell" (Basler V:184). Coming at the end of a long paragraph detailing the movement of troops away from protecting Washington, Lincoln forcefully reminded McClellan that McDowell had lost his command for such actions. In two sentences, Lincoln used the word of "*all* the commanders" (emphasis Lincoln) and the rather stark reminder that leaving Washington unprotected could get McClellan fired.

As if that were not enough, Lincoln continued the same thought that climaxed with a long rhetorical question: "Do you really think I should permit the line from Richmond *via* [emphasis Lincoln] Mannassas [*sic*] Junction, to this city to be entirely open, except what resistance could be presented by less than twenty thousand unorganized troops? This is a question which the country will not allow me to evade" (Basler V:187). The very length and detail should have excited McClellan to action.

But Lincoln had still another complaint: the persistent problem of McClellan's asking for more troops before he could act. Again, Lincoln detailed all the troops that he had sent McClellan and wrote: "You now say you will have but 85, 000 [men], when all *enroute* [emphasis Lincoln] to you shall have reached you. How can the discrepancy [between my count] of 23,000 be accounted for?" (Basler V:185). Being quite specific about the number of troops Lincoln had sent him, and then asking the question, brought force and energy to Lincoln's question. He followed that by asserting that not just Lincoln, but the entire country, wanted an answer.

Later in the same letter, Lincoln told McClellan that he must act: "I suppose the whole force which has gone forward for you, is with you by this time" (Basler V:185), a reminder that Lincoln had done all that McClellan had asked for; "and if so, I think it is the precise time for you to strike a blow" (Basler V:187). The verb that Lincoln chose was "strike," a transitive verb requiring an object, which Lincoln again very carefully chose as "a blow." The combination of a forceful verb and a noun object that itself could be a transitive verb adds great vigor to Lincoln's command. For as Lincoln asserted: "By delay the enemy will relatively gain upon you—that is, he will gain faster, by *fortifications* [emphasis Lincoln] and *reinforcements,* than you can by reinforcements alone [emphasis Lincoln]" (Basler V:185).

Interestingly, Lincoln wasn't finished. The emphasis Lincoln displayed suggests that he hoped to specifically motivate McClellan to move. In the very next paragraph, he began, "And, once more let me tell you, it is indispensable that you strike a blow" (Basler V:186), adding emphasis not only by repeating the same clause, but also by beginning the paragraph with "and," as though the first sentence in the next paragraph was a part of the same paragraph, only set aside with paragraph indention. The sentence that followed began with an italicized "I" and is a short, segregated sentence in comparison with the rest of the sentences in the paragraph: "*I* am powerless to help this" (Basler V:185), almost pleading with McClellan to "strike a blow."

The last paragraph continued the pleading: "I beg to assure you that I have never written you, or spoken to you, in greater kindness of feeling than now, nor with a fuller purpose to sustain you, so far as in my most anxious judgment, I consistently can. *But you must act*" (emphasis Lincoln) (Basler V:185). The repetition of the same command, to "act," the placement of the sentence at the very close of the letter, and the short length of the sentence—all speak of urgency for McClellan to move, but also contain a personal tone that veritably pleaded for McClellan to "strike a blow." In essence, all the devices Lincoln used come together to display Lincoln the writer at his best, while they also clearly show Lincoln's growing frustration, yet his seemingly "infinite" patience with McClellan.

The next letter to McClellan was dated May 9, 1862, while he was at Fort Monroe, Virginia. The matter Lincoln addressed was the reorganization McClellan had requested; but Lincoln wanted to "return to organization by divisions," leaving Lincoln to dismiss ineffective generals (2013, Woods, 71). Lincoln thus nixed McClellan's plan of reorganization. The primary purpose of this particular letter was to explain *why* Lincoln denied McClellan's plan, since he had already informed McClellan by telegraph of his ruling. Important to understanding the letter was the running feud McClellan had with generals Edwin Sumner, Samuel Heintzelman, and Erasmus Keyes, generals under McClellan's command (Basler V:208–209).

Lincoln dealt with McClellan in a more nuanced way, appealing to his ego. The letter began with Lincoln's saying that his dispatches had no doubt already preceded this letter, but Lincoln wanted "to say a few words ... privately on this subject," still another attempt of Lincoln to build some kind of personal rapport by appearing to address the issue on an individual basis with McClellan and explain why Lincoln made the decision he did: "I ordered the army corps organization not only on the unanimous opinion of the twelve generals whom you had selected and assigned as generals of divisions, but also on the unanimous opinion of every *military* [emphasis Lincoln] man I could get an opinion from, and every modern military book" (*ibid.*). Lincoln then curiously qualified his sentence with this: "Of course, I did not, on my own judgment, pretend to understand the subject" (*ibid.*). Lincoln thus explained the method he used to make his decision: the use of authority, good authorities that McClellan would regard as at least well chosen and that he was partially responsible for. But Lincoln did not say that.

Lincoln next turned to the reaction of others to McClellan's plan, informing McClellan of the ramifications, political and otherwise, of McClellan's reorganization: "I now think it is indispensable for you to know how your struggle against it, is received in quarters which we cannot entirely disregard" (*ibid.*). Here Lincoln turned the letter into an important message that McClellan, the person, and his professional judgment had been called into question. He then reported the tenor of the reactions: "It is looked upon as merely an effort to pamper one or two pets, and to persecute and degrade their supposed rivals" (*ibid.*). In other words, some had said that McClellan's decision-making was based on petty feelings, not sound judgment.

Lincoln quickly asserted that he had not talked to Sumner, Heintzelman or Keyes; they were not the source of the accusations against McClellan: "I have no word from [them]," but, Lincoln reminded McClellan, that they "are of course the three highest officers with you, but I am constantly told that you have no consultation or communication with them." Again, Lincoln reminded McClellan that rumors are in particular: that "you consult and communicate with nobody but General Fitz John Porter, and perhaps General [William] Franklin," with Lincoln quickly demurring: "I do not say these complaints are true or just; but at all events it is proper you know of their existence." In fact, these rumors concerned Lincoln and cast McClellan in a less than flattering light. Here, once again, Lincoln was speaking to McClellan on a personal basis and he quickly asked rhetorically: "Do the Commanders of the Corps disobey your orders in anything?" (Basler, V, 208). Lincoln wrote in such a way to allow that McClellan was correct in not talking to the three generals; asking, in other words, for McClellan to account for his lack of communication with these three generals. Perhaps McClellan had justifiable reasons for not communicating with the three generals. Once again, Lincoln did not make direct accusations or assign responsibility to McClellan, but the upshot of the letter again called into question McClellan's ethos indirectly.

Hammering away upon the same theme, Lincoln told McClellan,

"When you relieved General [Charles] Hamilton of his command, the other day, you thereby lost the confidence of at least one of your best friends in the Senate." Lincoln again reminded McClellan that the image he had with other people in power had diminished because of his actions, but Lincoln did not directly attack the character of McClellan. Lincoln continued: "And here let me say, not as applicable to you personally, that Senators and Representatives speak of me in their places as they please, without question," a reminder to McClellan that any criticism is protected in this country. Lincoln went on: "and that officers of the army must cease addressing insulting letters to them for no greater liberty with them." Lincoln did not directly accuse McClellan of writing any letters, but the implication was that such conduct was unbecoming of an officer in the army (Basler, V, 188).

Lincoln next returned to an earlier subject: the matter of the three generals McClellan did not communicate with: "But, to return, are you strong enough—are you strong enough with my help—to set your foot upon the necks of Sumner, Heintzelman and Keyes all at once? This is a practical and very serious question for you." Lincoln thus used a rhetorical question to ask if McClellan had the courage—with Lincoln's help—to deal with the three generals, a direct challenge to McClellan's ethos. To close, Lincoln reminded McClellan that the "success of your army and the cause of the country are the same; and, of course I only desire the good of the cause" (Basler, V, 209).

Much of the letter subtly represented a challenge to McClellan's ego, a way of acknowledging that McClellan had problems without directly accusing McClellan of creating any of the problems. He approached McClellan's narcissism carefully without assigning fault, maintaining that Lincoln himself would assist him without alienating him. For Lincoln knew how important McClellan was to the war effort, but he also knew that McClellan had problems.

It is indeed a masterful letter, a way of dealing with an individual Lincoln saw as a source of great frustration, but at the same time someone Lincoln had to get along with in spite of McClellan's egotism, an approach that was more nuanced than his previous letters.

After a series of short telegrams that briefly discussed strategy and McClellan's constant insistence on needing more troops (Woods 2013, 95–97), Lincoln spoke more plainly about supplying additional forces. His June 26, 1862, letter was quite direct: "The later one [dispatch] of 6:15 P.M., suggesting the probability of your being overwhelmed by two hundred thousand, and talking of where the responsibility will belong, pains me very much" (Basler V:286).

Lincoln's reaction to personally accepting the blame McClellan said would come if McClellan did not get the troops he requested, Lincoln described in personal terms: "pains me very much." Lincoln went on to explain: "I give you all I can, and act on the presumption that you will do the best you can with what you have," a presumption that Lincoln felt was quite reasonable. But he didn't stop there, adding, "while you continue, ungenerously I think, to assume that I could give you more if I would. I have omitted, and shall omit, no opportunity to send you reinforcements whenever I possibly can" (Basler V:286). Lincoln did not close with anything but his signature, clearly incensed at McClellan for suggesting that Lincoln was "holding out" on him. If McClellan was defeated and men were killed, it would be Lincoln to blame.

The tone of the letter was in direct contrast with the letter that succeeded it. Lincoln continued to address troop supply and strength in the letter that followed on July 2, 1862. By then, Lincoln had returned to using reason to deal with McClellan: "In this hope allow me to reason with you a moment. When you ask for 50,000 men to be promptly sent you, you labor under some gross mistake of fact" (Basler V:301). Lincoln then turned to numbers: "Recently you sent papers showing your disposal of forces made last spring for the defense of Washington, and advising a return to that plan. I find it included in and around Washington about 75,000 men" (Basler V:301). Then Lincoln listed all the men he had dispatched and to whom. Lincoln wrote: "Thus, the idea of sending you fifty thousand, or any other considerable force promptly, is absurd" (Basler V:300).

But ever more patient, Lincoln then qualifies his criticism: "If in your frequent mention of responsibility, you have the impression that I blame you for not doing more, please be relieved of such impression. I only beg that in like manner, you will not ask impossibilities of me" (Basler V:301). Lincoln then qualified his resentment even farther: "If you think you are not strong enough to take Richmond just now, I do not ask you to try just now. Save the Army, material and personal; and I will strengthen it for an offensive again, as fast as I can" (301). Indeed, the latter part of the letter seemed to acquiesce to McClellan's "impossible" demands. But looking closely at the letter yields some information not obvious at first. Surely, Lincoln wanted to "save the Army," but only for "the offensive again, as fast as I can." Lincoln would provide the troops, but he expected action as soon as possible. Again, Lincoln signed the letter with no complimentary close, just his signature: A. Lincoln. McClellan would have little difficulty understanding that if he were to satisfy Lincoln, he had "to strike a blow."

The next few pieces of communication in letter form and telegrams are rather mundane messages that acknowledged McClellan's needing even more troops, Lincoln's insistence that he had none to offer, and questions about the location of troops.

The next letter to McClellan told McClellan that Lincoln had sent more troops to him and congratulated him on his recent successful ventures, a rather mundane message that like many other letters was necessary communication, but hardly more than that (Basler V:303). The letter that followed the next day discussed strategy and again related the troops Lincoln was sending McClellan, but added that the president could not "send another man within a month" so "[to] reinforce you so as to enable you to resume the offensive within a month, or even six weeks is impossible" (Basler V:305). The letter was evidence that Lincoln was earnestly trying to supply McClellan with all the troops he "needed," and not supposing that McClellan's being cut off from communication could have escaped McClellan's "attention." The carefully worded letter showed Lincoln being as patient as he could be with McClellan. There are no bitter recriminations coming from Lincoln.

By now, Lincoln had tried appealing to McClellan's personal relationship to Lincoln, McClellan's patriotism, his sense of duty, Lincoln's providing for McClellan's wishes, and McClellan's persistent call for more troops. But Lincoln soon grew weary of McClellan's seemingly constant call for more men. Lincoln had kept track of the number of troops he had sent him, but McClellan's figures and Lincoln's did not match. Lincoln seemed to suggest that perhaps the more precise language of mathematics would help Lincoln get his message across. On July 13, 1862, Lincoln wrote him a letter whose undertones were obvious, but whose words were designed to use simple arithmetic to determine how many troops McClellan actually had: "I am told that over 160,000 men have gone into your army on the Peninsula. When I was with you the other day we made out 86,500 were remaining, leaving 73,500 to be accounted for" (Basler V:322). Lincoln then cited some additional figures: "I believe 23,500 will cover all the killed, wounded and missing in all your battles and skirmishes, leaving 50,000 who have left otherwise." Lincoln's counting was a clear indication

5. Letters to His Generals

that "[n]ot more than 5,000 of these have died, leaving 45,000 of your Army still alive, and not with it" (322). Clearly, there were vast discrepancies between the number of troops Lincoln had sent him and those that McClellan said he had. But characteristically, Lincoln appeared to be willing to listen to McClellan's own accounting. But his rhetoric was carefully selected. On one hand, he gave McClellan a chance to answer pertinent questions. On the other hand, these same questions could serve as rhetorical questions, a way of creating "an effect" (D. Hendrix 1996, 608–609), a tactic, then, of directing criticism at McClellan in a less direct manner. Lincoln begins with the first question: "Have you any more perfect knowledge of this as I have? If I am right, and you had these men with you, you could go into Richmond in the next three days. How can they be got to you, and how can they be prevented from getting away from you in such numbers for the future?" (Basler V:322).

The strategy is clever. If you "lost" 45,000 men, where did they go, because I sent you at least that many? Are you that incompetent that you lost 45,000 men? But if you have the men I sent you, then you can attack Richmond "in three days." McClellan would have to admit that he "lost" 45,000 men, or he would have to attack Richmond. He had no other choices. Lincoln was at his best here, using his rhetorical skills to push McClellan "into a corner" from which he had a limited number of avenues of action.

The several telegrams that followed were of a procedural nature, short questions, news of the movement of troops, and military advice. It was not until mid–October that Lincoln again addressed McClellan in letter form (Basler V:460–461). This time, Lincoln tried a final tactic: appealing to McClellan's ability to do what the enemy seemed to be able to do, but McClellan didn't. The letter challenged McClellan as he had not been challenged before, for if McClellan wasn't able to do what the enemy was able to do, McClellan admitted his own fate. Lincoln, then, used two rhetorical questions to focus on the thesis, stated a thesis, provided detailed evidence to support the thesis, re-stated the thesis, gave more particulars, stated the thesis again and cited still more particulars. The strategy is age-old, using a controlling thought, employing particulars to support that thought, and repeating the same strategy two more times. First the questions that contain the thesis.

> You remember my speaking to you of what I called your over-cautiousness. Are you not overcautious—when you assume you cannot do what the enemy

is constantly doing? *Should you not claim to be at least equal in prowess, and act upon that claim?*

As I understand, you telegraphed General Halleck that you cannot subsist your army at Winchester unless the railroad from Harper's Ferry to that point be put in working order. But the enemy does now subsist his army at Winchester, at a distance nearly twice as great from the railroad transportation as would have to do, without the railroad last named. He now wagons from Culpepper-Courthouse, which is just about twice as far as you would have to do from Harper's Ferry. He is certainly not more than half as provided with wagons as you are. I certainly should be pleased for you to have the advantage of the railroad from Harper's Ferry to Winchester, but it wastes the remainder of autumn to give it to you, and, in fact, ignores the question of time, which cannot and must not be ignored [Basler V:46] [italics added].

Here Lincoln stated the thesis and then used specific details to support that thesis, detailing how McClellan could do what the enemy was, wagoning at a distance "twice as far as you," and reminding the general that waiting for "railroad transportation as you would have to do" "wastes the remainder of autumn" and "ignores the question of time." By comparing what the enemy was able to do at "twice the distance" as McClellan, Lincoln argued rather forcefully that McClellan should easily be able to do what the enemy was able to do.

Arguing that the general should concern himself with communication, Lincoln urges McClellan to "[c]hange positions with enemy, and think you not he would break your communication with Richmond within the next twenty-four hours," another reminder that McClellan ought to be willing and able to do what the enemy would do (Basler V:460). While the import of the remark may be understood as argument as well as advice, Lincoln reminded McClellan that he and his men should be able to do what the enemy would or was able to do.

The next paragraph of the letter reiterated to McClellan that in fact he was "nearer Richmond than the enemy is by route that *can* and he *must* take. Why can you not reach there before him, *unless you admit that he is more than your equal on a march*" (italics added) (Basler V:460). Once more, Lincoln appealed to McClellan's pride in himself as a general, wondering why McClellan thought he could not do what the enemy appeared to be able to do, a re-statement of the thesis and the use of particulars to support that thought (Basler V:460).

The next to the last paragraph laid out a detailed strategy that McClellan should follow to deal with the enemy and a justification of that strategy. The last paragraph continued the movement of troops in order to engage the enemy. The last sentence of the letter, placed in a highly emphatic position, and should have left McClellan with a sufficient challenge to his abilities as a general in charge of the largest army of the nation: "it is all easy if our troops march *as well as the enemy; and it is unmanly to say they cannot do it*" (italics added) (Basler V:460).

Typically, Lincoln softens the criticism: "This letter is in no way an order," but the challenge to McClellan is real: *Are you the general you think you are, or are you not equal to the enemy? Prove it.* And he issued that challenge by repeating the thesis two times and expanding on it by using specifics that supported that thesis (Basler V:460).

But by November, Lincoln ran out of patience and seemingly, rhetorical strategies to motivate McClellan to act. So on November 5, 1862, "in spite of tremendous pressure from many political figures and private citizens, as well as the majority of his cabinet" (Basler V:486), Lincoln relieved McClellan of command. Lincoln had tried every rhetorical strategy he could muster, but they had not motivated McClellan to act. That is not to argue that Lincoln fired McClellan because Lincoln ran out of rhetorical strategies he could use to entice McClellan to act. But Lincoln felt that using various rhetorical strategies was at least part of what he could do to motivate the recalcitrant McClellan.

Lincoln was also not happy with General Don Carlos Buell, who Lincoln thought was being much too casual in carrying out a military mission in what was then called the West. Lincoln was quite concerned that Union supporters in East Tennessee were unhappy with General Don Carlos Buell, the commander of the Army of Ohio, "being hanged and driven to despair" by the Confederate forces occupying that area. Lincoln's letter of January 6, 1862, began with a bit of alliteration and a stark, clear description of his feeling: "Your dispatch of yesterday has been received, and it disappoints and distresses me." Again Lincoln used a tactic he used with McClellan, in which he told Buell that Buell's tactics were not just ineffective but rather a personal affront to Lincoln. It was not only Lincoln that Buell was disappointing, but other people, too. Lincoln wasn't shy about naming the people that Buell was letting down: "But my distress is that our friends in East Tennessee are being hanged and driven to despair, and, even now, I fear, are thinking of taking rebel arms for the sake of personal protection. In this, we lose the most valuable stake we have in the South." If letting those people down wasn't enough, Lincoln told Buell, "My dispatch ... was sent with the knowledge of Senator Johnson and Representative Maynard of East Tennessee, and they will be upon me to know the answer.... They would despair, possibly resign to go to save their families, or die with them" (Basler V:90).

But at this point in Lincoln's knowledge, he did "not offer them [his suggestions] as orders, and while I am glad to have them respectfully considered." Yet Lincoln very carefully offers an analogy with "the [First] Battle of Manassas" that Lincoln mentioned "to illustrate and not criticize." But Lincoln acknowledged, "[It] is a matter of no small anxiety to me, and which I am sure you will not overlook, that the East Tennessee line is so long and over so bad a road." Lincoln then tempered his remarks in such a way as to allow Buell to believe that if he fulfilled Lincoln's "suggestions," he would less likely cause the president the "disappoint[ment] and distress" (Basler V:90).

Overall, the strategy was to appeal to Buell by naming all the people he would disappoint if Buell did not carry out the mission that Lincoln suggested. It was a personal appeal once again, for at this point in the war, Lincoln felt that his knowledge of military tactics was not complete enough to warrant giving a direct order; besides, at this point in the war, without a clear understanding of military tactics, he needed trained generals like Buell.

But earlier in the war, Lincoln was faced with an order by one of his generals that could have had catastrophic consequences. A seasoned military leader and the first candidate of the Republican party, General John C. Frémont, operating in Missouri and dealing with Confederate guerrilla fighters, declared martial law in the state and freed all the slaves of rebel sympathizers. Frémont also planned to shoot all Confederate supporters in the state. Thus, Lincoln was faced with the possibility that if he allowed Frémont's edict to stand, it would convince many tentative Union supporters that the war itself was all about abolition of

General Don Carlos Buell. Lincoln wrote a scathing letter to encourage Buell's efforts.

slavery, and not, as Lincoln had said earlier, about preserving the Union. Given the political status of the general and the nature of the edict, Lincoln had to approach writing a letter cautiously and use his rhetorical skills with acumen.

In his first sentence, Lincoln wrote that two aspects of Frémont's proclamation of August 30, 1861, bothered Lincoln, so Lincoln walked on rhetorical eggshells in dealing with Frémont. In fact, his next sentence did not deal with the most alarming aspect of Frémont's proclamation. Lincoln at the outset deliberately explained that shooting dissenters in Missouri as Frémont planned to do had serious implications: "First, should you shoot a man, according to the proclamation, the Confederates would very likely shoot our best men in their hands in retaliation, and so, man for man, indefinitely. It is, therefore, my order that you allow no man to be shot under the proclamation without first having my approbation or consent" (Basler IV:506). The order did not display the ire of a commander-in-chief who can't believe what one of his underlings was about to do; the order was straightforward, direct, but lacking a tone of authoritarianism— a kind of gentle, yet firm command that Lincoln seemed always to be able to effect in his letters to his sometimes recalcitrant generals.

The next section of the letter contained what Lincoln thought was the most explosive implication: the possibility of the "border states" leaving the Union because of the proclamation's plan to emancipate the slaves in Missouri. Again, Lincoln approached the offending aspect of the proclamation with delicate language: "Secondly, I think there is a great danger that the closing paragraph [of Frémont's proclamation], in relation the confiscation of property and the liberating of slaves of traitorous owners, will alarm our Southern Union friends, and turn them against us." Finally, at the end of the sentence, Lincoln placed his overwhelming fear of losing the border states, and especially, Kentucky, a state politically important to the president as well as his birth state: "[And] ... perhaps ruin our rather fair prospects for Kentucky" (Basler IV:506).

Lincoln then followed this rather significant order with a sentence designed to lessen the embarrassment Frémont would feel: "[A]llow me, therefore, to ask that you will, as of your own motion, modify that paragraph so as to conform to the first and fourth sections of the act of Congress entitled 'An act to confiscate property used for insurrectionary purposes,' approved August 6, 1861, and a copy of which I herewith send you." The order surely did not have the sting other commanders might have inflicted—even reminding Frémont that part of the authority Lincoln was using came from Congress itself. Lastly, Lincoln closed the letter with considerate language: "This letter is written in a spirit of caution, and not of censure" (Basler IV:506), closing the letter with language that was clear but courteous, as much of the rest of the letter displayed.

One of the most interesting letters that Lincoln sent his generals was his letter to "Fighting" Joe Hooker, who had been appointed to the same position as George McClellan in Lincoln's long search for a general who would do more than ask for more troops and equipment. Hooker succeeded General Ambrose Burnside, who had been Hooker's immediate commander. Hooker, a man with supreme confidence in his own abilities, was, as the letter revealed, a commander that Lincoln did not have the most confidence in, but the President was willing to go along with Hooker's appointment as long as Hooker understood some of Lincoln's misgivings.

The letter is quite interesting rhetorically because of the arrangement of ideas. It opened with Lincoln's announcement, followed by a statement of Lincoln's reservations. Surprisingly, the next section was quite complimentary of Hooker as a general and person. Then Lincoln followed with a listing of aspects of Hooker's conduct displeasing to Lincoln. Lincoln then confronted the general with Hooker's call for a dictator, which the president quickly refuted, and returned to a section with Hooker's job at hand. The letter ended with a reminder that Hooker must watch his tongue and a call for the general to "give us victories" (Basler VI:78–79).

One of Lincoln's most powerful letters, it rested on several rhetorical devices. For example, Lincoln boldly stated his reservations about Hooker: "I think it best for you to know that there are some things in regard to which I am not quite satisfied with you" (Basler VI:78). The reader would expect that Lincoln would then list those qualities that Lincoln was "not quite satisfied." But instead the letter next listed all those qualities that Lincoln liked about Hooker in two pairs of similar grammatical structures:

> I believe you to be a brave and skillful soldier, which of course I like.
> I also believe you do not mix politics with your profession, in which you are right.

Then the next pair also repeated a grammatical structure, with the second sentence ending with a qualification that led immediately into the serious reservations that Lincoln had about Hooker:

5. Letters to His Generals

You have confidence in yourself, which is a valuable if not an indispensable quality.

You are ambitious within reasonable bounds which does good rather than harm, but I think that during General Burnside's command of the army you have taken counsel of your ambition and thwarted him as much as you could, in which you did a great wrong to the country and to a most meritorious and honorable brother officer [Basler VI:78].

Next, Lincoln particularized the reason for him to be critical of Hooker: "I have heard, in such a way as to believe it, of your recently saying that both the army and the government needed a Dictator." Apparently such a notion was quite insulting to the politics of the president: "Of course, it was not for this, but in spite of this, that I have given you the command" (Basler VI:78).

General Joe Hooker. Lincoln angrily replied to a letter from Hooker when Hooker suggested that Lincoln become a dictator.

Lincoln had a clever retort: "Only those generals who gain successes can set up dictators." Lincoln then returned to the business of war, but added a stinging retort: "What I now ask of you is military success, and *I will risk the dictatorship*" (italics added) (Basler VI:78–79).

Lincoln reassured Hooker that the government would support him to its "utmost ability." But then Lincoln returned to those qualities he disliked about Hooker: "I much fear that the spirit that you have aided to infuse into the army, of criticizing their commander and withholding confidence from him, will now turn upon you.... Neither you nor Napoleon, if he were alive again, could get any good out of an army while such spirit prevails," a veiled reference to Hooker's lack of support for General Ambrose Burnside, Hooker's most recent commanding officer. Lincoln then wrote a stern warning in which he used repetition as a means of driving home his message: "And now beware of rashness. Beware of rashness, but with energy and sleepless vigilance go forward and give us victories" (Basler

The Rhetoric of Lincoln's Letters

VI:78). Lincoln was certainly stern and direct, but one reason the letter is interesting is Lincoln's use of certain rhetorical devices that made it the memorable letter it is, and reinforced the sternness and directness Lincoln meant.

Lincoln sent other letters to his generals that had a somewhat nonmilitary purpose: one to help secure votes in Indiana, and the other to secure a place for military service for his son, Robert. The first was a letter to General William Sherman to ask if his men from Indiana could be excused to return home to vote in state elections a few weeks before Lincoln's own presidential election. The first sentence acted as controlling sentence: "The State election in Indiana occurs on the 11th of October, and the loss of it to the friends of the Government would go far towards losing the whole Union cause." At this point in time, Lincoln was not convinced that he would win re-election, and he needed all the votes he could gather. The votes of Indiana soldiers really mattered then. He then explained why he needed the vote of Sherman's men from Indiana to return home to vote: "The bad effect upon the November election, and especially [turning over] the State government to those who will oppose the war in every possible way was too much to risk if it can be avoided" (Basler VIII:11). Of course, Lincoln was hopeful that the majority of Indiana soldier would support him, something quite evident in the letter itself.

But Lincoln had still another problem: Indiana had a highly unpopular *draft*: "The draft proceeds[,] not withstanding its strong tendency to lose us the State." Lincoln felt that the results of the state election would indeed affect the presidential election. He explained further complications: "Indiana is

Robert Lincoln. He served briefly under Grant.

5. Letters to His Generals

the only important State voting in October whose soldiers cannot vote in the field." Lincoln had pointed out the problem, and his next move was to provide a solution to the problem: "Anything you can safely do to let her soldiers or any part of them go home and vote at the State election will be greatly in point." Then Lincoln offered a caveat to Sherman: "They need not remain for the Presidential election, but may return to you at once" (Basler VIII:11).

Lincoln, of course, for political reasons, realized that he could not order Sherman to carry out this course of action: "This is in no sense an order, but is merely intended to impress you with the importance to the Army itself of your doing all you safely can yourself being the judge of what you can safely do." Lincoln had then provided himself a defense in which the "request" was not a direct order, but equally he also alerted Sherman about the importance of his political party winning the state election, hoping that it would influence voters to cast votes in his favor in the presidential election. In the end, the letter was quite informal, was carefully organized, and rhetorically sound in the way it attempts to get Sherman to do what he wanted him to do, with "safety" (Basler VIII:11).

Another letter Lincoln wrote, on January 19, 1865, was to General U.S. Grant concerning Lincoln's son's serving in the war; Lincoln feared, perhaps less so than his wife, that his son would put be put in harm's way. The strategy Lincoln used was to try to reduce for a time the ethos Lincoln possessed in relationship to Grant's, but

General William T. Sherman. Lincoln wrote him asking him for a "political favor."

simultaneously still underlay Lincoln's ethos as commander-in-chief. Lincoln seemed to be saying: "Forget I'm the boss, but do me a favor as though I am your boss." Lincoln began the letter this way: "Please read and answer this letter as though I was not President, but only a friend" (Basler VIII:223). Then Lincoln explained: "My son, now in his twenty-second year, having graduated at Harvard, wishes to see something of the war before it ends." So far it seemed like a fairly straightforward request. Perhaps, all Lincoln was requesting was for his son to serve under Grant.

But the request became a little more complicated than just asking Grant to accept his son as a soldier: "I do not wish to put him in the ranks, nor yet give him a commission." At this point Lincoln was asking Grant for more than accepting his son as an ordinary soldier with low rank, perhaps as a private, but accepting him at a higher rank, Lincoln continued, "to which those who have already served long and hard are better entitled and better qualified to hold" (Basler VIII:223).

Then Lincoln turned his request into a question: "Could he, without embarrassment to you, or to the detriment to the service, go into your military family with some nominal rank...." At this point Lincoln wished to take personal responsibility for the assignment of rank and membership in the "family." He continued: "I, and not the public, furnishing his necessary means?" (Basler VIII:223). Lincoln then offered a way out, a means of Grant's turning down the president's request: "If no, say so without the least hesitation, because I am as anxious and deeply interested that you shall not be encumbered as you can be yourself."

General U.S. Grant. Lincoln wrote Grant asking that Grant give Robert Lincoln a "safe" military assignment.

Lincoln's request was indeed honored by

Grant, who offered Robert Lincoln the rank of captain (Woods 2013, 259). Without a doubt, Lincoln probably answered critics who wondered why his son had not served, and yet placated himself and his wife that Robert would be out of harm's way but still be a part of the army.

Lincoln, of course, wrote other letters to his generals, although as the war continued he more frequently used the telegraph to send messages. Once he placed Grant in charge and Lincoln was at least settled in his mind about who the military leaders would be, he had fewer reasons to send the kind of letters he had to McClellan, Buell, and Hooker. Instead, his letters contained a variety of purposes that were unlike those to his earlier "recalcitrant" generals. Sometimes, the letters were letters of introduction like the March 1, 1864, letter to General Lorenzo Thomas introducing a "Mr. Lewis" who would help in "facilitating the introduction of the free labor system on the Mississippi plantations" (Basler VII:217). Another letter, of March 13, 1864, to General Carl Schurz told him, "[W]ith a Major General out [of the service], it is next to impossible for even the President to get him in again" (Basler VII:217). Still another letter, to General Frederick Steele on June 29, 1864, concerned an administrative matter in the "new State government there [in Arkansas]" (Basler VII:418). There was a September 22, 1864, letter to General Grant in which Lincoln apologized for pursuing a policy that the general "had protested against" (Basler VII:17). These later letters Lincoln wrote were not as "rhetorically rich" as some of Lincoln's previous letters. They were, instead, general missives designed to transmit information rather than to persuade the reader. Since the war effort looked brighter, Lincoln possibly felt that there was little need to try to persuade military figures to act as he thought he had to in previous letters to McClellan, Buell, and Hooker.

In sum, Lincoln's letters to his generals represented either the everyday transmittal of information, or they acted as attempts to have generals McClellan, Buell, and Hooker move to action, what Douglas Wilson called "Lincoln's sword." In such letters to these three generals, perhaps out of necessity, Lincoln displayed the rich variety of rhetorical strategies he was capable of using, realizing that personal letters had the ethos of the president contained within them and directed at the reader himself. Unlike in present day politics, Lincoln did not have a variety of methods with which to speak to his generals. But when he needed to, he relied on personal correspondences to goad, apologize, and order his generals to pursue courses of action that would lead to Union victories.

6

The Logician

Background and Letters Exchanged Between Carl Schurz and Lincoln

In a number of letters, Lincoln tried to show his ability to argue logically, an ability fundamental to any lawyer's repertoire of persuasive skills. What follows are examinations of first, one set of letters that found Lincoln in a "battle of logic" in which he came up short, and the second, a "public" letter showing Lincoln at his persuasive best.

In the first exchange of letters, Lincoln displayed the intent, at least, to debate a political matter by using logical reasoning to prove his point. Logic is just one tool used to persuade an audience in rhetoric, the larger category. While many definitions are associated with it, as it is generally conceived, rhetoric refers to, either in written or oral form, the art of persuasion.

In its many forms, in Ancient Greece and Rome, rhetoric was a set of many persuasive techniques applied to audiences to convince them of guilt or innocence, or a certain course of action. But the use of logic quickly became vastly important. Surely, as a lawyer, Lincoln had to possess a clear ability to be persuasive using logical support. Arguing cases before a judge and jury often meant that he must sway them in his favor using clear lines of reasoning.

Where did Lincoln, a master communicator, learn these logical appeals? While there is evidence, discussed earlier, that Lincoln read Hugh Blair's *Lectures on Rhetoric and Belle Lettres*, a popular book that taught rhetorical skills based on models, Blair pays little attention to the fundamentals of logical appeals. The work itself is more an extended treatise on the use of models to imitate than it is a primer for those who want to

6. The Logician

learn the fundamentals of argument, for example. Blair himself admits as much when he introduces his work as "originally designed for the imitation of Youth into the study of Belles Lettres, and of Composition" (2005, 1). Lincoln must have found what he read in Blair's book reassuring since the probability is that Lincoln himself, in the main, learned the fundamentals of writing *style* in imitation of the writers he read closely, including legal writing.

Lincoln was introduced to formal legal writing by pure happenstance, acquiring a volume of Blackstone's *Commentaries* from the bottom of a barrel of "junk" he bought as a storekeeper from a man anxious to get rid of the barrel since he did not have room for it in his westward-bound wagon (Woldman 1936, 7–8).

Commentaries was the dominant law book in England and America in the century after its publication (in 1765) "and played" as Stanley Katz says, "a unique role in the development of the fledgling American legal system," the scholar concludes in his introduction to *Commentaries* (1979, iii). Katz explained that Blackstone wrote *Commentaries* "to serve two general purposes. One was to popularize the notion of university education. The other was to educate the landed class in the character of the law." In other words, it was not an introduction to logical thinking. Certainly, it was a serendipitous find for Lincoln and the course of American history, for *Commentaries* was a work whose structure must have given Lincoln some sense of how the law was organized. For example, the book opened with an introduction followed by a section on "the study of the law," followed by "the nature of laws in general," and then a section on "the laws of England" and finally a part on the "countries subject to the laws of England" (Blackstone n.p.). Such tight organizational patterns probably provided Lincoln with the basics of logical arrangement and certainly were fundamental to good reasoning. But the work isn't a study of logical appeal.

Lincoln read other legal works besides Blackstone, but as Woldman in *Lawyer Lincoln* notes, "[so] assiduously did Lincoln read the elementary principles of law explained therein, and [it] so impressed [his] naturally analytical mind with the logic and reasoning of the great English jurist, that from the chance finding of this book of law arose one of the most momentous decisions in all of Lincoln's epoch-making career—the resolve to make law his life's calling" (1936, 7). The work provided the young Lincoln with the fundamentals of the study of law, but offered little advice on logical thinking.

What seemed to be the case was that no single work seems to be the source of Lincoln's acquisition of the foundations for logical thinking. He probably acquired an understanding of logical appeal gradually and slowly, as was his wont, as he studied the way legal writing was done and probably paid close attention to format and wording in the course of his self-taught legal education. He learned then by what rhetoricians call "imitation": by studying the legal documents that used logical appeals and imitating them. In the end, Lincoln was able to acquire an impressive ability to follow the conventions not only of legal writing, but concurrently to use various persuasive techniques in the courtroom and transport them even to the political arena. Some biographers have noted his skills. For example, Ronald White in *The Eloquent President* speaks of Lincoln's "logical mind" in his First Inaugural Address and his reply to Horace Greely (2004, 156–157). Lincoln, then, was no stranger to the use of logical appeal in his writing, whether in a legal setting or a political one.

Carl Schurz. He and Lincoln engaged in a battle of logic.

So it was not surprising that Lincoln would muster the confidence to engage in a display of his logical writing abilities in a political setting with somebody who obviously reflected a similarly logical mind. This first set was an exchange of two letters from both Lincoln and Carl Schurz, an early political supporter who sought to explain to Lincoln why the Republican Party had lost seats in the U.S. Congress during the 1862 midterm elections. In the letters, both Schurz and Lincoln took particular positions and then defended those position using logical support. Noteworthy is that Lincoln used terms familiar to any student of logic: "assertion," "premise," and "fact."

6. The Logician

Carl Schurz, a German immigrant friend and political advisor, who had had training in ancient rhetoric (Horner 1952–53, 90), told Lincoln that the "defeat of the Administration is owing neither to your proclamations, nor to the financial policy of the Government, nor to the desire of the people to have peace at any price.... The defeat of the Administration is the Administration's own fault. It admitted its professed opponents to its counsels. It placed the Army, now a great power in this Republic, into the hands of its enemies.... It forgot the great rule that if you are true to your friends, your friends will be true to you, and that you make your enemies stronger by placing them upon an equality with your friends." Expanding on that idea, Schurz maintained, "Many of your friends had no longer any heart for the Administration as soon as they felt justified in believing that the Administration had no heart for them" (Schurz quoted in Horner, 94). Schurz then criticized Lincoln for appointing military leaders that were not Lincoln's administration supporters.

Lincoln's November 10, 1862, reply was a clear demonstration of his deep disagreement with Schurz. After some preliminary niceties of greetings and acknowledgment of receipt of Schurz's letter, Lincoln first very carefully laid out his position on why the Administration did so poorly in the recent election:

According to Schurz, the main causes were: "1. The Democrats were left in a majority by our friends going to war. 2. The Democrats observed this and determined to reinstate themselves in power, and 3. Our newspapers, by vilifying and disparaging the administration, furnished them with all the weapons to do it with."

Lincoln, then, like a good logician, tried to dismantle the opposition's argument by attacking Schurz's major assertions, quoting them verbatim as Schurz wrote them, and then labeling them as mere opinions or weak assertions:

> The defeat of the administration is the administration's own fault (*Opinion*) It admitted its professed opponents to its counsels (*Asserted as* fact). It placed the Army, now a great power in the Republic, into the hands of its enemies. (*Asserted as fact*). In all personal questions to be hostile to the party of the Government seemed to be a title to consideration (*Asserted as* fact) [Horner 1952–53, 95] [italics Lincoln].

In essence, Lincoln had laid out the basics of Schurz's entire argument that supported Schurz's contention that Lincoln himself was to blame for the party's defeat in the midterm elections, and labeled them as "opinion" or "assertion of facts." But, curiously, rather than point by point vigorously refuting Schurz's argument as he implied he would, Lincoln instead merely defended his position. For example, Lincoln asked to see the evidence from Schurz that supported his contentions: "On the three matters (stated as facts) I shall be glad to have your evidence upon them when I shall meet you." In other words, Lincoln is not going to refute Schurz's argument at this time, but Lincoln will refute them only when "I [Lincoln] shall meet you" (Horner 1952–53, 95)—in spite of implied promises he made earlier in the letter. But there is no evidence that Lincoln fulfilled this promise; it smacks of a delaying tactic on Lincoln's part.

Instead, Lincoln defended the reason *he* saw for the loss of seats in the Congress. For example, Lincoln noted, "[T]he administration came into power very largely in a minority of the popular vote." The facts do support the contention that his administration was elected into office by less than 50 percent of the popular vote. Based on those figures, Lincoln further asserted that he "distributed to its party friends as nearly all the civil patronage as any administration ever did" in these pre–Civil Service days of governmental jobs. In other words, Lincoln said that he appointed as many Republicans as possible, thus questioning how could Schurz see the election as Lincoln's fault. He then chided Schurz for what Lincoln assumed was Schurz's belief that all Democrats were "enemies of the government": "Mr. Schurz, ... I do not recollect that [Schurz] then considered all who were not Republicans were enemies of the government, and that none of them must be appointed to military positions." Lincoln seemed to imply that Schurz was guilty of the logical fallacy of the hasty generalization by claiming that *all* who are not Republicans were "enemies of the government" (Horner 1952–53, 95).

Lincoln followed that with an attack on Schurz's implication that all military leaders should be appointed leadership positions because they were Republicans: "It would have been a question whether the war should be conducted on military knowledge or on political affinity." He enlarged that point by observing, "I have scarcely appointed a Democrat to a command, who was not urged by many Republicans and opposed by none." He used General George McClellan as an example, noting that McClellan "was first brought forward by the Republican Governor of Ohio" as well as "the Republican delegation in Congress" and "a majority of Democrats" (Horner 1952–53, 95).

In summary, Lincoln tried to refute Schurz's point that Lincoln had

6. The Logician

appointed too many "enemys" to positions of authority. Lincoln argued that he had to do that because his was a minority party. Besides, Lincoln averred, he only appointed Democrats to high-ranking positions, such as that of general, when they were recommended to him by fellow Republicans. Lincoln concluded his letter in answer to Schurz by noting that Republican military leaders have not had any more success than Democratic ones: "I do not see that their superiority of success has been so marked as to throw great suspicion on the good faith of those who are not Republicans" (Horner 1952–53, 95).

At this point, Lincoln must have thought that he had successfully answered Schurz's criticism. Yet as Horner pointed out: "Schurz loved debate" (Horner 1952–53, 95). So on November 20, 1862, Schurz answered Lincoln. First, though, Schurz spent a great deal of time in the first part of the letter, reassuring Lincoln that Schurz understood the position he was in: "I do not know how many friends you have faithful enough to tell you things which it may be unpleasant to hear." And: "I throw myself upon your patient kindness in replying to your statements" (96). Schurz probably attempted to create a climate that would make Lincoln more receptive of Schurz's arguments.

To Lincoln's belief that Schurz would have him only appoint Republicans to military leadership, Schurz first admitted that Lincoln was correct in his observation that his was a minority party, but Schurz reminds Lincoln that "at the commencement of the war, you were sincerely and even enthusiastically sustained by the *masses* of the people and the Administration party was not confined to the Republican ranks" (italics Schurz). In Schurz's mind, the people would have supported Lincoln in almost every way: "All they wanted was merciless energy and speedy success," Schurz maintained. In the end, even Republicans were "disturbed and confused by the almost universal feeling that there must be a change, either against you or withhold their votes. I *know* this to be a fact" (Horner 1952–53, 96) (italics Schurz).

Then Schurz turned his attention to Lincoln's belief that the press participated in Lincoln's party's unpopularity in the last election: From the newspapers, "I have seen little else than a moderate and well-measured criticism. I know of none that impeached your good faith or questioned your motives." In the end, Schurz asked, could the administration have "been able to set up against it [the criticism]" as "evidence of great successes?" (Horner 1952–53, 142–143).

After that, Schurz clarified what he meant by "friends" of the administration: "I meant those who, fully [understand] and [appreciate] the tendency of the great revolution in which we are engaged, intend to aid and sustain you honestly in the execution of the tremendous task which has fallen on your lot" (Horner 1952–53, 143).

Schurz then did not blame Lincoln for appointing Democrats to high military positions, as Lincoln assumed he did; they were not the "enemies" Schurz talked about. "[B]ut it is unfortunate that you sustained them in their power and positions with such inexhaustible longaminity [sic] after they had been found failing." Schurz pointed particularly at generals George McClellan, Don Carlos Buell, and the general in charge of the Western theater, Henry Halleck, pointing out particular incidents where these men had failed and Lincoln had kept them in their positions in spite of their ineffectiveness as commanders. And in frustration, Schurz asked: "Was I really wrong saying that the principal management of the war had been in the hands of your opponents?" And more particularly, Schurz concluded with another question: "Did not McClellan, Buell, and Halleck and their creatures and favorites claim, obtain, and absorb everything?" (Horner 1952–53, 143). By using questions to elicit obvious answers, Schurz presented his argument indirectly. He thus cultivated the respectful relationship he had with Lincoln as the commander-in-chief and presented himself as subject to Lincoln's authority. But at the same time he argued that Lincoln should accept the obvious answers to his questions as tenets that both Lincoln and Schurz could agree on.

Schurz also was careful not to equivocate, that is, to change the definition of key terms. Schurz avoided any ambiguity that would have changed the meaning of a key term in the middle of an argument, "friends," by which Schurz meant "those whose sympathies you can rely as securely as their ability." These were the people who "had sown confidence and reaped disaster and disappointment" (Horner 1952–53, 143). These same people were the initial supporters Schurz saw as being grossly disenchanted with the Lincoln administration: "You must re-conquer the confidence of the people at any price, or your administration is lost" (144). In other words, his friends, regardless of party affiliation, who supported him, had lost faith in him as their leader, Schurz maintained.

The writer then ended the letter with a pathetic appeal, a way of inserting a level of emotion into his argument: "I see their familiar faces amid the campfires and to think of it, that tomorrow they may be called

6. The Logician

upon to die"; and "I hear the wailings of so many widows and orphans, and remember the scenes of heartrending misery and desolation I have already witnessed"; and finally, "I do not know whether you have ever seen a battlefield. I assure you, Mr. President, it is a terrible sight" (Horner 1952–53, 144).

The pathetic appeal was an interesting way to end the letter. It contrasts sharply with the logical flow of the argument before it, yet it also had some power of persuasion, appealing to Lincoln's sympathy for the soldiers he commanded and ending with a rhetorical flourish in the most emphatic position in the letter.

Perhaps surprisingly, Lincoln answered Schurz's letter only four day later. Lincoln opened his letter to Schurz by summarizing Schurz's position, concluding with a stylistic device: "You think I could do better; therefore you blame me already. I think I could not do better: therefore I blame you for blaming me" (Horner 1952–53, 144). This stylistic device of balancing clauses provided a summary of his understanding of Schurz's position, and as a persuasive device, subtly asked for sympathy from someone who had been critical of Lincoln's course of action.

Lincoln then attacked Schurz's charge that Lincoln had the support of the large part of the public, but squandered it with generals who were Democrats who were generally ineffective and were too long kept in their positions, generals who were at first judged by Lincoln as having their "hearts in it." Lincoln's reply asked: "But who is to be the judge of hearts, or of 'heart in it'"?—an impossibility, Lincoln implied. Lincoln then answered his own rhetorical question by asserting, "For be assured, my dear sir, there are men who have 'heart in it' that think you are performing your part as poorly as you think I am performing mine" (1952–53, Horner, 144), shifting the blame in part to the accuser. Lincoln then diverted the argument away from criticism of Lincoln's appointing ineffective generals and reminded Schurz that some were critical of how Schurz performed, too. It was a way of shifting attention away from Lincoln's handling of certain generals and placing the blame partly on Schurz, too, a kind of red herring in which Lincoln attempted to diverted attention away from the argument Schurz had presented. Next, Lincoln explained why he had not replaced McClellan, Buell, and Halleck, even though they proved to be ineffective over a long period of time. Lincoln averred, "I certainly have been dissatisfied with their slowness…, but before I relieved them I had great fears I should not find successors to them who would do any better" (*ibid.*). Lincoln had thus set up an either-or dilemma that reduced his decision to either having McClellan, Buell, and Halleck or having no successors at all. But, of course, Lincoln did have other generals he could have appointed, like Burnside, Hooker, and eventually Grant.

Lincoln then appealed to the quality of the friendship that he and Schurz had by asserting his need for sympathy: "I must say I need success more than I need sympathy" (*ibid.*, 144–145), a clever way to ask Schurz to soften the criticism and recall the friendship they had with one another, once again avoiding the real crux of the argument. Then Lincoln closed the letter. In essence, Lincoln's answer to Schurz's criticism seems more like excuses and attempts to blame Schurz rather than artful refutation of Schurz's argument.

In many ways, in terms of the sheer ability to argue logically, Schurz had gotten the better of Lincoln: asserting propositions, supporting those, carefully defining the terms of his criticism, backing those up with particulars, and making use of a number of effective appeals to cement his arguments. What is quite clear is that Schurz could argue quite effectively when circumstances demanded it.

It is obvious also that Lincoln was no match for a trained logician like Schurz. In the end, in this competition of two logicians, Lincoln had come up short. Horner says as much: "Lincoln must have felt that Schurz had the best of the argument, [for] shortly after writing his letter..., he summoned Schurz to Washington" (*ibid.*, 145). When Schurz arrived, after exchanging pleasantries in which Lincoln asked Schurz if he thought Lincoln had done his job as poorly as Schurz had made it out to be, Lincoln advanced a curious assessment of their exchange of letters: "Then, slapping [Schurz's] knee again, he broke out in a loud laugh and exclaimed: 'Didn't I give it to you hard in my letter? Didn't I?'" (146), which seemed to say that he, not Schurz, had gotten the better of the other in the argument.

Lincoln then reassured Schurz that in spite of Schurz's rather stinging criticism, they would remain friends (*ibid.*, 146). Lincoln had picked a worthy opponent, gone head to head with him, but was not willing to openly admit that that opponent had been victorious in the battle of wits. It is a side of Lincoln that does not appear in his many biographies. Did Lincoln feign the comment he made to Schurz, knowing full well that Schurz did "get the best of him"? Or did Lincoln actually feel that in this exchange of letters that he did "get the best of Schurz?" (145). It is not entirely clear.

Almost always we think of Lincoln as a humble man, not given to displays of self-aggrandizement, but the exchange of letters showed a side of Lincoln that most are not likely to see.

Lincoln's Letter to James Conklin

Yet, in another instance, in the fall of 1863, Lincoln exhibited a more impressive display of logical reasoning and rhetorical power, in a letter to a political friend, James Conklin, in Springfield, Illinois, to be read aloud, "slowly" at Lincoln's instruction, to his other supporters back in Illinois. The epistle was an example of one of Lincoln's "public letters" in which he addressed the major aims of the Civil War, since he lived when television press conferences were not possible. Other letters of its kind included "public letters" to Horace Greeley, Albert Hodges, Horatio Seymour, Erastus Corning and Matthew Richard (Carwardine 2005, 264).

Knowing his audience in Springfield would include a number of learned lawyers, he employed extensive logical thinking as a persuasive technique. In fact, one of Lincoln's secretaries, John Hay, said the letter as a whole "takes its solid place in history as the great utterance of a great man.... He can snake a sophism out of its hole better than all the *logicians* of all schools" (Nicolay 2006, 371) (italics added). Lincoln biographer David Herbert Donald called the letter "a hard-hitting defense of his administration's policies" (1996, 456), but doesn't extensively dissect the letter's reasoning and persuasive power. In his biography of Lincoln, Richard Carwardine, too, complimented the writer and said that Lincoln often used "carefully crafted" letters like this one when he needed to explain his aims carefully (2005, 264), yet the biographer also left out any careful and deliberate analysis of the letter's power. On the whole, as Helen Nicolay said, the letter is an example of Lincoln's "close reasoning, innate perception of political conduct, wit, sarcasm, and that picturesque eloquence which abounded in his earlier and more careful oratory" (371–372), but again she was not specific.

Looked at as persuasive writing, this often-quoted letter represented Lincoln at his persuasive best. Few, however, have looked at the letter's reasoning with its basis in effective organization, or as the rhetoricians call it, arrangement. Arrangement is defined as "the art of dividing a discourse into its parts and the inclusion, omission, or ordering of those parts according to the rhetor's [the speaker's or writer's] needs and situation and the constraints of the chosen genre" (1996, Fahnestock, 320). Lincoln realized that in order to convince his audience, he had to carefully present certain bits of information before he discussed others; otherwise, the audience would likely not have accepted his ideas. He then relied on this arrangement to compose a letter sequenced in such a way as to make the ideas most persuasive, or "ordering of those parts according to the rhetor's needs and situation" (*ibid.*).

The letter began (like many others of the era) by acknowledging that he had received the letter, but politely declining the invitation to speak, saying, "I cannot, just now, be absent from here, so long as a visit there, would require" (Basler, IV, 406). In explaining his reasons for not traveling to Springfield, Lincoln cast himself as both valuing those who invited him and building a relationship with the readers or audience: "The meeting is to be of all who maintain unconditional devotion to the Union; and I am sure my old political friends will thank me for tendering as I do, the nation's gratitude to those other noble men, whom [*sic*] no partisan malice, or partisan hope, can make false to the nation's life," an attempt to use such compliments as groundwork, enabling Lincoln to present his ideas to a sympathetic audience *(ibid.)*. In other words, Lincoln seemed to recognize that because what he later said in the same letter later would be difficult for his audience to accept, he strove to put the audience in a more "receptive spirit." In that way, Lincoln effected a kind of ethos that presented himself as a reasonable man behind the prose, and indicated that he was someone who was willing to take his audience in careful consideration. He effected, then, something *Style* by Joseph Williams defines as *ethos*, "the character that readers infer from your writing [that makes] them think you are difficult or accessible? Amiably candid or impersonally aloof? Trustworthy or deceitful...? [W]e tend to trust most a writer with a reputation for being thoughtful, reliable, and considerate of her reader's needs" (2007, 215).

Lincoln's next sentence rather boldly followed from the one before it: "There are those who are dissatisfied with me" (Basler IV:406). He did not try to pretend that his audience had approved of what he had done since becoming president, including the issuance of the Emancipation Proclamation, an edict which provided for the use of African American soldiers who were freed in all states "in rebellion" against the Union at that time. The Emancipation Proclamation was a particularly thorny issue

6. The Logician

in the Midwest, settled in a significant part by people from slave-holding states like Lincoln's native state, Kentucky (1988, McPherson, 142). In particular, the issuance of the proclamation became the "elephant in the room" that Lincoln would deal with in his letter only when he felt that he had sufficiently prepared his audience to accept his thinking. In other words, the organization of the letter seemed specifically designed to prepare his audience to accept his arguments.

Accordingly, Lincoln first commented on the more general topic of Lincoln's handling of the Civil War: "You desire peace, and you blame me that we do not have it," a statement that acted as background so that he could later arrive at a point where he could discuss the proclamation itself as a way of obtaining the peace his listeners so desired. Lincoln then named three ways to gain peace: "by force of arms," pointing out that he was "trying to do" that. He then used the rhetorical question: "Are you for it?" And then answered the question with: "If you are, so far we are agreed" (Basler IV:406).

He then offered two other alternatives: the first was to "give up the Union," and he averred, "I am against it" (Basler IV:406). He then followed that with another pointed rhetorical question: "Are you for it? If you are, you should say so plainly" (407). Such a question was probably intended as a way to disarm the opposition, assuring them that giving up the Union was not an option for him either.

Lincoln then presented the third alternative to ending the war: "some imaginable compromise." He dismissed that alternative, saying, "I do not believe any compromise, embracing the maintenance of the Union, is now possible," because "the army dominates the country" (the Confederacy). Such conditions made any pact involving compromise impossible: "because [no men have the power] to enforce their side of the compromise." He asked rhetorically, "[C]an that compromise be used to keep Lee out of Pennsylvania?"—a question Lincoln has already answered. But Lincoln assured his audience that any compromise that met the standards that Lincoln had outlined "shall not be rejected, and kept a secret from you," for Lincoln recognized that he was a "servant of the people" and, of course, at the same time, he wanted to project the ethos of a "reasonable man." (Basler, IV, 407).

At this point, Lincoln had dismissed other courses of action, other than his use of the force of arms to maintain the Union, his first way to win the war. He thus had presented all the other alternatives, refuted each, and then settled, and trusted his audience had settled on this course of action; that is, win the war militarily.

But how was he planning to win the war and save the Union? Lincoln now must lay more groundwork for his argument for this arrangement to work. He did so by being direct: "But, to be plain, you are dissatisfied with me" (Basler, IV, 407). He continued by noting, "I wish all men could be free, while I suppose you do not. Yet I have neither adopted, nor proposed any measure, which is not consistent with your view, *provided you are for the saving the Union*" by military means (italics added). He admitted, in essence, that he tried and failed using one approach: "I suggested compensated emancipation, to which you replied you wished not to be taxed to buy Negroes" (408). As far as Lincoln was concerned, he had exhausted other means of dealing with slavery and winning the war militarily.

So Lincoln was ready to offer a solution to the problem he said was the main concern of his audience, too: preserving the Union and confronting the "elephant in the room" now that he had anticipated and dismissed as not workable or desirable all other arguments for saving the Union through military force: "You dislike the Emancipation Proclamation; and, perhaps, would have it retracted. You say it is unconstitutional—I think differently. I think the constitution invests its commander-in-chief, with the law of war, in time of war, [that] property, both of enemies and friends, may be taken when [we] need to destroy enemies, [and] property they cannot use" (*ibid.*), an elementary strategy in time of war that he assumed his audience would have agreed with to.

At this point, Lincoln argued that the freeing of slaves, which the South regarded as property, was then a military measure to deprive the enemy of property he could use to make war. Lincoln offered a solution to the problem of winning the war militarily and saving the Union, but first he had to deal with the "elephant in the room": the Emancipation Proclamation, its legality and the arguments against it.

Anticipating the argument that the Emancipation Proclamation was not constitutional, Lincoln next engaged in a bit of logical gymnastics: "But the proclamation, as law, either is valid, or is not. If it is not valid, it needs no retraction. If it is valid, it cannot be retracted, any more than the dead can be brought to life" (*ibid.*). Either way, Lincoln said, it doesn't make any difference; it was a bell that couldn't be "unrung,'" as he said it, "a promise [of freedom] made" must be kept, since to ask freed slaves to return to slavery after the war was won would have been an impossibility.

6. The Logician

Lincoln then returned to a shared premise he had articulated earlier: that the war was being fought militarily to save the Union. How then was Lincoln to save the Union that seemed to be in such peril earlier in the war?

Lincoln then answered his own question, arguing that the war effort was not successful *before* the proclamation, but was *more* successful *after* "colored" soldiers, that is, ex-slaves who were freed by the Emancipation Proclamation and became a part of the Union's military. To support his contention that "colored" soldiers were effective in winning the war, he used a series of techniques. One method was to use an effective rhetorical flourish: "You say you will not fight to free negroes. Some of them seem willing to fight for you" (*ibid.*, 409), making his argument plain and forcing his audience to consider the import of his assertion.

He then reiterates the idea that the proclamation was to aid in putting down the rebellion. "I issued the proclamation on purpose to aid you in saving the Union"; and followed that with a rhetorical question: "Do you think differently?" (*ibid.*, 408). Wasn't saving the Union your aim, too? he asked, reminding his audience.

And then he advanced a commonsensical argument for issuance of the proclamation: "I thought whatever Negroes can be got to do as soldiers, leaves just so much less for white soldiers to do." He followed that by still more rhetorical questions: "Does it appear otherwise to you?" "Why should they do anything for us, if we will do nothing for them?" he asked.

If Lincoln's letter was to be effective, he must at this point cite still other specifics that showed that the "colored" soldiers had made a difference in winning the war. That, of course, was indeed what followed: "The Father of Waters [the Mississippi River] again goes unvexed to the sea" (Basler, IV, 408). There have been major victories at "Antietam, Murfreesboro, and on many fields of lesser note" (408). "...Uncle Sam's Webfeet [must not] be forgotten" (409). He summarized that "[p]eace does not appear so distant as it did" (409), Lincoln argued, due to the use of "colored soldiers." He even argued that the opposition, the Confederate States of America, had begun to learn to choose the "ballot" over the "bullet" (410), an apt metonymy that provided a summary of the great progress being made in the war with the addition of "colored" troops.

He then turned to a warning to those who had opposed the liberation of Negro soldiers: "[T]hen, there will be some black men who can remember that, with silent tongue, and clenched teeth, and steady eye, and well-poised bayonet, they have helped mankind on to this great consummation; while, I fear, there will be some white ones, unable to forget that, with malignant heart, and deceitful speech, they have strove to hinder it," cautioning, perhaps, those who opposed to his use of "colored" soldiers. Lincoln ended the letter cautiously: "[L]et us not be too sanguine of a speedy triumph," and added an appeal to their religious belief: "[N]ever doubt that a just God, in his own good time, will give us the rightful result" (*ibid.*).

The argument then is that if the listeners wanted to save the Union by putting down the rebellion, they must accept African American soldiers who had, in Lincoln's mind, made a difference in the war, which was made possible by issuing the Emancipation Proclamation. Lincoln had purposely arranged the letter in such a way so as to not begin too abruptly in defense of the Emancipation Proclamation and the freeing of slaves of those states "in rebellion," but rather by establishing first that his purpose was to save the Union. The addition of "colored" soldiers aided in reaching that goal, but at the same time he also warned his readers that these same "colored" soldiers would remember those who did not support their inclusion in the war effort.

Lincoln evidenced a keen understanding of presenting his argument in the most effective way, understanding that the audience objected, in part, to some of his policies. Rather than refuting their objections haphazardly, Lincoln carefully arranged his arguments in the most effective manner, expertly guiding his audience toward his own thinking.

Examination of Lincoln's power of persuasion in these letters provides a firm basis upon which to reach generalizations about his strength as a writer, a weapon in his arsenal that Lincoln wielded as way to win the war.

7

The Problem of Clemency

During the Civil War, the lack of a consistent policy for adjudicating cases of various crimes, civilian and military, created widespread confusion in the country. In the military, for example, sometimes a soldier would win clemency for a crime, while another soldier would be punished by the same military commander for seemingly the same offense. In a word, ambiguity reined. President Abraham Lincoln himself displayed great difficulty dealing with the problem. Lincoln's acts of clemency in general as they applied to both soldiers and citizens could be described as quite unpredictable. Lincoln himself, then, was probably the source of the ambiguity about who should receive and who should not receive pardons, as his policies became the model for those beneath him. Generally, perhaps inadvertently, Lincoln by his lack of consistency spread much confusion among the ranks of those who made decision about pardons for military and civilian personnel.

Looking at just one offense, the problem of desertion alone in the Union army illustrates how inconsistent commanders were, for commanders were at a loss for just what to do about the military offense, and they received little guidance from President Lincoln. It is no wonder, then, that often military commanders were quite confused and thus referred the toughest cases to President Lincoln who, in turn, might inconsistently pardon even the worst offenders.

But first some background. To begin with, in many ways, things were quite different during the Civil War. The tendency is to apply today's standards to an earlier time, and believe that the war was, as is so often pictured, a united effort on the part of all those in the North and the South. In truth, desertion, in particular, the act of leaving the army, hiding out and absenting oneself from duty, was much more common than what we have been led to believe by tradition and by many history books. Only one extensive study of desertion during the Civil War has ever been done, and that book is sadly outdated. *Desertion in the Civil War* by Ella Lonn, a noted scholar in 1928, is a thoroughly researched book using sources available to the author at the time. In Lonn's study, 104,428 Confederates deserted, while 278,044 Union soldiers deserted (1928, 234–235); the Union army was much larger than the Confederate army and the titular punishment for desertion was shooting by a firing squad.

Seeking to update much of Lonn's work, Joan Cashin, writing in *The War Was You and Me*, published in 2002, says of the whole subject of desertion: "The story is messier than that" and "commitment to the Union cause among some white Northerners was quite tenuous" (263). Cashin argues that many of the soldiers and civilians were products of a "decentralized, small town, rural society where the bonds of family and community were still powerful and beliefs in white supremacy were taken for granted. Just as community expectations could encourage men to enlist, they could even encourage men to avoid military service" (266–267).

To illustrate that the problem also existed in the Rebel army, at the very important Battle of Antietam, on September 17, 1862, as a part of Confederate general Robert E. Lee's invasion of Maryland, Lee estimated that a "third of his force" was absent, according to Sheehan-Dean in *Encyclopedia Virginia*, a figure startling enough to make students of the war wonder what the outcome of the battle would have been had Lee had that other third of his soldiers. The battle ended in a quite tentative Union victory and spurred Lincoln to issue the Emancipation Proclamation. What would have happened if Lee had actually won the battle because all of his forces were on the field? So the problem of desertion was a problem for both the North and the South.

Speaking just for the Union cause, Cashin notes that Northern support of the war was not as widespread as previously has been assumed. She relates example after example in which families actively encouraged their sons to desert since families felt no need for their sons to continue their services to their country—especially since many felt, as the war dragged on, that the war was more about freeing the slaves than preserving the Union as it originally had been presented to them. In fact, many saw military service as a form of slavery, not a call to duty and patriotism. Cashin cites as an example Clinton Wasson of Cincinnati, who deserted his unit in the winter of 1862 and lived unbothered with his family until

7. The Problem of Clemency

the spring. In fact, recruiters both North and South were also often vilified by locals, seen as objects of ridicule, and subsequently run out of town as invaders of that particular local community. Cashin cites the *Chicago Tribune,* which estimated that in 1863 there were 500 communities in Indiana and Illinois "where men could be apprehended without military force," but were not. Women often threw eggs at provost marshals in pursuit of the many deserters (2002, 273).

In fact, late in the war, the problem of desertion was so acute that the government of both North and South offered amnesty to those who would return to their units. In the North, toward the last month of war, on March 11, 1865, Lincoln issued a proclamation which granted a general pardon to "all who have deserted the military or naval service of the United States" if they return to "their proper posts" (Basler, VII, 349–350).

Besides those factors mentioned, what were other causes of all this desertion? One problem was that citizens both North and South saw enlistment more as a contractual agreement between the government and the enlistee. According to this way of thinking, the government agreed to provide food, clothing, arms, and pay, and the soldier in return agreed to fight. If, however, the soldier felt that the government was not living up to its end of the contract, the fighting man felt no compunction to stay in the army. If the soldier did not like his commanding officer, he felt no real duty to continue his services. Many units, to bypass this problem, elected their own officers, but even that did not stop certain men from deserting (Cashin 2002, 268). Another problem, a far more onerous one, was "bounty jumping." Since a man of means, say a factory owner in the North or a plantation owner in the South, could pay a rather large sum of money for a replacement for him, some rather unscrupulous men would accept the "bounty," enlist in a unit, quickly desert, move to another place, assume a new identity, collect another bounty, and desert again. As a result of this practice, the desertion rate was not as accurate as the figures reflect (267). For the bounty jumpers, it was quick, easy money. Since the practice was widespread on both sides of the Mason-Dixon Line, it became so commonplace that many didn't see it as a serious crime, especially since the common parlance was that the war itself for both sides was "a rich man's war and a poor man's fight." What was so wrong, many reasoned, since the money was going to those who needed it the most (267)?

Still another common problem was that many potential soldiers did not come from a strong military tradition where the federal government could tell them what to do. Being true to the family and the state were much more important to them. Some even feared that they would give their lives to a cause they didn't believe in, or as Cashin notes, "Ultimately, they didn't see losing their lives for a cause that was often very confusing to them as all that worth it" (2002, 265).

A look at Kentucky illustrates the desertion problem. In fact, Kentucky was Lincoln's birth state and Lincoln realized how important Kentucky was to the war, concluding that to "lose Kentucky is nearly the same as to lose the whole game.... Kentucky gone, we cannot hold Missouri, nor, as I think, Maryland. These all against us, and the job on our hands is too large for us. We would as well consent to separation at once, including the surrender of the capital" (2009, Harrison, 300). Writing in the *Civil War in Kentucky*, Lowell Harrison notes that the Bluegrass State "then ranked ninth" in population in the United States, and "she occupied seventh place in the value of farms and fifth in the value in the value of livestock." In addition, the state "ranked fifteenth in both capital invested in manufacturing and the value of products" (2). Kentucky was important geographically, too, with its northern border next to Illinois, Indiana, and Ohio (3). If the state supported the South, Kentucky could be a launching station to raids in the North. If she stayed in the Union, Kentucky could be used as a buffer state to the South. Lincoln realized how important it was to keep Kentucky in the union.

Kentucky was, after all, a slave state, with about 20 percent of its people in bondage. Kentucky then depended to a great degree on those slaves for its economy. Many felt that by not seceding from the Union, Kentucky would eventually be able to retain its slaveholdings and continue its usual way of life. Even the Emancipation Proclamation exempted Kentucky and the other border states from the abolition of slavery. Kentucky also furnished soldiers for both the Union army and the Confederate army, with as many as 40,000 soldiers wearing gray. Parts of Kentucky were staunchly Union, and other parts, especially around the Bluegrass and in western Kentucky, were quite loyal to the Confederacy. Many other Kentuckians didn't really have a dog in the fight and just wanted to be left alone.

Truly, Lincoln had to be quite careful when dealing with the problem of desertion in Kentucky. Not surprisingly, he had to devote careful attention to the issuance of pardons in the state of his birth rather than drive Kentucky into the hands of the opposition. Since the state had loyalties North and South, military commanders had to handle desertions delicately.

7. The Problem of Clemency

P.S. Ruckman, Jr., and David Kincaid, who updated Dorris' work on clemency, concluded that Lincoln systematically "used a relatively wide variety of clemency actions and strategically employed clemency powers in the border states." In the end, they assert, "Lincoln was sympathetic toward petitioners from Kentucky" (1999, 95).

The figures for desertion in the state, based on the evidence available, was that 3,482 soldiers from Kentucky deserted from the Confederate army, while 7,227 soldiers from Kentucky deserted the Union army. Converting those figures to percentages, 3.31 percent of the Kentucky Confederates deserted, while 2.59 percent of the Kentucky Union soldiers deserted, figures fairly close together when all things are considered. But Kentucky's population was less than, say, New York, which had an unbelievable 44,913 deserters, for a 16 percent desertion rate (1928, Lonn, 234–235), so the desertion rate for soldiers from Kentucky, for both North and South, was relatively low, considering all the factors mentioned. In contrast, Kentucky soldiers in both the War of 1812 and the Mexican War joined up in large numbers and served honorably, creating a tradition that affected the desertion rate in the Civil War on both sides.

Union and Confederate soldiers from Kentucky set themselves apart from other soldiers from other parts of the country in the intensity of their deep devotion to the family. The Confederacy handled Kentucky troops differently. For example, Confederate general Humphrey Marshall in two letters to his commanders pointed out the "problem" of many Kentucky soldiers. In one letter, General Marshall admitted that recruiting for the Confederate cause in Kentucky "was a signal failure," a problem the Union forces also had. Kentuckians who didn't support the war just wouldn't join up, in spite of those who eagerly supported one side or another (United States War Department, 1880–1901, series 1, vol. XX, Part II, 408).

In another letter from Marshall, he outlined the problem of getting Kentuckians to fight outside of Kentucky. He wrote: "[A]fter the retreat from Kentucky was determined on, and they were called upon to pass their homes, to leave their families to the tender mercies of the Union men of Kentucky, it was more than they were willing to stand and they vanished day after day" (*ibid.*, 390). To combat this problem, in the same letter, Marshall commanded one of his officers to "remain in Kentucky with his soldiers until further notice." Marshall's reasoning seemed to be that he could get his Kentucky soldiers to fight in Kentucky, but not outside the state, as the ties of the family and community were too strong.

An even larger problem in handling desertions among Kentucky soldiers was the gross inconsistency in the form of punishment by commanders. Some deserters were shot, but that wasn't always the case. For example, a particular regiment of Union soldiers aptly illustrates how the Twenty-Seventh Union Infantry handled desertion. On September 4, 1863, five men (James Anderson, Frazier Carmen, Christopher Coffey, John Coffey, and James Pointer) were all executed in Munfordville by a firing squad, for desertion, ordered by a general court-martial (Kentucky Adjutant General's Office 1866, vol. 1, 250–251). Yet Company G of the same unit listed fifteen men who had deserted who apparently were not executed. In fact, while something was known about where they deserted, there is no evidence that they were ever punished. In Company D William Mitchell deserted, was arrested on January 6, 1863, and was "sentenced to serve the residue of his time in military prison," before being "restored to duty on November 15, 1864" (242–243). Similarly, in the same company, Thomas Kelm is reported as "deserted on February 5, 1863; arrested on June 26, 1863; sentenced to forfeit all pay and allowances to December 31, 1863" (*ibid.*). Still another deserter, Thomas Caswell, from the same unit, who deserted on July 28, 1862, "was arrested and returned to duty April 4, 1863; sentenced by the General Court Martial to be dismissed from out of service" (256–257).

What these examples point to is the gross inconsistency of punishment for desertion for this particular Union military unit. Some soldiers were shot; some deserters were never pursued and punished; some were sent to military prisons but later restored to duty; some had to forfeit pay; and some were dismissed from service. It seems, as far as this unit was concerned, the army didn't know just what to do with deserters.

In most of the country, for the Union, Lincoln's liberal policy for granting pardons was not helpful for commanders in deciding punishment for their recalcitrant soldiers and civilians who had broken laws. In fact, it may be true that Lincoln's policies added to the problem for both generals and government officials. General William T. Sherman wrote, "[T]oo many spies and villains [mean] time consumed by trial, review and remission to Washington, and we know that it is very hard for the President to hang spies, even after conviction, when a troop of his friends follow the sentences with earnest and ex-parte appeals" (1998, Dorris, 550). Secretary of the Navy Gideon Wells wrote in his diary that Lincoln was "always disposed to mitigate punishment, and to grant favors. Sometimes this is a weakness" (551).

7. The Problem of Clemency

To his credit, Lincoln did not see all requests for pardons for soldiers and civilians. Edmund Stedman, Attorney General William Bates' pardon clerk, kept all but "the most deserving cases from coming before the kind Mr. Lincoln at all; since there was nothing harder for him for him to do than to put aside a prisoner's application and he could not resist it when it was urged by a pleading wife and a weeping child" (Dorris 1998, 550). Of those convicted in civil court, Lincoln pardoned 375 people and denied pardon for 81 (548). According to the *Abraham Lincoln Encyclopedia*, the figures for military pardons are 225, but they only cover from March 1861 to April of 1863 (Neely, 1982, 60). In the main, besides his favoritism toward the border states (especially Kentucky), and his pardons for young soldiers, his pardons didn't seem to follow any pattern, but his pardons served a number of purposes.

First, Lincoln used military pardons to "boost the morale" of the fighting men in the Union army. He recognized that if he were perceived as a man of mercy, they would realize that he cared about their welfare. Since they endured the most hostile conditions, being in danger of losing limbs and even their lives, Lincoln knew that boosting the morale of Union soldiers could lead to their voting for him in the next election, votes he probably needed to be returned to office (Ruckman and Kincaid 1999, 84).

Lincoln also was quite forgiving to those young soldiers who deserted because they had been persuaded to do so by a "political agitator." "Must I shoot a simple-minded soldier, while I must not touch a hair of a wily agitator, who induces him to desert?" (Dorris 1998, 553). Lincoln was also quite willing to pardon young soldiers who were charged with sleeping while on guard duty. If the soldier was under eighteen, he was likely to win Lincoln's favor. He wrote General George Meade, "I am not willing for any boy under eighteen to be shot" (551). While older men charged with the same offense could not count on Lincoln to grant clemency, Lincoln himself, who had a young son, must have felt that these young men had not experienced much of life and lacked the experience to be responsible for such crimes.

As already mentioned, Lincoln often granted pardons to those living in the border states, believing that being merciful would pay off in keeping those states in the Union. That is not to say that the border states stayed in the Union solely because of Lincoln's liberal issuance of pardons, but granting pardons was one of many measures that Lincoln used to win the favor of these states.

On occasions, although not consistently, the president granted clemency to those who had political power. For example, in civilian court, Lincoln pardoned three New Yorkers who seemed to have been granted clemency because of their partisan politics in a state threatening to go against Lincoln in the 1864 election. As was many times the case, he required the petitioners "to endorse his pardon in writing before he commuted the sentence, relieving him of the sole responsibility of the pardon" (Dorris, 555). In addition, especially in the early years of the war, Lincoln was quite generous with his pardons of Confederate soldiers in Union prison camps. As president in the early part of the war, he felt he should do all he could to encourage Rebel soldiers to sever their former ties to the Confederacy and take an oath of allegiance to the Union cause. By doing so, he realized that a soldier who had switched sides dealt a blow to the Confederate army already outmanned (558).

In 1864 and beyond, Lincoln issued a number of pardons because the "Declaration of Amnesty and Reconstruction" granted amnesty to deserters already in prisons if their generals thought they would be of some use in the war (Ruckman and Kincaid 1999, 86). Of course, the number of deserters was quite high, since many were disenchanted with the conduct of a war that seemed to drag on well past their ability to endure the suffering they had felt. These cases are not usually counted as a part of the pardons that Lincoln granted, since the act, granted by Congress itself, was not directly in Lincoln's purview. Dorris says that the policy also applied to the ordinary citizen of the South as a way of establishing some approach to the "dissatisfied countryman" that would become a part of reconstruction, expressed most nobly in Lincoln's Second Inaugural Address—"with malice toward none, with charity for all"—words that signaled that the Lincoln administration would be merciful in dealing with the states in rebellion.

Relevant to any discussion of Lincoln's pardoning is a listing of the crimes he pardoned. These included, from the most frequent to the least frequent pardons: "counterfeiting; postal violations; theft, burglary and larceny; murder and manslaughter; assault and battery; conspiracy; treason; violation of revenue laws; forgery; rebellion; mutiny; holding confederate office; arson; fraud; perjury; rape; embezzlement," and a host of other crimes of lesser severity (Ruckman and Kincaid 1999, 91). In essence, Lincoln did not seem to avoid pardoning those who had committed relatively lesser infractions or were indicted for more serious crimes. All in all, Lincoln's

7. The Problem of Clemency

tenderness was applied to those who faced a punishment of death. A contemporary summarized Lincoln's many pardons as "a man clothed in almost absolute power, who never abused it except on the side of mercy" (Dorris 1998, 551).

Even Lincoln's pardons, in their own way, subtly reveal insights into Lincoln the writer. Lincoln's pardons are, after all, in the rhetorical sense, arguments for a particular course of action. So studying the pardons rhetorically seeks to answer key questions such as these: What effect is the writer trying to create? How does the writer get ideas to persuade the audience? What choice of words or diction is going to be the most persuasive for a given audience? In the end, those questions may be quite important to the overall effectiveness of the writer to persuade a given readership. Sometimes a writer makes use of a single course of action in persuading a particular audience.

Joseph Colavito in *The Encyclopedia of Rhetoric and Composition* suggests a way that writers answer these questions and clarifies just how the writer is to proceed (1996, 492–493). Sometimes the writer will appeal to an audience using the character of the writer himself as persuasive, or what may be called the ethos of the writer. For example, the writer may consider what effect the writer wants to create using his ethos. Granted, the writer may also use the language employed and the arrangement of ideas to supplement his ethical appeal.

At other times, the writer may use logic, facts, or reasons to persuade the audience. While ethos is always important, what may be more important to another audience are the facts and reasoning the writer uses. For example, an audience of physicians may be more convinced by the statistics surrounding a particular drug than by the reputation of a researcher. However, if the person citing statistics is grossly inept at presenting those statistics, the presentation may be unsuccessful simply because the audience is not able to extract or accept the necessary information due to the ethos (in the form of abilities) of the presenter.

Still another appeal may use emotion to convince an audience of a certain course of action. While the writer may use a mixture of ethos and logos, the main thrust of the argument may be a pathetic appeal. In such an appeal, the writer attempts to sway the audience to his position by appealing to the reader's feelings and emotions. For example, a particular charity describing a young child who may starve to death if a certain amount of money is not raised makes use of a pathetic appeal. The audience is persuaded then to move in a particular direction and donate money to keep the child from starving. While it may seem that the pathetic is a weak appeal, it is used much more often than it may seem, especially by legitimate charity groups trying to raise money. Colavito remarks, "The place of pathos in the rhetorical tradition is a significant one; emotional appeals constitute a crucial intersection among audience, [writer], and subject matter, so the connection between audience analysis and rhetorical purpose comes to be an important component of the construction of emotional appeals" (1996, 494). Consequently, rarely is the persuasive act solely based on a pathetic appeal; instead pathos may be mixed with some justifiable parts of ethos and logos to render an effective argument. If the pathetic appeal is the only appeal, the reader has a right to be suspicious, since a pathetic appeal alone discounts or ignores evidence in arriving at a decision, such as in the case of Lincoln during the Civil War, to pardon the individual.

Using this information about the three different kinds of appeal may seem unimportant in examining Lincoln's pardons, but closely examining his clemency requests for all offenses reveals that Lincoln often used the three different appeals generously, and perhaps unknowingly, thus adding to his generals' own confusion about granting or not granting pardons. Sometimes Lincoln issued par-

Civil War soldiers. Lincoln wrote pardons for many soldiers—critics believed too many.

7. The Problem of Clemency

dons based on his position alone, that is, his ethos as president. At other times, Lincoln made use of evidence in granting pardons; that is, Lincoln used logos in issuing clemency. At still other times, he seemed to grant clemency for crimes military and civilian based on a pathetic appeal only; in other words, Lincoln at times granted pardons merely on an emotional appeal.

Generals, recognizing Lincoln was the commander-in-chief of all the military forces, were occasionally confused about when to grant pardons and when not to grant pardons, since Lincoln's policies for granting pardons, they thought, served as a "model" for military leaders to follow. Yet sometimes in a case, when it seemed that the soldier or civilian was obviously guilty, Lincoln unpredictably would pardon the soldier or civilian. Besides Lincoln's policy in issuing pardons for predictable patterns for those young boys under eighteen and those from the border states, it was anyone's guess whether a soldier or civilian would be granted clemency. The model, then, that he provided was wrought with confusion and contradiction.

Lincoln, at times, seemed desperate for any way to pardon a soldier or civilian. And in these attempts he made use of the three appeals of ethos, logos, and pathos as argumentative patterns that seemed to justify the pardons he issued. This is not to say that Lincoln was an astute student of Greek and classical rhetoric, but he did carefully model in his writing the rhetoric of his contemporaries through, among other places, the letters where he practiced extensive composition, the most important influences in Lincoln's age. As a sign of the times, Lincoln in some cases used facts, expert testimony from his generals or the accusers, or other logical appeals. In other instances, he found little evidence to justify pardons, so he used emotional appeals, being swayed by his feelings instead of logic. In the third category, he used his authority as president to justify his pardoning of some offenders, relying on his own ethos as justification for granting clemency. He wasn't swayed by evidence or emotions; he quite simply granted a pardon because he felt a pardon was justified—for whatever reason he felt appropriate.

Truly, Lincoln struggled and agonized with each decision. As Edmund Stedman, the pardon clerk in the Lincoln administration, says, "There was nothing harder for him to do than put aside a prisoner's application, and he could not resist it when he was urged by a pleading wife and a weeping child" (1982, Neely, Jr., 61). In the end, Lincoln's inconsistency in meting out justice may have had an effect on those below him, such as in the military and civilian ranks, and that lack of consistency spread confusion among them. While we cannot be certain that such inconsistency on President Lincoln's part spread confusion in the civilian and military ranks, it seems likely that the model for the confusion among generals could have been Lincoln himself and his pardons. Whatever his motivation, Lincoln's use of the three appeals were convenient tools to help him issue pardons, perhaps never realizing that he was spreading confusion at the same time.

What follows illustrates Lincoln's confusing pardon policy and his use of the rhetorical appeals of logos, pathos, and ethos to stimulate his thinking and generate the pardons for civilians and soldiers. (I have drawn from only the main text of Roy Basler's *Collected Works of Abraham Lincoln*; those pardons contained in the appendix to volume 8 were not considered since they may not be Lincoln's work and they contain little or no text.)

In this first group, Lincoln renders pardons for no other reasons than his own authority or ethos as president of the United States. He offers no tangible testimony, reasons, or witnesses other than his own belief that the applicant should be pardoned. Lincoln is saying to his readers that he believes that the applicant should be pardoned. In other words, the strength of his argument to pardon resides in his own authority: He doesn't have to explain his reasons for granting the pardon; his ethos is enough. Obviously, the very fact that he alone grants the pardon strengthens his ethos, too, for soldiers and civilians alike realize that he does have mercy, and he is not the hard disciplinarian they might imagine he could be. After all, he probably knew that soldiers and civilians would view him more favorably if he did occasionally pardon a perpetrator based solely on his own ethos without hard evidence. It is also important to understand that ethos was by far the most frequent means by which he granted pardons, far beyond logos and pathos.

The first case is that of Robert Sutton from the South Carolina Volunteers, who was convicted of mutiny. The pardon is composed of only eight words, with no references to those who might have spoken on Sutton's behalf except an allusion to Judge Advocate General Joseph Holt, who presumably forwarded the case to Lincoln:

July 21, 1863
   Let the sentence of Sergeant Sutton be remitted [Basler VI:340].

It's entirely possible that Sutton was pardoned because he was from South Carolina, the first state to secede from the union, acting as an impetus to remind the South of his being one of their own residents.

The second example concerns a soldier named William Blake, under sentence for murder. In the message, Lincoln asked for and later received additional records on Blake:

December 21, 1863
It is said that William H. Blake is under sentence of death at Fort Magruder, in your Department. Do not let him be executed without further orders from me. In the meantime have the record sent to me. He is said to belong to the 1st or 2nd Pennsylvania Artillery [Basler VII:82].

Later, on April 27, 1864, Blake received a pardon from Lincoln with no further explanation, nor reference to further material to be examined in the case that may have exonerated him. All that is said is that he was pardoned.

Another case, that of John Burnam, a "Kentucky rebel," illustrates Lincoln's special mercy for those from Lincoln's birth state, in spite of the person's support for the Confederacy:

December 19, 1863
Attorney General, please make out a pardon for Mr. Burnam, in this case [Basler VII:80].

Again, Lincoln offered no extenuating circumstances that might have had some bearing on the case. Lincoln appears to have pardoned Burnam because he was from Kentucky.

In all three cases, Lincoln uses his ethos to decide the cases, not using testimony, witnesses, or any other factors that may have some bearing on deciding the cases. His argument to his readers was that as president and with the ethos of that office, he had a right to pardon the individual without offering any reasons, witnesses, or outside sources; his own position was sufficient.

Many pardons fitting in this category contain some sort of stipulations attached to them. It is as though Lincoln wanted to make sure that if he granted pardons, there would be some sort of assurance or qualifications to go along with them. Usually it was a simple statement that they who received the pardon agreed to return to their units, or swore allegiance to the United States, for example.

The first pardon is that of Jacob Bowers, illustrating Lincoln's stipulation that he "returns to duty," given on December 30, 1863:

> Jacob Bowers is fully pardoned for past offences, upon condition that he returns and reenlists for three years or during the war [Basler VII:98].

The assumption is that Bowers would take the pardon and the stipulations rather than being shot for desertion.

The second pardon like this is that of a private who is under sentence for "offenses prior to this," whatever they are:

> January 15, 1864
> If Private William G. Toles, of 59th, Ohio Volunteers, returns to his regiment and faithfully serves out his term, he is fully pardoned for all Military offences prior to this [Basler VII:130].

Again, the assumption is that there are certain qualifications attached to the pardon.

The third pardon is to an unidentified soldier, serving in a unit, also unknown to the editor. Presumably, the pardon got to the appropriate soldier:

> November 16, 1864
> Upon rejoining his regiment as soon as practicable & faithfully serving out his term, this man is pardoned for any overstaying of time or desertion heretofore committed [Basler VIII:112].

In all three of these cases, Lincoln cites no evidence that would argue for the pardon of the individual soldier; instead he relies on his own believability as justification for granting the pardon.

Other pardons, however, do use evidence before declaring any decision. It may be on the recommendation of a commanding officer, a prominent figure in public office or well-known member of a particular community; Lincoln in these cases grants a pardon based on some sort of evidence other than his own feelings about the individual soldier.

Perhaps the most detailed set of pardons by Lincoln surrounded the Sioux uprising in Minnesota in August of 1862, after the Native Americans attacked white settlers in the area because promised money, food and supplies, according to treaty, had not arrived to the Native Americans as a result of corrupt agents and traders (Burlingame 2008, vol. II, 480). To deal with the uprising, H.H. Sibley headed an investigating committee that condemned to death 303 Sioux, motivated in large part by angry settlers who demanded retribution for the "barbaric actions" of the Native Americans. After consulting his cabinet, Lincoln asked for suspension of the hangings until he had time to study the sentences. Pressured by, among others, the

7. The Problem of Clemency

governor of Minnesota who demanded the Native Americans be punished, and those such as Bishop Henry Whipple, a Methodist Episcopal who argued for restraint, Lincoln was barraged by white settlers who claimed they were totally surprised by the attacks by the Sioux, but still demanded justice even after the facts of the case were known. Lincoln realized that the situation was also political, since the whites were voters whose voices would reverberate throughout the rest of the nation. In the end, Lincoln ordered that 38 Native Americans be hanged, specifically those who had committed murder and participated in rapes. In a present-day analysis of the incident, David Martinez argues that Lincoln "was less concerned with any of the victims of the 1862 war and more interested in quelling the unrest among belligerent Minnesotans threatening rebellion" (2008, 21). As a result of his decision, Burlingame says that after the rest of the country learned of Lincoln's action of reducing the number of hangings, he gained a reputation for mercy (vol. II, 480–484). What is significant about Lincoln's only hanging 38 Native Americans and not 303 as requested was that in issuing the pardons, Lincoln did consult the advice of a large number of people on both sides of the issue, and only made his decision after careful and deliberate study (Basler VI:6–7):

> Washington, Dec., 16, 1862
> As you suggest, let the executions [be] fixed for Friday, the nineteenth (19th) instant, be postponed to, and be done on Friday the twentysixth [sic] (26th) instant [Basler VI:6].

Lincoln thus displayed an organization pattern, logos, to organize his thoughts and argument when he consulted other sources outside himself, unlike the ethos he displayed using only his own thinking in deciding on pardons.

The second pardon of this sort was granted to William Martin on January 9, 1862:

> This man William Martin, it seems, has been imprisoned on some charge of suspicion of kidnapping and as Senator Pomeroy and Hon. Green Adams ask for his release, let him be released [Basler V:6].

Here Lincoln is relying on the ethos of Senator Pomeroy and Hon. Green Adams to reach a decision about whether or not to pardon Martin. Lincoln decided to pardon Martin based on the testimony of prominent individuals assumed to have substantial enough ethos to justify it.

The third pardon is for manslaughter, a serious crime, and again based on the testimony of reliable figures, Bernhardt Weiss and H.P. King, identified in the notes of the pardon as recommending Henry Williams from Baltimore for a pardon:

> February 10, 1863
> Let a pardon be made out in this case [Basler VI:98].

In another case, the two prominent figures who recommend a pardon are not named in the pardon, but are provided by the editor. Trusting in the ethos of those who recommend a pardon, Lincoln accepts their testimony as sufficient reason to issue a pardon (Basler, IV, 389).

Fourth, the following pardon names a Dr. Charles T. Ratcliffe for consideration by Lincoln:

> December 14, 1863
> If upon examination of this case you find that the facts are in accordance with the statement of the petition and that Dr. [Charles T.] Ratcliffe took the oath of allegiance at the invitation of our military authorities & has since kept it inviolate, let him be pardoned for any treasonable practice previous to such recantation, and freed from the penalties now overhanging him [Basler VII:62].

What makes this interesting as a pardon is that not only does the pardon rest upon certain stipulations—that the facts are borne out, and that he has taken the oath of allegiance from military authorities—also, Lincoln wants to be absolutely clear that those stipulations must be adhered to if he is to grant a pardon.

The third category lists pardons granted based on pathos, that is, emotional appeals. In other words, Lincoln doesn't argue from his authority as president or the testimony or recommendation of certain individuals, but instead he grants appeals based on purely emotional pleas, the seemingly weakest form of argument in most cases, but convincing as far as Lincoln is concerned:

> April 20, 1863
> I have promised this lady to ask your attention to the application for her husband, James E. Dunawin, for a pardon—the application said is now before you [Basler VI:180].

Although not specifically mentioned, Lincoln issues the pardon simply because Mr. Dunawin's wife asked for it. No evidence or testimony is offered, and there is no indication that Lincoln's ethos as president is referred to or cited.

The second example of pardoning using pathos is based on a combi-

7. The Problem of Clemency

nation of logos, particularly, "officers of his regiment," and the fact that the subject of the pardon has "already suffered much":

> Feb. 8, 1864
> In consederation [sic] of the recommendation referred to, and that the party has already suffered much he is hereby pardoned for the rest [of his enlistment?] [Basler VII:173].

This combination of appeals redoubles Lincoln's argument: an appeal from logos in the form of the officers' testimony, and an emotional appeal that the man has suffered enough.

The third example of a pathetic appeal is a pardon of Charles Brady, who was pardoned twice: once for desertion with a stipulation that he served "out his time faithfully," and another time, six days later, after receiving a cruel form of punishment that Adjutant General Joseph Holt termed "excessively harsh." Lincoln appears to be moved by Brady's unusually harsh punishment:

> January 17, 1865
> Pardon on condition of serving out his time faithfully in his regiment [Basler VIII:233].
> January 23, 1865
> Pardon for unexecuted part of sentence [Basler VIII:219].

The notes submitted by Joseph Holt and interpreted by Roy Basler say that Brady had been "branded on his left hip the letter 'D' three inches high in addition to receiving a sentence of three years of hard labor." The sheer magnitude of the harshness must have moved Lincoln to remit his sentence quickly.

In these three cases, Lincoln decided upon pardons based upon an emotional or pathetic appeal. He then granted pardons based not on the use of ethos or logos, but upon the emotions he must have felt when he read the soldiers' files and found them moving.

In the end, Lincoln used pardons in a unique situation: a civil war involving states in rebellion against the democratically elected government. It is undeniable that some of the pardons were given for political purposes, especially those of soldiers from Kentucky and other states, to curry their favor and to keep those states in the Union. It is difficult indeed to measure the political effectiveness of that strategy, except that no border states or any other states seceded from the Union after he granted pardons. But it is also possible that President Lincoln used pardons as opportunities to show mercy toward soldiers and civilians, the kind of altruism that he is known for. Indeed, some in his cabinet thought he was *too* merciful. James Speed, attorney general at the time, said, "His love of mankind ... was so boundless, his charity all-embracing and his benevolence so sensitive that he sometimes was as ready to pardon the unrepentant as the sincerely penitent offender" (Dorris 1998, 567). For example, Lincoln was by all accounts sympathetic to young soldiers who had been charged with very serious crimes, especially sleeping on guard duty or desertion, granting pardons simply because as president he had that right. In that way, his pardons were oftentimes difficult to understand by military and civilian alike.

In the minds of many, he may have been wrong, but Lincoln did have that power in the Constitution, and he often used that power. In a word, he had the ethos to pardon those he wanted to pardon. At other times, Lincoln relied on evidence and the testimony of prominent figures and generals. He used various facts and testimonies outside of himself in support for granting pardons. In those cases he made use of the evidence to justify to his readers why he granted pardons. At still other times, Lincoln was swayed by the emotions surrounding a case, and he assumed that his readers would understand and be touched by the emotions. To summarize, then, Lincoln used ethical appeals, logical appeals, and pathetic appeals to sway his readers to understand why he granted pardons.

At the same time, he used these three appeals not only to help him organize why a particular individual should receive a pardon, but also to express opinions or orders in language his readers would understand. In that way, he employed the three appeals to hone his skills as a writer, for they assisted him in arriving at a decision about whether or not he should grant a pardon and determine what language to use. For when he did reach a decision, Lincoln was quite careful to use the word "pardon" or another form of the same word, making perfectly clear his intentions. His decisions were also often written in short sentences, but the brevity of his sentences doesn't mean that Lincoln didn't struggle over his decisions and the language in which to express himself. He seemed to know that convincing various audiences of the appropriateness of a pardon required that they were swayed, too, by the same line of thought he felt appropriate. In fact, his careful use of the appeals—which he somehow learned on the road to acquiring his great facility with the use of the written word—helped him arrive at a decision and the language appropriate to the situation.

No doubt Lincoln, alone in the power he possessed, agonized over whether or not to grant certain pardons and struggled over just what the right language was in which to write those pardons. In doing so, he displayed what Francis Bacon had said so many centuries earlier: "Writing [makes] an exact man." Bacon pointed out that all writers—and especially effective ones—struggle with just what words to use to best express themselves. So the angst that Lincoln felt as he wrangled over just the right words to convey his decision is time-honored and universal. In other words, Lincoln's grappling to find the right language in which to express an idea is the same kind of angst that all writers agonize over when they attempt to be the "exact" person Bacon was talking about. Lincoln was no different, except perhaps in his decisions; he knew well that he had to write in a clear voice, guided by the use of the appeals, for his pardons did indeed save the applicant's life—a responsibility Lincoln rightly found extremely important. But as far as pardons themselves were considered, much can be said, for Lincoln added to the confusion within the government over clemency.

8

The Love Letters

Aristotle's discussion of rhetoric's "available means of persuasion" may seem unrelated to any study of love letters in nineteenth century America, but, in fact, rhetoric did indeed provide an appropriate lens to study the love letters that Lincoln and his contemporaries wrote during midcentury America (Aristotle 1932, 7). As noted earlier, Aristotle makes plain that persuading the audience (in this case, the loved one) means that the words used by the writer of the letter (particularly, the lover) must be believable. Or more to the point, what Aristotle would describe as the ethos of the epistles. As Aristotle says, the ethos, that is, the speaker of the prose, "is a cause of persuasion when the speech is so uttered as to make him worthy of belief" (8). For as he sees it, ethos is "the most potent of all means of persuasion" (9).

But building ethos is not all there is to persuasion. Specifically, this means focusing, too, on the loved one, for Aristotle's notion is that for an argument to be effective, it must also carefully consider the audience (9). So, indeed, the love letter should not only project an appropriate ethos, but also focus on the audience for it to be effective. It must do both.

According to William Merrill Decker's comprehensive study of letter writing in America, young men eagerly bought various writing and etiquette guides to composing effective love letters and other writings needed to enhance their status and gain acceptance by the middle class. These included guides to middle class predilections like playing whist, and books on preparing certain mixed drinks popular in this segment of nineteenth century American society. Specifically, those buyers, in the main, eagerly sought guides so that they could learn to write in acceptable nineteenth century prose, which meant in this particular case, those necessary letter-writing skills to ultimately earn "middle class status" (1998, 60).

8. The Love Letters

This is not to say that learning writing skills for composing love letters was all that was necessary to be a member of the middle class, or that acquiring the appropriate writing skills was the only subject of these various manuals. But at the time, society offered few educational opportunities to mature young men seeking to acquire various skills that reflected middle class values. It is no surprise then that these guides of all kinds were quite popular in their time.

Lincoln, of course, like many of his generation, was self-educated and sought to improve his middle class skills by acquiring, among others, certain skills related to writing and rhetoric. Douglas Wilson's study of Lincoln during his formative years devotes a whole chapter to Lincoln's quest for the kind of knowledge he needed to know to "improve" himself, concluding that young Lincoln "educated himself by a determined program of nightly instruction after the day's work was done, systematically consuming all the books in the sparsely inhabited neighborhood where he grew up" (1998, 54). In the end, the Rail Splitter no doubt believed that he could "better himself" by acquiring those skills that members of the middle class valued. Such intensive study surely affected how he viewed the writing act, in particular, with its emphasis on supporting an argument by the various "means of persuasion" available to him.

Yet with so many of these manuals extant in the United States, no direct evidence exists that Lincoln did in fact refer to any of these various guides or manuals. But as Decker notes, "The authority of letter writing manuals ... would have played a secondary role of encouraging an unquestioned acceptance of certain structures and phrasing" (1998, 90). In the main, the writers of these manuals were intent on teaching a certain kind of contemporary writing etiquette to their readers who sought entry to the middle class. In other words, there were societal norms for expressing oneself.

But guides to letter writing have a long history that stretches back to the ancient writers, including Aristotle. As Poster and Mitchell observe: "Letter writing instruction has existed in a well-attested tradition from the earliest known cultures and the literature of Western cultures to the present" (2007, 1). Consequently, it is quite difficult to imagine that Lincoln, who read widely from the classics, too, would have escaped the influences of manuals on writing love letters from antiquity to his own age, as he considered such matters as style in the broadest sense and inevitably absorbed their content. If Lincoln did not directly use love letter manuals when he composed his love letters, the manuals no doubt had an *indirect* influence on Lincoln the love letter writer, even in so simple a matter as the words of the salutation and the complimentary closing.

What were some of these tenets of writing love letters that may have influenced Lincoln's composing them, and what elements of the lover letter in his day did Lincoln follow? Karen Lystra in her study of love letters in nineteenth century America, "The Pen Is the Tongue of the Absent: Reading and Writing Nineteenth-Century Love Letters," cites a number of characteristics that love letters of that day displayed. She begins by arguing, "Love letters were perused more intently and re-read more frequently by ordinary Americans than any other form of written expression" (1989, 13). Obviously, then, there must have been an eager audience for these types of manuals, since learning to write in the college classroom was not an option for most people. This left the aspirants with only one option: using the many writing manuals of the day.

In particular, Lystra notes that these manuals "provided model love letters" (*ibid.*, 13), prompting the obvious question of how often the readers of these manuals, intent on moving up to the middle class, copied the model letters word for word, only changing the names, date, and addresses. Her surprising response is that such copying occurred "very little," since copying love letters was seen to be quite unacceptable behavior by the members of the middle class (13–14). At the same time, Lystra also concludes that the manuals spent more time on the "difficulties and anxieties of persons in love than celebrating the pleasures of the heart," something that may have been off-putting to readers anxious for words of encouragement. In fact, Lystra says that these nineteenth century advisors devoted "more attention to losing than gaining love" (14).

In essence, the manuals argued for using "the most simple, natural and unaffected way" to express oneself in a love letter (*ibid.*, 14–15), noting that the nineteenth century emphasis on reserved behavior was relegated to other areas in the culture of the middle class. Candor prevailed in the letters themselves. The manuals instead advised that those whose education may be "very slight" needed to work at "natural expression in intimate relationships" as a more important element in the love letter.

Lystra observes that letters that resulted must be "natural and sincere … [even though] nineteenth-century guides required an increasingly complex series of adjustments in gesture, tone, style, and substance for different audiences and contexts" (*ibid.*, 16–17). This made the writing act much

8. The Love Letters

more sophisticated than the manuals at first seemed to be, following the Aristotelian dictum that the writer of love letters had to adjust to the audience; for indeed, suiting the text to the audience is an elementary principle of almost any type of writing.

It was the writer of love letters who also assumed that his letters were expressions of "private" matters rather than "public" issues (*ibid.*, 17), meaning love letters must be sincere and natural in language, quite different from that language used in public places. The writer of effective love letters was to assume that the same tone and style suitable for public audiences would in fact not produce the sincerity and naturalness writers of love letters wanted to effect. The writer of love letters realized then that expressing himself in these epistles in language was highly private, for "[p]rivate words were written and read in private places, reflecting the crucial relationship between words and space" (*ibid.*). It was assumed then that the recipient of a letter would withdraw alone to private places to read the letter. "This public-private division," Lystra maintains, "was a basic organizing of nineteenth-century middle class culture" (*ibid.*). Such a distinction made possible the intimate revelation of feeling in love letters of this era. In that way, only if the writer knows that his or her feelings are entirely private matters does the writer of love letters feel able to be sincere and natural: that "[p]rivacy was essential to nineteenth-century middle-class romantic love because the meaning of love was so deeply rooted in acts of protected and exclusive self-revelation" (18). Thus, love letters allowed the extended effusions of emotions as an essential part of their very nature, because the writers knew that such letters were private and their contents were known only to the recipient of the letter.

In an ironic way, with the emphasis in the middle class on self-control as a clear sign of public middle class values, the "advice books could urge expressive control and a tightly reined role performance in one social space, the opposite in another" (*ibid.*). Such a distinction allowed for sincerity and natural expression in love letters while it maintained the middle class idea of self-control in other matters. Lystra concludes that such a stance "was one of the more crucial boundaries of Victorian culture and a guiding principle of all aspects of middle-class life" (19).

But to conclude that love letters were nothing more that bathetic and flowery expressions of the lover's feeling and nothing more would be to ignore that most love letters contained much more, and were "chatty and colloquial and ranged over a wide spectrum of topics from business to

The Rhetoric of Lincoln's Letters

sex." In fact, Lystra maintains that "correspondents employed a conversational language, tone, and rhythm" as well as the more familiar literary tropes, metaphors, and romantic figures of speech" (*ibid.*).

Love letter-writing manuals of the day also usually taught the love letter as having a rather predictable structure. One particular guide to writing love letters from that era, *Chesterfield's Letter Writer*, notes that the love letter should have a definite characteristic and structure. This guide notes that even though love inspires passion, "no creature, man or woman can be guilty of a mean or a base passion" (1857, 54). For if the young man is struck by the beauty of the loved one, he must not put himself forward in any bold way, or he must have his friend to introduce him to her. If that is not possible, he must resort to a letter. Even dispensing advice on the type of paper the lover should use in the letter, the guide writer maintains that the paper should be "that of costly quality, gold-edged, perfumed, or ornamented in the French style"; in addition, "the letter should be carefully enveloped, and nicely sealed with a fancy wafer" (*ibid.*). Advice is also given on the salutations, grammar, and postscripts, calling a post script "*old womanish*" (66–67). How the letter is presented is important, too, for the love letter writer, because the writer obviously wants to reflect middle class values.

The guide then goes on to matters of the heart, saying, "I will hazard the assertion that [passion] applies accurately only to such love letters, as the writer is most likely acquainted with: 'things that are of the earth earthly.'" Then the writer should close the letter, but the guide advises the writer to remember that he or she should include more than just "Cupids and Venuses" (*ibid.*, 54–55), for "[no] subject can be too exalted for the pen of an intellectual lover" (55) "for *love*, true love, is the inspirer, the creator of all our noblest virtues" (53). The advice then was to say what you have to say "as plainly as possible" and "without any flourishes, as they tend not in any way to add to the harmony" (67).

The following letter in tone and style serves as an example of the type of love letter the *Chesterfield* advises readers to emulate. Notice that the language reflects the elevated style of the day, although it is more conversational than other works:

Chester, October 15, 18____,

My Dearest Fanny—If there is one thing that can console me for my unavoidable absence from your side, it is the pleasure of being able to pen a few lines to express, however feebly, my continued and increasing affection for you. It

is indeed a painful and irksome change from our rambles about the fields, our evening duets, and the stolen conversations to a dull routine. Happy, however, of mercantile accounts, and the never-ending confusion of business. Happily, however, my affairs are in a state of retirement, and I shall hope once more soon to bask in the sun light of Fanny's sweet countenance and to feed my imagination with thought of the happiness which her placid and sincere disposition will hereafter shed around a home! I need hardly say how eagerly I watch for the post and how I cherish every line that bears of any dear girl's affection and how gratefully every sentiment that flows from her pen is treasured in my memory. God bless you, my dearest Fanny, and believe me, with most respectful and affectionate remembrances to your parents, and all friends.
Your ever affectionate and devoted _____ [Chesterfield 1857, 57]

Notice the recall of events in the relationship, the emphasis on the lover and loved one and happiness, and the small secrets they both shared. While the tone is quite conversational, the letter also displays metaphorical language ("bask in the sun of Fanny's sweet countenance," and "how gratefully every sentiment that flows from her pen is treasured in my memory." Accordingly, the lover reassured the loved one that his accounts "are in a state of retirement," and thus they are not subject to the "never-ending confusion of business," a re-assurance that she will be well taken care of. The writer then tells her that he has an "increasing affect" for her. The sample letter then is a model for the lover to follow as he composes his own letter.

The next letter also can serve as a model and supposedly contains elements that make for a good love letter in the time.

Dear Miss_____,
It is with no small degree of apprehension, as to the manner in which you may receive the following avowal, that I take up my pen to address you; but I have so long struggled with my feelings, that they have now got the better of my irresolution; and throwing aside all hesitation, I have ventured, although alarmed at my own boldness in doing so, to lay open my whole heart before you. For months past I have been oppressed with a passion that has entirely superseded every other feeling of my heart—that passion is *love*—and *you—you alone* are the object of it. In vain have I endeavored to drive the idea from my mind, by every art that I could possibly think of: in vain have I sought out every amusement that might have a tendency to relieve my mind from the bias which it has taken, but I am unable to entertain but one idea, one thought, one feeling, and that is always yourself. I neglect myself, my business, and can neither hear nor see any one thing, but you bear the chief part therein. Believe me, I am sincere, when I assert, that I feel it totally impossible to live apart from you; when near you, I am in paradise—-when absent, I feel in torture. This, I solemnly assure you, is a true description of the feelings with which my breast is continually agitated, and it remains only for you to give a reality to those

hopes, or at once to crush them, by a single word, say but that word, and I am the happiest or the most miserable of mankind.
Yours, till death,
_____ [Chesterfield 1857, 61]

The letter's situation calls for a "small degree of apprehension, as to the manner in which [the loved one] may receive" his "avowal," but he is willing to venture forth and "lay open" his "whole heart" and express his "passion" for her, in spite of his unsuccessful attempts "to drive the idea from" his mind. He has "neglect[ed]" his business but he can't "entertain but one idea, one thought, one feeling," and that is "always" of her. The letter in fact is an elaborate plea to the loved one to offer some relief of his passion for her. Indeed, it is "totally impossible to live apart from" her, for when he is near he is "in paradise" and when he is "absent," he feels "torture." He closes his plea: "it remains only for [her] to give to a reality to those hopes, or at once to crush them, by a single word, say that word, and [he would be] the happiest or the most miserable of mankind." The lover is not only asking the loved one to relieve him of his misery but also to then swear allegiance to him so that he can think of other things besides the relationship and the questions he has with her. In a rhetorical sense, then, the lover is offering an argument that essentially says that his pleas, his available means of persuasion, are intended to offer proof for the assertion that the lover is, indeed, in misery without her. In response to him, the lover is essentially asked for some kind of measure that is unassailable proof of her devotion to him or rejection of his plaintive cries. Thus, to accomplish this, the writer seeks to create an appropriate voice by detailing all the heartache he feels. If he were flippant or humorous, that would not be the kind of ethos he seeks to display.

The next letter is a sample love letter from another source, this time an entire book from this period, composed of some 140 sample love letters, seemingly to fit practically every situation the lover might be in; "suitable for lovers of any age and condition and under all circumstances," the cover of *Love Letters: How to Write Them and When to Use Them* says. However, the book contains more than just sample letters, offering advice on how to write love letters. For example, the book says that the lover should display what the author calls "the utmost candor" when writing love letters, a warning that without candor "permanent happiness is impossible" (North 1867, 10). The author then reassures the lover that "there is nothing to be ashamed of in a love letter, provided it is sincere" (11). But he warns

8. The Love Letters

the lover that no receiver has a "right ... to communicate [the contents of a love letter] to others, except, of course, where the advice, sympathy, or sanction of proper persons is desired in respect to an engagement." If by chance, the loved one rejects the lover, then "the return of the letters is indispensable, and their retention dishonorable, on both sides" (12).

According to this manual, the letter should begin with an appropriate salutation on the order of "My dearest Kate" and avoid pet names like "Poppet and many others that have been put on paper" (*ibid.*, 16), seeking to display the appropriate ethos necessary for his purpose. The writer should end a letter with "yours sincerely," warning of extremes in both the salutation and the complimentary closing (16–17). The sample letter follows:

> DEAR MADAM,
> The long friendship which you have allowed to subsist between us, and which is a source of the most sincere pleasure to me, leads me to hope that I may address you upon a subject which I have very much at heart. I have always admired you, dear madam, with the real and settled admiration which one of my age is best capable of feeling. It has grown steadily in depth and strength, until I realize to myself the truth that a warmer sentiment inspires me which I cannot overcome, and that all my hopes have become centered upon yourself. In saying this, believe me, I use no empty compliments, such as younger men might employ. There are many who would say much better what I would express, but they could not speak more directly from the heart than I do, when I declare that I esteem, admire and love you. If I thought that this letter would cause you any painful surprise, it would not, I assure you, [it should not have] been written. On the contrary, I am not without hope that you may receive it without disfavor. We are both able to judge of what circumstances are most likely to conduce to our happiness, and the worldly position and history of each is well known to the other of us. You may rest assured that your welfare and comfort will be the constant study of my life, if you will consent to reward my devotion by giving me your hand. I shall await your reply with great anxiety, and pray that it may not be unfavorable to my dearest hopes, and, meanwhile, with every wish that true respect and affection could dictate, I remain, dear madam,
>
> Respectfully yours,
> OLIVER OLDCASTLE [*ibid.*, 16–17].

Another letter begins by reminding the loved one of the long and enduring friendship the lover and loved one have had, reminding her of his past "admiration" for her. But this letter has as its purpose something more than friendship, seeking instead to raise the level of friendship to love and devotion. The lover hopes that the loved one will receive his announcement of love for her: "You may rest assured that your welfare and comfort will be a constant study of my life, if you will consent to reward my devotion by giving me your hand" (*ibid.*, 17). The letter closes with a wish that the reply would not be "unfavorable" but he wishes that "every wish [for] true respect and affection could dictate" and signs it "[r]epectfully yours" (*ibid.*, 27), which, according to this letter-writing manual is appropriate, especially for the initial love letter. This first letter to the lady is not filled with hyperbolic claims about his devotion to her, but assumes a rather conversational tone, while also reporting to her that his devotion to her is something more than friendship. To that end, he tells her that his letter is composed without the elaborate hyperbolic language that "young men might employ." He acknowledges that "he speaks from the heart" and prays that her reply would not be "unfavorable." He hopes his wish is for "true respect and affection" and hopes his offer will be accepted. In a very real way, the writer of the letter is refashioning his ethos, since he seeks to move from the ethos of a friend to the ethos of a lover. Perhaps that is why he takes such great pains to "re-define" the role of the letter and his role in relation to her.

Again, the purpose of the letter is to offer a subtle argument for the writer to be accepted as a lover by offering support for that argument by pledging his love and devotion, spelled out in appropriate language. The lover then hopes that the loved one will accept the proof of his argument and raise the level of the relationship from admiration to love.

Examining the love letter as a genre in mid–nineteenth century America provides the background necessary for studying the love letters of Abraham Lincoln, written on a number of occasions to at least two different women. While Lincoln had other romantic relationships, letters from him to other women are either not extant or were perhaps never written. For reasons ripe with speculation, Lincoln felt quite ill at ease in the company of women (1996, 55), says biographer David Herbert Donald. Donald explains, "With the wives of old friends, he could be courtly and even affectionate, but he froze in the presence of eligible girls" (*ibid.*). Wilson describes Lincoln as awkward around women—even in adulthood: "Unaccustomed to its proprieties, he probably found the prescribed forms and manners an awkward fit, if not down-right difficult and burdensome, for someone with his temperament and social background" (D. Wilson, 1998, 181).

This awkwardness around women could be traced to a number of psychic problems involving women, so it is not surprising that the first

8. The Love Letters

woman to show any romantic interest in him was essentially rebuffed. In the fall of 1827, Lincoln was sued for violating a franchise held by the Dill brothers, John and Lin, who operated a ferry on the Kentucky side of the Ohio River, near Lewisport. Lincoln was asked to appear in front of a magistrate. While Lincoln's legal defense impressed magistrate Samuel Pate, who had encouraged Lincoln to study law, Lincoln also attracted the attention of Pate's wife's niece, the young and vibrant Caroline Meeker, who was then living on the Pate plantation. As young Lincoln walked back to the river through an orchard, Miss Meeker was there to give him an apple. A woman used to the fruits of the higher class, she saw something in Lincoln that others from his class had not. She told him of a corn husking party at the neighboring Eli Thrasher farm and asked if he would take her to the event. He agreed, and came to pick her up on the agreed-upon night.

According to the rules of the event, if someone found a rare red ear of corn, then that person was entitled to kiss anyone he or she liked. As the night wore on, Caroline happened upon a red ear and slyly shoved it over to the bashful Lincoln. When the corn husking was over, he walked her home and shyly produced the red ear and claimed his prize.

But Samuel Pate's wife, Arretta, objected to this budding romance. She instead hoped that Caroline would marry her brother, Eli Thrasher, the host of the corn husking party. To Mrs. Pate, on the surface, young Lincoln appeared to be a man who had no promise to support Miss Meeker in the fashion to which she was accustomed. Her aunt's discouragement worked because even though Lincoln returned on "Law Days" for trials at Squire Pate's courtroom, Lincoln showed little further interest in Miss Meeker (Myers, 1990, 30).

Did he realize that their difference in social rank, as Mrs. Pate observed, would be an unsurmountable barrier to him and his relationship to Miss Meeker at his present station in life? The Meeker-Lincoln romance ended in much the same way for Lincoln on at least two other occasions. It is not surprising then that no love letters exist between Miss Meeker and Mr. Lincoln, if, indeed, any were ever written (Myers, 1990, 40).

As *Herdon's Informants* (Wilson and Davis 1998) makes plain from interviewing villagers from New Salem and the surrounding area during this period in Lincoln's life, the Lincoln–Ann Rutledge romance is more than the stuff of legend, but at the same time, the truth of the relationship is difficult to sort out. She and Lincoln met while he was living in the now defunct New Salem, Illinois, where her father ran a tavern and where Lincoln boarded for a time. Betrothed to a merchant named John McNamar, who had returned East to take care of family business, Miss Rutledge was left behind to wait for him.

Like Lincoln, she was curious about a number of different areas of knowledge, and the two spent many evenings discussing what they had read. Even after her family moved seven miles from town, Lincoln continued to see her and soon the two were deeply in love. Realizing that her station in life was quite like his own, Lincoln received encouragement from her in his nascent interest in politics. But their love for one another ended when she developed "brain fever" and died in 1832. After her death, Lincoln reeled into a deep depression, an illness that haunted him all his life (*ibid.*, 13ff).

What makes the relationship significant is that Lincoln did not assume his characteristic shyness around women since she, like him, lacked much formal schooling; Miss Rutledge then was a woman from his same social and educational class. Later in life, asked about his relationship with Miss Rutledge, Lincoln replied, "I loved that woman dearly and soundly: she was a handsome girl—would have made a good wife—I did honestly and truly loved the girl and [I think] of her often" (Donald, 1996, 57–58). In spite of an elaborate hoax that claimed to have letters from Lincoln to her, no genuine letters between the two exist, according to Mark Neely (1982a, 265) and Donald Winkler (2004, 75).

While other women may have shown an interest in Lincoln, none of the letters he wrote except those from two women have survived—if he wrote them at all.

For the most part, the women Lincoln showed an interest in were far more educated than he. Perhaps he was looking for a woman like Miss Rutledge who shared his curiosity and social class, while accepting his hard-scrabble economic status. But all the women Lincoln showed a romantic interest in shared certain characteristics. All were slightly plump. All were relatively short in stature. Every one of the other women in one way or another, except Miss Rutledge, had made him feel a bit insecure about providing for them financially. And they were all from Kentucky. Shortly after Miss Rutledge's death, a visitor to New Salem to whom Lincoln wrote letters fit those categories herself. But quite frankly, she was not really interested in him. In fact, from the letters he wrote to her and from the letters she wrote to Herndon in 1866, neither party seemed deeply attracted to each other (Wilson and Davis, 1998, 55).

8. The Love Letters

There were a number of reasons. To women in his day, Lincoln was not exactly a promising husband. In the company of educated women, he often stumbled around trying to think of something to say to women who felt at least comfortable in the presence of eligible bachelors. Lincoln, of course, did not exhibit the same kind of ease around women that he felt around men (Donald, 1996, 55). Around males, Lincoln had thousands of stories and jokes to tell, some a bit on the risqué side, and hardly suited for cultured young women who would have taken offense at any suggestion of impropriety.

His choice of clothing also reflected his rustic roots. He often appeared at parties and other social gatherings dressed in an ill-fitting suit whose trousers hit well above the ankles, what teenagers today call "high waters." Such pants often showed his long underwear and many times, even when he did wear suitable sartorial garb, the clothes looked much like he had slept in them the night before. He often appeared with mud on his enormous boots. His ill-fitting suit covered a chest often described as much like a birdcage. Fond of wearing a hat, the hat grossly exaggerated his six-foot-four-inch height all out of proportion. At such a height and weighing only about 180 pounds, most of his clothing did little to enhance his appearance.

Perhaps part of his lack of attractiveness to women was that Lincoln was not a very handsome man. Besides having large ears and a prominent nose, Lincoln's neck was long and thin. He had coarse black hair that rarely was neatly combed, what some called later his "wild hair," that often showed up in formal portraits. His gray, pensive eyes belied the high speaking voice some described as "squeaky," a voice often accompanied by awkward gestures made with large, sinewy hands (Wilson and Davis 1998, 115–116). If that weren't enough, he spoke in a backwoods Kentucky drawl that contrasted sharply with the ladies he courted, who spoke with careful attention to educated speech. He used phrases like "yonder way," and "cheer" for "chair," that reflected his lack of formal education.

Lincoln, in many ways, realized his less than dashing good looks—and made it the subject of self-deprecating humor. According to what may be an apocryphal story, once while riding the circuit as a young lawyer in central Illinois, he happened upon a woman in her yard staring intently at him. Curious, he stopped to see what she had to say. After some time, she looked him over, and announced, "You are the ugliest man I ever saw."

Lincoln, searching for an apt reply, said, "I know, madam, but there's not much I can do about it."

The woman replied curtly, "Well, you could stay at home more!"

In spite of his appearance, Lincoln persisted in his attempts to win a mate. The fact that he was thirty-three years old when he finally found someone to marry him attests to his struggle to find a life partner. He must have thought that he would never find another Ann Rutledge. And perhaps he never did.

Yet with the encouragement of his fellow residents, Lincoln, after a time, bounced back and began a curious relationship with a woman who had visited her sister in New Salem, in 1833, while Lincoln was still reeling from the romance and subsequent death of Ann Rutledge.

Her name was Mary Owens, born September 29, 1808, in Green County, Kentucky, the daughter of Nathaniel Owens and Nancy Grayham Owens. Records indicate that the decidedly round Mary S. Owens, called Polly, was from a prominent family, one of five children. Her father shows up on the tax rolls of the county as early as 1795; later information puts the size of the Owens land at 7,500 acres, a sizeable plot of land for anyone to own (Myers, 2012, 37–38).

Although Baptist, Miss Owens had received a good education at Nazareth, a Roman Catholic school near Bardstown, Kentucky in Nelson County, now Nazareth College. Records indicate that she entered Nazareth Academy at about eight and a half years of age and probably left at about seventeen or eighteen. Years later, speaking about her father, Miss Owens remarked in a letter to William Herndon that "few persons placed a higher estimation on education than he did" (Wilson and Davis 1998, 256). Her formal schooling and Lincoln's lack of it, like so many times before, was a factor in his not winning her hand.

By those who knew her, she is described in various ways, with large variations in her height and weight. But most seem to agree on two words that picture her best: "handsome" and "smart." "Handsome," of course, is not a word we use now to describe a woman; we reserve it exclusively for men who fit the category. But "handsome" meant something different in Lincoln's day than it does today. *Webster's Dictionary*, published in 1828, defines "handsome" as "moderately beautiful," continuing with further delineation as "less than beautiful or elegant." That sense seems to be an accurate picture of Miss Owens. One source says "she was tall, pretty, had large blue eyes and the finest trimmings I ever saw. She was jovial, social, loved wit and humor, had a liberal English education, and was considered wealthy" (Lamon, 1872, 173). Another friend of Lincoln described her as having a "symmetrical face—features roundish—a very intellectual woman ... with even teeth, [given to] mirthful" (Wilson and Davis 1998, 243). Several years later, in 1866, in a letter from Lincoln's biographer, Mary Owens herself says she is five feet, five inches and weighs about 150 pounds (265). "Tall" for a woman in the early nineteenth century seems to have meant something different than it does today.

The other word often used to describe her was that she was "smart." Other similar labels included "sensible" and "very intellectual," terms befitting a woman who had had a very good education for the times, when sending women to school seemed to most fathers not a necessity at all. But one of her acquaintances, years later, said, "She was a very superior woman but like some other pretty women (God bless them) she loved Power and conquest" (Wilson and Davis 1998, 81). But he seems to be the only one who had that judgment.

At any rate, Miss Owens had a number of relatives in New Salem, and apparently she made enough of an impression on young Lincoln that her sister, Mrs. Betsy Abell, in the fall of 1836 told Lincoln that she was going back to Kentucky and returning with Mary Owens. Was Lincoln interested? Curiously, Betsy Abell went one step farther: She asked Lincoln if he would marry her. Surprisingly, Lincoln said he would.

Mary S. Owens did return with her sister to New Salem. But Lincoln commented that she had lost some of her beauty in the three years since he had seen her, gained some weight, and seemed to him, at least, too anxious to get married. Perhaps Lincoln's reaction to her was that since he last saw her, she had changed in looks and desirability, a fact he could probably not ignore.

Fact and legend swirl around two particular episodes in their relationship that may explain what she meant. As she relates it, one time she, Lincoln, and some others were out for a ride when they came upon on what Miss Owens characterized as "a very bad branch to cross."

She continues: "The other gentlemen were very officious in seeing that the partners got safely over. We were behind, he riding in, never looking back to see how I got along. When I rode up beside him, I remarked, 'You are a nice fellow! I suppose you did not care whether my neck was broken or not!' He laughingly replied (I suppose by way of a compliment), that he knew I was plenty smart to take care of myself." For a woman of her breeding, Miss Owens thought this marked Lincoln as not the gentleman she was looking for in a life mate (Wilson and Davis 1998, 262).

There was still another incident, although Mary Owens disputes that it ever came to words. She, her cousin Mrs. Bowling Green and her large baby, and Lincoln were walking over some rather rough country to the Abell's home, a distance uphill of nearly a mile. While Mrs. Green struggled to carry the oversized and fussy child, Miss Owens noticed that Lincoln never even offered to help carry the baby. As some tell the story, Miss Owens and Lincoln had an exchange of harsh words, but Miss Owens said she "gave little heed to the matter. We never had any hard feelings towards each other that I know of." Lincoln seemed unable to garner sympathy for Mary Owens and the baby, either. It is probably significant that Mary Owens remembered the incident in such detail (Wilson and Davis 1998, 262–263).

Lincoln and she continued to see each other from time to time. But he had his doubts about the relationship, and she did, too. He managed to explain his feelings for her in very interesting letters whose strategy seemed to be "You-want-all these-things, and-I-can't-provide-them-for-you, but-if-you-really-want-to-get-married, well, all-right, I'll-marry-you."

But what were Lincoln's letters to her like? Did he obey many of the conventions of the love letter of that time for a man who had set about to raise his social status? Below are the extant letters Lincoln wrote to Miss Owen:

> Mary, Vandalia, Dec. 13, 1836
> I have been sick ever since my arrival here, or I should have written sooner. It is but little difference; however, as I have very little even yet to write. And more, the longer I can avoid the mortification of looking in the Post Office for your letter and not finding it, the better. You see, I am mad about that *old letter* yet. I dont [sic] like very well to risk you again. I'll try you once more any how.

While the letter opens with a less than romantic salutation (Mary), Lincoln must have assumed that to address her by anything other than her given name would be too presumptive. The letter is also dated for convenient reference by him and her. As the letter says, Lincoln opens by saying that he would like to hear from her, since he has sent letters and received no reply from her. Instead of assuming that Miss Owens has not written him, Lincoln composes another letter to her: "I don't like very well to risk you again. I try you once more anyhow" (Basler, I, 78–79). However,

8. The Love Letters

his intolerance of not receiving a letter from her is not enough to discourage him from writing her.

Assuming a conversational tone, as the manuals for writing love letters instruct, Lincoln launches into a lengthy narrative about the controversy over the movement of the Illinois state capital to Springfield. The letter here becomes a report on the proceedings about that issue:

> The new State House is not yet finished, and consequently the legislature is doing little or nothing. The Governor delivered an inflamitory [sic] political Message, and it is expected there will be some sparring between the parties about [it as] soon as the two Houses get to business. Taylor [deliv]ered up his petitions for the *New County* to one of [our me]mbers this morning. I am told that he dispairs [sic] [of its] success on account of all the members from Morg[an C]ounty opposing it. There are names enough on the petition[,] I think, to justify the members from our county in going for it; but if the members from Morgan oppose it, which they [say] they will, the chance will be bad.
> Our chance to [take th]e seat of Government to Springfield is better than I ex[pected]. An Internal Improvement Convention was held here since we met, which recommended a loan of several milli[ons] of dollars on the faith of the State to construct Rail Roads. Some of the legislature are for it[,] and some against it; which has the majority I can not tell. There is great strife and struggling for the office of U.S. Senator here at this time. It is probable we shall ease their pains in a few days. The opposition men have no candidate of their own, and consequently they smile as complacently at the angry snarls of the contending Van Buren candidates and their respective friends, as the Christian does at Satan's rage [*ibid.*, 53–54].

The reason Lincoln wrote in so much detail about the events transpiring in the capital might have been that he wished to enhance his image to Mary. In other words, after all, he was seeking status as a "public man," indeed, even as a legislator. He may have reasoned that he would be more impressive to her as not just an ordinary man, but a legislator. In his own way, he may have been reminding her, too, of his stature among what may have been rivals, known and unknown. Including such details may have cemented in her mind just how "important" he was in the political world.

He next becomes quite personal:

> You recollect I mentioned in the outset of this letter that I have been unwell.
> That is the fact, though I believe I am about well now; but that, with other things I can not account for, have conspired and have gotten my spirits so low, that I feel that I would rather be any place in the world than here. I really can not endure the thought of staying here ten weeks [*ibid.*, 55].

Lincoln then asks her to cure him of his anxiety and lonesomeness, which he never assigns to being away from *her personally*, but says that hearing from her would relieve him of his problems with staying there ten weeks. He says:

> Write back as soon as you get this, and if possible say something that will please me, for really I have not [been] pleased since I left you. This letter is so dry and [stupid] that I am ashamed to send it, but with my pres[ent] feel[ings] I can not do any better Give my respects to M[r. and] Mrs. Abell and family.
> Your friend,
> LINCOLN [*ibid.*, 55].

The upshot of this request Lincoln wrote to Mary Owns seems to be: "Please relieve me of my anxiety and lonesomeness I am suffering from by writing to me." The relief from anxiety by swearing allegiance to her is a common theme in love letters. But Miss Owens must have concluded that *anybody* who wrote to Lincoln would satisfy his request—as long as it was a letter. Indeed, the letter seems to be also saying to her that she was not special in his eyes. In essence, then, little about the letter Lincoln wrote to Miss Owens meets the criteria for the love letter genre in his time, except a muted relief-from-anxiety theme. Mary Owens must have been a bit disappointed with what he wrote.

A later letter to Mary Owens takes on a more personal tone, beginning with the date and a salutation that is a little more personal than his last letter, "Friend Mary," but not, at the same time, striking the reader as a resolute declaration of true love:

> Friend Mary   Springfield, May 7. 1837
> I have commenced two letters to send you before this, both of which displeased me before I got half done, and so I tore them up. The first I thought wasn't serious enough, and the second as on the other extreme. I shall send this, turn out as it may [*ibid.*, 78].

As she read the letter, Miss Owens may have decided that Lincoln was frustrated by his inability to express his love for her at this point; after all she probably realized that he was uncomfortable around young women like her. But instead, in a bit of a surprise, he seems to be using details to explain why she would not be happy to move to Springfield, his home by now, and presumably be his wife:

> This thing of living in Springfield is rather a dull business after all, at least it is so to me. I am quite lonesome here as [I] ever was anywhere in my life. I have been spoken to by but one woman since I've been here, and should not have been by her, if she could have avoided it. I've never been to church yet, nor probably shall not be soon. I stay away because I am conscious I should not know how to behave myself [*ibid.*, 78].

8. The Love Letters

The dullness of Springfield may have been enough discouragement, but Lincoln adds that he is not active in any church, a possible source for fellowship for her or them as a couple. Yet there are still more reasons not to move there:

> I am often thinking about what we said of your coming to live at Springfield. I am afraid you would come and not be satisfied. There is a great deal of flourishing about in carriages here, which it would be your doom to see without shareing [sic] in it [ibid., 78].

In a small town, not only the sophistication of a large city life would be missing for a future Mrs. Lincoln. Lincoln then details that he himself would offer his wife a rather frugal way of life:

> You would have to be poor without the means of hiding your poverty. Do you believe you could bear that patiently? [ibid., 78].

Lincoln explains that he would do all he could to make her happy, but he warns her that he would not be able to support her in the life she was accustomed to:

> Whatever woman may cast her lot with mine, should any ever do so, it is my intention to do all in my power to make her happy and contented; and there is nothing I can imagine, that would make me more unhappy than to fail in the effort. I know I should be much happier with you than the way I am, provided I saw no signs of discontent in you [ibid., 78].

So Lincoln, in an attempt to be brutally honest with her, explains just what marrying her means:

> What you have said to me may have been in jest, or I may have misunderstood it. If so, then let it be forgotten; if otherwise, I much wish you would think seriously before you decide. For my part I have already decided. What I have said I will most positively abide by, provided you wish it. My opinion is that you had better not do it [ibid., 78].

Then Lincoln reminds her:

> You have not been accustomed to hardship, and it may be more severe than you now imagine. I know you are capable of thinking correctly on any subject; and you can deliberate maturely upon this, before you decide, then I am willing to abide your decision [ibid., 78].

Lincoln has mustered a rather complete list of the liability of being married to him, and includes the familiar theme in Lincoln's love life of not being able to support her at an economic level she is accustomed to. In light of detailing just what the liabilities for marrying him are, Lincoln wants to know what her plans are:

You must write me a good letter after you get this. You have nothing else to do, and though it might not seem interesting to you, after you had written it, it would be a good deal of company to me in this "busy wilderness." Tell your sister I dont [sic] want to hear any more about selling out and moving.
That gives me the hypo whenever I think of it.
Yours, &c. LINCOLN [ibid., 78].

It seems that Lincoln probably was truthful about getting "the hypo," that is, clinical depression, an illness that had haunted him all of his life and would continue to do so. He realized that he had made a promise to marry Miss Owens. With his reputation for honesty on the line, he realized that the worst thing a person could do was break a promise. The residents of New Salem had been impressed by his honesty; two of them concluded that Lincoln was "obliging and honest" and another was convinced that Lincoln was "honest" (Donald 2003, 11, 24). With his friendship with Mrs. Abell at risk, and in light of the promise he had made to her to marry Miss Owens, Lincoln concluded that in this relationship, he had to be completely honest to Miss Owens about just what marrying him would entail, including self-deprecating details that would lead her to the conclusion that he was probably a poor catch for a woman of such breeding.

But that is not all Lincoln wanted to say. In the last letter he wrote to Mary Owens he tries to clear up just how she feels about him. On one hand, he seems to want to continue the relationship; but on the other hand, he is uncertain whether she wants to continue the relationship in light of what he had said being married to him would mean. He expresses his growing affection for her, telling her that he could not think of her with "entire indifference," yet he was uncertain how she felt about him.

He begins the letter using the same salutation, "Friend Mary," choosing to remain rather distant, and somewhat lacking in passion, probably by design until he knows just how she feels. He certainly does not want to jilt her, especially since he had a reputation for honesty:

Friend Mary,   Springfield Aug. 16th, 1837
You will no doubt, think it rather strange, that I should write you a letter on the same day on which we parted; and I can only account for it by supposing, that seeing you lately makes me think of you more than usual, while at our late meeting we had but a few expressions of thoughts. You must know that I can not see you, or think of you, with entire indifference; and yet it may be, that you, are mistaken in regard to what my real feelings toward you are.
If I knew you were not, I should not trouble you with this letter. Perhaps any other man would know enough with further information; but I consider it *my*

8. The Love Letters

peculiar right to plead ignorance, and your bounden duty to allow the plea [*ibid.*, 94].

Attesting to the anxiety he feels, Lincoln then intends to build the kind of ethos he thinks appropriate: He is an honest man who wants to understand just how she feels about him. At the same time, if she would choose to marry him, he would do all he could to please her. After all, having promised to marry her, he would do all he could to add to her "comfort." But she may not feel enough affection for him to continue the relationship. So he calls on her to make her feelings for him known:

> I want in all cases to do right, and most particularly so, in all cases with women. I want, at this particular time, more than any thing [*sic*] else, to do right with you, and if I *knew* it be doing right, as I rather suspect it would, to let you alone, I would do it. And for the purpose of making the matter as plain as possible, I now say, that you can now drop the subject, dismiss your thoughts (if you ever had any) from me forever, and leave this letter unanswered, without calling forth one accusing murmur from me. And I will even go further, and say, that if it will add any thing [*sic*] to your comfort, or peace of mind, to do so, it is my sincere wish that you should. Do not understand, by this, that I wish to cut your acquaintance. I mean no such thing. What I do wish is, that our further acquaintance shall depend upon yourself [*ibid.*, 94].

He then turns the decision of whether or not to continue the relationship entirely over to her. He explains that if she is interested in continuing the relationship, he would give his all to make her happy, adding that her happiness is his sincere aim, whatever that may mean:

> If such further acquaintance would contribute nothing to your happiness, I am sure it would not to mine. If you feel yourself in any degree bound to me, I am now willing to release you, provided you wish it; while, on the other hand, I am willing, and even anxious to bind you faster, if I can be convinced that it will, in any considerable degree, add to your happiness. This, indeed, is the whole question with me. Nothing would make me more miserable than to believe you miserable—nothing more happy, than to know you were so [*ibid.*, 94].

In fact, he again stresses that he wants to know whether or not she wants to continue the relationship:

> In what I have now said, I think I can not be misunderstood; and to make myself understood, is the only object of this letter [*ibid.*, 94].

He suggests that she can make her wishes known by merely not answering his letter:

> If it suits you best to not answer this—farewell—a long life and a merry one attend you. But if you conclude to write back, speak as plainly as I do. There

can be neither harm nor danger, in saying, to me, any thing [sic] you think, just in the manner you think it.

My respects to your sister. Your friend LINCOLN [ibid., 94–95].

He then signs his letter to her, pledging his respect for their acquaintance, using "friend" as his complimentary closing. Lincoln suggests that the continuance of the relationship is in Mary Owens' hands. If she does not see Lincoln anymore, if she has no feelings for him, all she has to do is not answer his letter and the matter is done. The letter has a ring of finality about it, and she probably did not answer his letter, choosing the option that Lincoln suggested in his last letter. When asked why she and Lincoln ended their relationship, she later explained herself to William Herndon gruffly: "I found him lacking in smaller attentions" (Wilson and Davis, 1998, 262).

In a letter written two years later, on April Fool's Day of 1838, to the wife of a close friend, he pokes fun at himself, but there are elements in his letter to Mrs. Browning that have a distinctive ring of regret about them. He handles that regret by making himself the butt of the joke, concluding that Mrs. Browning would see the humor in it all. He told Mrs. Browning about how he got into such a mess by promising to marry Miss Owens without seeing her for some time, a decision that he admits found him acting like a "blockhead." His honesty, though, had been the source of his troubles since he had made a promise to marry her. Honesty was a trait Lincoln worked hard at maintaining as the "public man" he was to become. William Lee Miller stresses how important honesty was to Lincoln: "The Lincoln of reality seems to match the Lincoln of this regard: that he tried to be scrupulously honest and honorable in personal dealings, and cared a great deal about his reputation for being so" (2002, 218). Jilting a well-bred lover such as Mary Owens certainly was not a charge he wanted to be attached to his name. He later admitted that his early ambiguity about breaking such a commitment was quite a matter of concern, containing "much more truth" than what would at first appear (Tripp 2002, 100). With his honesty of great concern, Lincoln goes to great trouble to write Miss Owens and ask just how she felt about him, rather than leave the relationship she had with him in question and risk his reputation for honesty.

In his letter to Mrs. Browning, Lincoln describes Mary Owens as a "fair match for Falstaff," a corpulent, comic character out of one of Shakespeare's plays, who is described as being so fat that he "lards the lean earth

8. The Love Letters

as he walks along"—not much of a compliment for a lady Lincoln was considering marrying. No doubt he was exaggerating her lesser qualities for comic effect, but he never mentioned her by name, an attempt, albeit a weak one, to avoid embarrassing Miss Owens, and keep their relationship private as writing the love letter manuals advise, although surely many would have known about it (Basler, I, 118).

In the next part of the April Fool's Day letter, Lincoln describes Mary Owens' "withered features, for her skin was too full of fat to permit its contracting into wrinkles; but from her want of teeth, weather-beaten appearance in general, and from a kind of notion that ran in my head, that *nothing* could have commenced at the size of infancy, and reached her present bulk in less than thirty-five or forty years." But he vowed, he would make her his wife after all and live up to the bargain he made with her sister: "At once I determined to consider her my wife; and this done, all my powers of discovery were put to rack, in search of perfection in her" (*ibid.*).

In the letter, though, Lincoln says that when he saw her that "through life I have been in no bondage, either real or imaginary from the thralldom of which I desired to be free." Honor-bound, he says he asked her to marry him, and she turned him down. He then attests that "my vanity was deeply wounded ... that I had so long been too stupid to discover her intentions." He then closes with: "Others have been made fools of by the girls; but this can never be with truth said of me. I most emphatically, in this instance made a fool of myself" (*ibid.*, 117–119).

It seems, though, that Lincoln didn't walk away unwounded. In fact, the last word Mary Owens ever received from Lincoln was in a message he told her sister, Mrs. Betsy Abell, to deliver to her: "Tell your sister that I think she was a great fool because she did not stay here and marry me." When Mary Owens heard the message, she grumped, "Characteristic of the man!" (Wilson and Davis 1998, 263).

Their romance, if it can be called that, was grounded in rather thin soil, lacking the passion necessary for a relationship to grow and blossom. She clearly had her expectations of how a potential husband should act, and he saw her as less than attractive, but he was still willing, because he had made a promise, to marry her. It was, then, best that each went their different directions. Both probably suffered a bruising, but probably neither would have been happy with the other one.

Mary Owens went back to Green County, Kentucky, married Jesse Vineyard, moved to Weston, Missouri, had five children, and died there

July 4, 1877. Two of her sons fought for the Confederacy (Wilson and Davis 1998, 531). But in his letter to Mrs. Browning was Lincoln lampooning the relationship with Miss Owens purely as an April Fool's Day joke? If that was all there was to it, why did he ask her to marry him even after he realized that she was no longer attractive to him? Why did he go to such lengths to spell out just what marrying him would mean? Lincoln, it seems, was not going back on his promise to marry her, if that was what she wanted. But he felt that Miss Owens had to know what she was in for. With his reputation for honesty on the line, and knowing he *had been painfully honest to her*, he had to know for certain how she felt. For his reputation really did matter to him. The last letter to her has all the earmarks of an attempt to ferret out just how Mary Owens felt about Abraham Lincoln in light of his attempts to be completely honest with her about the life she would lead if she were to marry him. According to Herndon, shortly before Mary Owens died, she was generous in her praise of Abraham Lincoln: "He was a man with a heart full of human kindness and a head full of common sense" (Wilson and Davis, 1998, 611).

The rhetoric of his letters to Miss Owens was more like letters of inquiry or essays, requesting, questioning, and disseminating information, than they were the love letters we would expect. In a word, he felt that in view of what he had said earlier about her to her sister, he had to be "honest" and make her aware of all that she would lose. If she still wanted to marry him, his honesty would dictate that he would indeed marry her. But his letters certainly are short on expressions of feelings, and long on information and requests.

Lincoln, of course, went on to have at least one more romance in which he wrote love letters to a woman. But this time, he composed letters that were more flattering to the loved one, and that projected more of the ethos of a man in a romance. Granted, most of the letters were more a report on just where he was and what he was doing, but that was the kind of information a husband would tell his wife. Yet there were occasions when he showed a legitimate affection for her. In other words, the tender moments between him and her are there, but they were not as obvious as many would expect. In many instances, his letters detail information she needed to know about her husband and, perhaps, their accompanying child, the stuff that she as a mother and a wife needed to know in order to rest more easily. After all, it must be said, that he *did* write her, evidence that he was indeed thinking of her.

8. The Love Letters

Lincoln struggled with his decision to marry Mary Todd. At first he broke off his engagement with her, but decided later, after a period of great anxiety, to fulfill his earlier promise to marry her. One contemporary described Lincoln as going "crazy" as he struggled with his conscience over the promise he had made to marry Miss Todd (Wilson and Davis, 1998, 475). Again, he had made a promise, this time to marry Miss Todd,

Mary Todd Lincoln. She was "difficult" at times, but she supported his political career.

and he felt "honor bound" to do so (*ibid.*). But this time, unlike with Mary Owens, Mary Todd did not release him from his promise, and Lincoln wrestled with his conscience and decided ultimately to marry Miss Todd. Promises obviously meant something to Lincoln, even though the decision to wed Mary Todd may have been the wrong one.

Mary Todd and Abraham Lincoln were a highly unusual couple, a match that would be unbelievable on paper, but quite understandable the more deeply we explore their complex relationship. Born December 12, 1818, to Robert Todd, a wealthy landowner and businessman in Lexington, Kentucky, she was given a rather extensive education in those topics that women were taught in those days. Lincoln, of course, was born nearly nine years earlier to a hardscrabble farmer and his wife, Thomas and Nancy Hanks Lincoln, in what is now Larue County, Kentucky. Because of a lack of opportunity out on the frontier, Lincoln attended school, "by littles," he said, amounting to about a year all told. Because of her background, Mary Todd was an accomplished conversationalist to both men and women. Lincoln, on the other hand, felt perfectly fine to tell his many stories, some too ribald for mixed company, especially for women from such a blue-blooded background as Mary Todd. She dressed in attractive fashion and moved gracefully across the dance floor, often dropping an apt French phrase into the conversation. She was impetuous; he deliberate in his thinking. To many close to the romance, the two hardly seemed a match. Mary was "high strung," described by twenty-first century psycho-biographer Jason Emerson as suffering from a "bipolar disorder" that must have made her a difficult person to live with (2006, 5). Lincoln was deliberate and plodding at times.

But they both liked politics; she often recalled seeing Henry Clay as a young girl. Lincoln's interest in Mary Todd may have become more intense, for Lincoln looked upon Clay as his "beau ideal," the man whose thinking inspired Lincoln to enter politics.

As Lincoln's wife, Mary worked tirelessly to do whatever she could to aid his campaign for the presidency—so much so that when Lincoln was elected president, he said to her, "Mary, we are elected." Her work for his campaign was dedicated and important, as she made their home a public relations center in those days when candidates did not openly campaign as they do today.

Both read and loved good literature, often quoting lines from the Bard's plays. He respected her mind, while she saw in him the buds of greatness.

8. The Love Letters

She had moved to Springfield partly to find a mate; he had moved to the Illinois capital to build his fledgling practice of law. Lincoln liked women on the short and plump side; she fit that description. While they differed in many ways, they shared enough to build a marriage on.

After Lincoln temporarily broke off their engagement, no doubt Mary's sister, Elizabeth, renewed her observation that Mary should snuff out the embers of such a fitful romance to a man beneath her station. As Elizabeth said of the romance: "I warned Mary that she and Mr. Lincoln were not suitable. Mr. Edwards and myself believed they were different in nature, and education and raising. They had no feelings alike. They were so different that they could not live happily as man and wife" (Baker 1987, 89). An earlier biography of Mary, *Mary Lincoln: Biography of a Marriage* by Ruth Painter Randall, assigns the temporary breakup to the Edwardses. As Painter says, "[T]he opposition of the Edwardses [to the marriage] was a cause of the breaking up of the engagement and Lincoln's great despondency which followed" (R. Randall, 1953, 64). Once again, like his feelings about Caroline Meeker and Mary Owens, Lincoln had to confront the idea that his background, lack of formal education, and social station may have prohibited him from being able to keep Mary in the manner to which she was accustomed. Yet after meeting secretly during the hiatus after their break-up, and despite the Edwards' objections to their romance, Mary Todd and Abraham Lincoln were married at the Edwards' home in Springfield on November 4, 1842.

The letters Lincoln wrote Mary are, in the main, merely short notes that told where he was, who was with him, and, perhaps, when he would be home—necessary notes between a husband and a wife, and, in their own way, expressions of his love. The tender moments would perhaps have their time when they were alone. Many letters or telegraphs (Basler does not distinguish them) took this form:

Mrs. Lincoln　　　　　　　　　　　　　　　　　　Executive Mansion
Philadelphia　　　　　　　　　　　　　　Washington, June 11, 1863
　　Your three despatches received. I am very well, am glad to know that you & "Tad" are so.
　　Lincoln [Basler, VII, 260].

Or his reporting his health and having repaired a vehicle that they both needed:

Mrs. Lincoln　　　　　　　　　　　　　　　　　　　　　　June 15, 1863
Philadelphia, Pa

Tolerably well. Have not ridden out much yet, but have at last got new tires on the carriage wheels, & perhaps, shall ride out soon.
A. Lincoln [Basler, VI, 277].

Or sometimes there was communication about the children:

The draft will go to you. Tell Tad the goats and father are very well—especially the goats.
A. Lincoln [Basler, VII, 320].

Sometimes, the letters contained news of the war:

Mrs. A. Lincoln   Executive Mansion
Manchester, N. H.   Washington, D.C., August 29, 1863
All quite well. Fort-Sumpter is *certainly* battered down, and utterly useless to the enemy, and it is *believed* here, but not entirely certain, that both Sumpter and Fort-Wagner, are occupied by our forces. It is also certain that Gen. Gilmore has thrown some shot into City of Charleston.
A. Lincoln [Basler, VI, 421].

At other times, Lincoln expresses concern for his wife:

Mrs. A. Lincoln   Washington
Continental Hotel   Dec. 24, 1864
Do not come on the night train. It is too cold. Come in the morning A. Lincoln [Basler, VIII, 174].

In three longer letters, Lincoln openly expresses how he feels about Mary:

Dear Mary: Washington, April 16–1848
In this troublesome world, we are never quite satisfied. When you were here, I thought you hindered me some in attending to business; but now, having nothing but business—no variety—it has grown exceedingly tasteless to me, and I hate to stay in this room by myself [*ibid.*, 467].

While the salutation is not a sure predictor of what the next part of the letter says, Lincoln soon launches into a "self-critical" mode, admitting that, in fact, he really did miss her. This approach helps to build an ethos in which Lincoln communicates to her that he misses having her around, effectively communicating to her that he is thinking of her, a thought that she must have found reassuring. In his own way, he is apologizing to her for not realizing how much he liked her being there with him, but he is also telling her that he really was sensitive enough to correct his former actions and to build an ethos that would be more aware of her needs. He emphasizes the point by using a short, segregating clause with enough punch to it to capture succinctly just how he feels with her gone: "and I hate to stay in this room by myself." This theme of the pain the lover feels because the lovers are apart is a frequent theme in love letters. He makes plain that in the future he has to modify his behavior when he and she are together. To him, it is ethos he has to work on.

The next part of the letter briefly alludes to the section before, but becomes much more an acknowledgment of his receiving three letters. The section then reflects the conversational tone a love letter should have when the writer speaks with "candor," by asking about his children, and discussing family business, along with appropriate allusions to acquaintances, Mary's recently widowed grandmother, and a reference to her uncle James Parker:

> You know I told you in last sunday's [sic] letter, I was going to make a little speech during the week; but the week has passed away without my getting a chance to do so; and now my interest in the subject has passed away too.
> Your second and third letters have been received since I wrote before. Dear Eddy thinks father is *"gone tapila"* [Lincoln and Mary's son mispronouncing of "capital"]. Has any further discovery been made as to the breaking into your grandmother's house? If I were she, I would not remain there alone. You mention that your uncle John Parker is likely to be at Lexington. Dont [sic] forget to present him my very kindest regards [ibid., 465].

Continuing in a more of a conversational tone, he again asks about family, and tells her about his sending a pair of socks for one of the children:

> I went yesterday to hunt the little plaid stockings, as you wished; but found that Mr. McKnight has quit business, and Allen had not a single pair of the description you give, and only one plaid pair of any sort that I thought would fit "Eddy's dear little feet." I have a notion to make another trial to-morrow morning. If I could get them, I have an excellent chance of sending them. Mr. Warrick Tunstall, of St. Louis is here. He is to leave early this week, and to go by Lexington. He says he knows you, and will call to see you; and he voluntarily asked, if I had not some package to send you [ibid.].

The next part of the letter changes direction and concerns itself with Mary and her world and other family matters, especially her relationship with the Wickliffe family, enemies of Mary's father (R. Randall, 1953, 127):

> I wish you to enjoy yourself in every possible way; but is there no danger of wounding the feelings of your good father, by being so openly intimate with the Wickliffe family?

Then the letter turns its attention to a woman apparently in the apartment building the Lincolns shared in Washington, D.C.:

Lincoln and family. Lincoln's letters reflect a deep devotion to family.

8. The Love Letters

Mrs. Broome has not removed yet; but she thinks of doing so to-morrow. All in the house—or rather, all with whom you were on decided good terms—send their love to you. The others say nothing.

Following that, Lincoln returns to the kind of conversation that two people committed to one another may in fact express:

Very soon after you went after you went away, I got what I think a very pretty set of shirt-bosom studs, modest little ones, jet, set in gold, only costing 50 cents a piece, or 1.50 for the whole.

Lincoln then comes back to family business and tells her whether or not to address him as "Honorable" when sending letters:

Suppose you do not prefix the "Hon" to the address on your letters to me any more. I like the letters very much, but I would rather they should not have that upon them. It is not necessary, as I suppose you have thought, to have them to come free [*ibid.*, 465–466].

As the letter nears a close, Lincoln then expresses his delight at her not having any "migraine headaches" as she has had in the past. He then articulates an expression of his jealousy. To Lincoln, Mary's restored health might mean that she may want to marry again:

And you are entirely free from head-ache? That is good—good—considering it is the first spring you have been free from it since we are acquainted. I am afraid you will get so well, and fat, and young, as to be wanting to marry again.

Indeed, he seems so concerned that he asks Mary to elicit the help of Louisa, a family "spy," to help him watch her should she develop a "wandering eye." He then gently teases her about weight:

Tell Louisa that I want her to watch you a little for me. Get weighed, and write me how much you weigh.

This is an interesting concern for him, because all the women we have knowledge of that Lincoln courted were at least somewhat rotund, so we assume that in fact he is gently poking fun at her, as he often did.

Lincoln next relates his fear for Robert because of a dream he had had about their son:

I did not get rid of the impression of that foolish dream about dear Bobby till I got your letter written the same day.

Lincoln paid attention to dreams, often seeing them as precursors of events in the future. The most famous one was that in the night before he was assassinated, he supposedly had a dream about being killed. In Mary's letter to him she must have alleviated his fears for his son's safety.

Lincoln then asks about his other son, Eddy, and Robert:

> What did Bobby [Robert] and Eddy think of the little letters father [sic] sent them? [sic] let the blessed fellows forget father [sic].

Lincoln continues this highly discursive format by asking her to write a letter and relate the news that Matilda Edwards would be coming to Washington, D.C., for a visit:

> A day or two ago Mr. Strong here in congress, said to me that Matilda would visit here within two or three weeks. Suppose you write her a letter, and enclose it in one of mine; and if she comes I will deliver it to her, and if she does not, I will send it on to her.
> Most affectionately, A. LINCOLN [Basler, I, 465–466].

Lincoln closes his letter with "most affectionately," an apt phrase for the separated lover and a loved one far away. The wandering nature of the letter is also characteristic of letters written from a married man to his wife. The drifting from one topic to another reads like a conversation on paper, and Lincoln's voice as a husband assures his wife of his many concerns about his family and his duties as a father and husband, exhibiting a believable and an appropriate ethos for such a situation.

The next letter is more businesslike; Lincoln apologizes for its brevity but explains that because of the setting at the post office where he is surrounded by men, the letter is brief. Lincoln asks her for an acceptance of his excuse:

> My dear wife: Washington, May 24–1848
> Enclosed is the draft as I promised you in my letter of sunday [sic]. It is drawn in favor of your father, and doubt not, he will give you the money for it at once. I write this letter in the post-office surrounded by men and noise, which, together with the fact that there is nothing new, makes me write so short a letter.
> Affectionately, A. LINCOLN [Basler, I, 473–474].

The business of the letter is about a money draft for Mary's father. Lincoln uses the salutation, "My dear wife," and assures her that there is "nothing new," which, because of that lack of information and the unusual setting for writing the letter, make for the short letter. His complimentary closing is entirely appropriate for a married man who is signing a letter to his wife. By writing her and pledging his love, Lincoln again reflects the ethos of a concerned husband and father.

The third of the four letters of Lincoln to Mary in the *Collected Works* details a more nuanced relationship between husband and wife, as Lincoln refers to his wife as "girl" and concerns himself with her welfare. He reminds her of what she must do to ready herself for the trip, as she returns to Washington, D.C. The letter begins by telling her that despite his "anxiety" at attending a Whig convention, he received the good news that she was returning to Washington:

> My dear wife: Washington, June 12, 1848
> On my return from Philadelphia, yesterday, where, in my anxiety I had been led to attend the Whig convention I found your last letter. I was so tired and sleepy, having ridden all night, that I could not answer it till to-day; and now I have to do so in the H.R. The leading matter in your letter, is your wish to return to this side of the Mountains [*ibid.*, 467].

Lincoln next teases her by asking if she will be "a good girl?" The phrase prompts questions about why he had reason to inquire. Granted, Mary was a notorious flirt. Baker, for example, mentions Mary's "flirtatiousness" as a "recurrent theme in their marital politics" (1987, 143). But the term "girl" may merely refer to their nine-year difference in age, or may be a pet name Lincoln had for his wife. Lincoln next expresses his excitement about her coming to Washington, D.C:

> Will you be a *good girl* in all things, if I consent? Then come along, and that as *soon* as possible.
> Having got the idea in my head, I shall be impatient till I see you [*ibid.*].

Then Lincoln returns to the practical matters of traveling in that day. Does she have enough money? Did she receive the fifty dollars he already sent? Where will she get the money? Will she be with just her uncle? Could she alter travel plans with him to make them more alluring for him?

> You will not have money enough to bring you; but I presume your uncle will supply you, and I will refund him here. By the way you do not mention whether you have received the fifty dollars I sent you. I do not much fear but that you got it; because the want of it would have induced you [to] say something in relation to it. If your uncle is already in Lexington, you might induce him to start on earlier than the first of July; he could stay in Kentucky longer on his return, and so make up for lost time [*ibid.*].

Next Lincoln returns to the mundane events in his life and asks her for reassurance that the letter is acceptable to her in spite of its brevity:

> Since I began this letter, the H.R. has passed a resolution for adjourning on the 17th. July, which probably will pass the Senate. I hope this letter will not be disagreeable to you; which, together with the circumstances under which I write, I hope will excuse me for not writing a longer one [*ibid.*].

No doubt he is quite pleased that she has decided to visit him:

> Come on just as soon as you can. I want to see you, and our dear-*dear* boys very much.

Every body here wants to see our dear Bobby [Robert, their son].
Affectionately A. Lincoln [Basler, I, 477–478].

The fourth letter is perhaps the most conversational of all, like the last letter including affectionate salutations and a complimentary closing along with a litany of concerns that a dutiful husband who learns that his wife is to visit him shortly might have. The tone of the letter is as though the couple has recognized that the days of romantic passages extolling their love for each other have passed and the business of the everyday is the present reality. One critic of love letters of this era sums up the letters of couples that had been married some time this way: "[they settled into] a routine and familiarity [that] would create a more matter of fact atmosphere between them" (Lystra 1989, 197).

In addition to finalizing Mary Todd Lincoln's plan for her trip to Washington, D.C., the letter is also filled with what may be called gossip about people familiar to the Lincolns. The first part of the letter is carefully crafted to make sure all the plans Mary has are complete. He wants to ensure that the trip to Washington is a smooth one. He then offers her a gentle reminder to have her greet her family in his name:

> My dear wife: Washington, July 2, 1848
> Your letter of last Sunday came last night. On that day (Sunday) I wrote the principal part of the letter to you, but did not finish it, or send it till tuesday [sic], when I had provided a draft for $100 which I sent in it. It is now probable that in that day (tuesday [sic]) you started to Shelbyville; so that when the money reaches Lexington, you will not be there. Before leaving, did you make any provision about letters that might come to Lexington for you? Give my kindest regards to your uncle John, and all the family [ibid., 495].

Then Lincoln names the people whom they both knew that he saw after his visit (apparently) to the Whig Convention in Philadelphia. He no doubt exaggerates his observation that one of the convention participants, Lincoln believed, voted three times. He then mentions his latest speech, followed by a return to a mention of her Uncle John:

> Thinking of them reminds me that I saw your acquaintance, Newton, of Arkansas, at the Philadelphia Convention. We had but a single interview, and that was so brief, and in so great a multitude of strange faces, that I am quite sure I should not recognize him, if I were to meet him again. He was a sort of Trinity, three in one, having the right, in his own person, to cast the three votes of Arkansas. Two or three days ago I sent your uncle John, and a few of our other friends each a copy of the speech I mentioned in my last letter; but I did not send any to you, thinking you would be on the road here, before it would reach you. I send you one now [ibid.].

8. The Love Letters

Next Lincoln mentions a bill that Mary had incurred that Lincoln did not know about. Throughout their marriage, Lincoln himself was often presented with his wife's clothing bills unexpectedly. Baker's biography of Mrs. Lincoln mentions that "Mary Lincoln bought things she did not need and sometimes returned purchases that did not suit." To explain Mary Todd Lincoln's buying habits, Baker notes that Mrs. Lincoln's extensive buying could be explained as "spending to make restitution for personal and political defeats" (1987, 157). In this letter, Lincoln's reference to a bill of hers appears to be an early version of her habit of spending money that he later found out about:

> Last wednesday [sic], P. H. Hood & Co, dunned me for a little bill of $5.38 cents, and Walter Harper & Co, dunned for $8.50 cents, for goods, which they say you bought. I hesitated to pay them, because my recollection is that you told me when you went away, there was nothing left unpaid. Mention in your next letter whether they were right [ibid.].

Turning next to other matters, Lincoln in a familiar tone mentions people that his wife might know and the news about them:

> Mrs. Richardson is still here; and what is more, has a baby—so Richardson says, and he ought to know. I believe Mary Hewett has left here and gone to Boston. I met her on the street about fifteen or twenty days ago, and she told me she was going soon. I have seen nothing of her since [ibid.].

Lincoln then reiterates what might be considered the gossip about a musical ensemble, and a man who was, in Lincoln's eyes, too familiar with members of a musical company of singers:

> The music in the Capital grounds on saturdays, or, rather, the interest in it, is dwindling down to nothing. Yesterday evening the attendance was rather thin. Our two girls, whom you remember seeing first at Carusis, at the exhibition of the Ethiopian Serenaders, and whose peculiarities were the wearing of black fur bonnets, and never being seen in close company with other ladies, were at the music yesterday. One of them was attended by their brother, and the other had a member of Congress in tow. He went home with her, and if I were to guess, I would say, he went away a somewhat altered man—most likely in his pockets, and in some other particular. The fellow looked conscious of guilt although I believe he was unconscious that every body around knew who it was that caught him [ibid., 496].

Lincoln then closes by asking for letters from Mary and by also assuring her that he understood her need of a house woman, and a reference to their "rascals"; that is, their children, and the father's strong desire to see them:

I have had no letter from home, since I wrote you before, except short business letters, which have no interest for you.

By the way, you do not intend to do without a girl, because the one you had has left you? Get another as soon as you can to take charge of the dear codgers. Father expected to see you all sooner; but let it pass; stay as long as you please. Kiss and love the dear rascals.

Affectionately, A. Lincoln [Basler, I, 495–496]

The above letter is perhaps one of his most familiar letters, where Lincoln scarcely mentions any political happenings and instead writes about with the "everyday news" that he wishes to share with his wife, the ordinary happenings in the life of a married couple. He closes the letter with "Affectionately."

After examining Lincoln's letters to Mary Owens and later those to Mary Todd, we find that they are remarkably lacking in what many would call "emotional passion." He, like many other great writers of his age, could create a kind of restrained passion without eliciting excessively emotional language and resorting to cheap sentimentality. Perhaps, in person, Lincoln expressed his deep and abiding affection—and sometimes, conditional love to various women—but this extensive sampling of Lincoln's love letters reveals that his letters are largely devoid of any "purple passages" when the writer soars into some sort of passion-produced land of roses and sunshine. In essence, then, his carefully crafted prose lacks the saccharine sentiments of his age, a fact that makes his writing so readable today and, at the same time, so unlike many of the things he was reading in his day. Stylistically, then, his prose is unlike much typical nineteenth century popular prose, written in a florid ciceronian style. In fact, Lincoln was a careful reader, even given to reading aloud, but Lincoln most assuredly dismissed the bathos of his contemporaries and, through practice and labor, learned the fundamentals of clear written expression.

When he wrote Mary Owens, he wanted to know how she felt about him and, and at the same time he wanted her to be aware that he had been honest with her about what married life would be like if she married him. If she was still committed to marrying him he would, indeed, marry her. The letter is a well-crafted and subtle—albeit perhaps difficult at times to interpret—query of just how she felt about him in light of her knowing what she should expect. If she could accept that kind of life, then he would take her as a wife—if that was what she wanted. But in order to proceed he had to know how she felt about him first. But the ethos of the letter is quite difficult to obtain: that of an honest man who, because he had promised

8. The Love Letters

to marry her, would indeed. Such an ethos was that of a man of unquestionable honesty and not an attempt to dissuade her from any interest she had in him. To achieve the ethos he sought required great skill.

Lincoln considered honesty in human relations to be of paramount importance. After breaking the engagement he had with Mary Todd, he fell into a deep depression, for she reminded him of his promise to marry her. His biographer, David Herbert Donald, describes Lincoln as having "his nerves snapped" (1996, 87). But his essential honesty prevailed. A promise was a promise, and, of course, he did marry her.

Writing to Mary Todd, with whom he traded Shakespearean quotations and whose heart he caught in some irreversible attraction, he composed a type of prose so that he projected clearly the ethos of the dutiful husband and father, concerned about her and their children's welfare, the money Mary needed, the routes she would take, while expressing at the same time his gentle and genuine affection for her and his children. In the main, Lincoln's prose that projects an ethos is quite believable, that of a deeply caring husband and father, those qualities that a wife looks for in a dutiful mate, and the kind of ethos he no doubt tried hard to achieve. Certainly, there were moments when he mirrored those qualities that were characteristic of the letters of the era: the pet names, the expressions of loneliness and desire to be with her, and, most assuredly, the conversational tone of the letters. But his letters are more definitively attempts to build a kind of ethos of an affectionate husband and father and win her heart.

Lincoln will be remembered as a nuanced and profound writer, with such documents as the Cooper Union Address, the Gettysburg Address, and the Second Inaugural Address projecting the ethos of a resolute and merciful countryman. No doubt he will receive the deserving attention of learned historians and sensitive rhetoricians for decades to come for these documents alone. But it is too easy to lose sight of where Lincoln learned the fundamentals of writing and the importance of his projection of his own believability in his prose. Students of Lincoln's most important documents also recall that his memorable prose evolved from, in large part, his letter-writing experience. Here he could practice what he had learned from his reading and study of model poetry and prose. Here he had learned the fundamentals of memorable prose, not only from others, but also, curiously, from himself. Here he set himself up for the joy, and the exhilaration, and the satisfaction that comes from writing well.

9

Letters to His Cabinet

On March 4, 1861, Abraham Lincoln swore to "uphold and defend the American Constitution" and assumed the awesome duties of the presidency of the United States. He was responsible, as the highest officer in the executive branch of the Constitution, to carry out the laws of the country.

But he was not to carry out his duties by himself. According the Constitution, he was to have a team of advisors to assist him and offer their opinion about various matters of importance to the duties of the president. While the American Constitution does not specifically name the various officers or their specific duties, it does say in Article II, Section II and Paragraph 1, that Lincoln was to have advisors that the president "may require the Opinion, in writing, of the principal Officer in each of the executive Departments, upon any subject relating to the Duties of their respective Offices."

Over the years, such officers quickly assumed the title of "Secretaries." During George Washington's administration, the first president had Secretary of State Thomas Jefferson, Secretary of the Treasury Alexander Hamilton, Secretary of War Henry Knox, and Attorney General Edmund Randolph, as well as the Vice President John Adams as advisors, all men devoted to helping make successful the first presidential administration. However, while Washington, generally speaking, remained neutral, a spilt quickly developed between Jefferson and Hamilton. Richard Norton Smith colorfully describes both: "Jefferson, the apostle of the yeoman, versus Hamilton, the mercantile prophet; one an aristocrat who lived on a mountaintop and considered himself a friend too; the other a self-made elitist with a Calvinistic belief in original sin" (2017, 13). Quite predictably, Smith says, "like fire and frost, they were temperamental opposites whom not

9. Letters to His Cabinet

Lincoln and his cabinet. Lincoln relied on letters to keep in touch with his cabinet members.

even George Washington could reconcile" (*ibid.*). Later, Jefferson would be elected as president and Hamilton was shot dead in a duel with Aaron Burr, another enemy of Jefferson. From the very first, cabinet members clashed with another, a fact that occurred during successive administrations.

During Lincoln's administration, he offered a twist on the clashing personalities of previous administrations. During the early days of the establishment of the Republican Party, the fledgling party had searched for politicians that could lead the party to victory after the defeat of its first candidate in 1856, John C. Frémont. While there were a number of good candidates in 1860, the Republican Party agreed on Lincoln, leaving a host of possible candidates behind, men such as William Seward, Salmon Chase, and Edwin Stanton, to name a few. Lincoln hoped to unite the party by appointing his political presidential rivals to office. Carl Brent Swisher, someone speaking as a constitutional expert, notes that apparently Lincoln believed that the country, the party, and he would be better served by "men who had been his competitors for the presidency and who were doubtless still convinced that they, rather than he, ought to have been placed at the head of the nation in the crisis" (1943, 275). Swisher goes further: "It was [Lincoln's] belief that it was better to have the assistance of these men and to compel them to share a portion than to leave them acting as critics from without the administration." What resulted was "an unusually strong cabinet, in spite of the difficulties involved in their divergent personalities." John Palmer Usher, active in the Lincoln administration, notes, "Mr. Lincoln, in the selection of his cabinet officers, named all his rival candidates in the convention" (2013, 25).

But selecting these men to serve their various offices was not enough. He had also to deal with their often quirky personalities, if each cabinet member was to be a successful member of Lincoln's administration. Part of that was knowing specifically what to write to each in the letters Lincoln wrote to each cabinet member. For example, what role should Lincoln assume in the letters? Should he be authoritarian? Should he coddle each to derive their best work? Part of the answer to these questions lies in the type of discourse he had to use. To approach some kind of analysis, Aristotle specifies that there are three types of discourse: forensic, epideictic, and deliberative (1932, 16–17). The first type, forensic rhetoric, concerns itself with matters of the past, concentrating on the discovery of arguments dealing with courtroom procedures to determine whether a person is guilty or innocent. The second type, epideictic rhetoric, is the type of writing that celebrates the achievement of an army or person, or the condemnation of an event or person that is publically recognized. In the United States, speeches on the Fourth of July are an example of epideictic rhetoric. The third type, deliberative rhetoric, concentrates on future matters; thus, it is the type of appeal that is present in legislative matters. Writing in the prestigious *Encyclopedia of Rhetoric and Composition*, James Benjamin maintains that deliberative rhetoric concerns matters such as "ways and means, war and peace, national defense, imports and exports, and legislation" (1996a, 171). In general, deliberative rhetoric "is aimed at expressing arguments about the expediency or harmfulness of a proposed act." Lincoln's letters, then, to individual cabinet members, discussing a political issue, fall under the category of deliberative rhetoric.

The types of argumentative patterns used in deliberative rhetoric are the enthymemes and examples (*ibid.*). Not every letter that Lincoln wrote

9. Letters to His Cabinet

is amenable to this type of analysis. While other letters display the need for other types of rhetorical analysis, the letters to cabinet members differ.

In spite a broad array of definitions, an enthymeme as used here refers to a rhetorical syllogism, in contrast to the more formal analytical syllogism. The enthymeme instead relies on the premise accepted as true by an audience. Sometimes the enthymeme uses a "because clause" and omits a premise, which is deemed unnecessary because of the sense of "connectedness between the reasoning proffered by an argument and the beliefs assumed to be shared with an audience" (Gage 1996, 225). For example, the writer may create a rhetorical argument that relies on an appeal that argues that *the Affordable Care Act should be continued because it ultimately saves on health care costs*. The premise *that programs that save money are good* is left out because this premise is widely accepted and is assumed to be known by readers. At other times, Lincoln uses what may be called hypothetical syllogisms in rhetorical form. These syllogisms usually contain "if clauses" that suppose that if A is true, then B is also true. Often the syllogisms contain evidence to support the assertions Lincoln made.

Examples, too, are often used in deliberative discourse. As Donald Bushman notes, the use of examples is in the main a process using induction, "arguing from particular instances to a general conclusion" (1996, 247). He goes on to point out that the use of an example represents "arguing from probabilities that known instances are parallel to and illuminating of those less known." In particular, the example used for argumentative purposes must be representative of the same class as other examples in that category if they are used for persuasive purposes. To generate examples for persuasive purposes, the writer might draw from historical examples or use various fables and other "invented examples" (*ibid.*). In a rhetorical use, the example can be a powerful persuasive tool when used effectively. For instance, a politician may narrate a story about a young family who would not have health insurance if the Affordable Care Act were repealed. If the writer picks a family that is representative of many others in this category, then the writer may have effectively used an example for persuasive purposes.

While it is a bit too ambitious to cover all the letters that Lincoln wrote to all thirteen men who served on Lincoln's cabinet, it is possible, to examine a representative number of letters Lincoln wrote to cabinet members that show the types and the themes of the letters Lincoln wrote. For the most part, the letters to cabinet members are presented as Lincoln wrote them, without careful editing for punctuation and spelling.

Secretary of State William Seward was the most frequent addressee of Lincoln's cabinet members. David Herbert Donald's *Lincoln* describes Seward as "an unquestionably able, experienced and adroit politician ... but he was seen as having an undeserved reputation for extremism because of his speeches proclaiming a higher law than the Constitution and predicting an irrepressible conflict between slavery and freedom" (1996, 236). John Palmer Usher described Seward as "one of the wisest statesmen we have ever had, and Mr. Lincoln ... would have had infinite trouble without him. The utmost confidence and kindly feeling between these two men" (12). In a very real way, Lincoln had great confidence in Seward, and his decision-making made him a very important advisor to the president. To Lincoln, Seward was his closest advisor, becoming a valuable friend. What that probably meant was that Lincoln handled much of his communication with Seward in person, for the letters Lincoln wrote to Seward were mainly short notes covering a variety of perfunctory day-to-day matters.

For example, Lincoln wrote letters of introduction to Seward:

> Hon. Sec. of State   Executive Mansion
> My dear Sir   October 26, 1861
>   This will introduce Judge A.D. Russell, of New York, who comes to me with a very kind letter of introduction from Mr. Bennett of the Herald.
>   Please give him a kind reception.
>   Yours truly
>   A. Lincoln [Basler, V, 5].

Sometimes, Lincoln used a note to recommend a person for a government office:

> As this recommendation is made by Bishop Janes & Simpson, I am anxious an appointment to a Consulship be made accordingly, if one could be found.
>   Nov. 2, 1861   A. Lincoln [Basler, V, 13]

Still another recommendation for a government post:

> Hon. Sec. of State   Executive Mansion
>   Washington, May 2, 1863
>   My dear Sir, Have you any committal as to the vacant consulate at Havvana [*sic*]? If we have not, I am for giving it to Hon. Caleb Lyon, and of doing it at once.
>   Yours truly. A. Lincoln [*ibid.*, IV, 195].

9. Letters to His Cabinet

Or Lincoln asks the advice on a particular issue:

> What thinks the Sec. of State, of the within? A. Lincoln [*ibid.*, V, 83].

Lincoln, especially as the war raged on, sent various dispatches to Seward informing him of the progress of a battle or campaign. This one is about Burnside at Knoxville:

Secretary of State William Seward. Seward and Lincoln carried on an important correspondence with each other.

> Executive Mansion
> My dear Sir:
> Washington, November 23, 1863
> Two despatches since I saw you—one not quite so late on firing as we had before, but given the points that that Burnside thinks he can hold the place, that he is not closely invested, and that he forges across the river. The other brings the firing up to 11 A.M. yesterday, being 23 hours later than we had before. Yours truly,
> A. Lincoln [*ibid.*, VII, 29].

Lincoln often asked Seward to see someone rather than formally introducing that person:

> Sec. of State, please see the bearer, Miss Alice Lightner.
> April 12, 1862   A. Lincoln [*ibid.*, V, 188].

Lincoln usually gave orders in asking Seward to do so in quite polite language:

> Hon. Sec. of State   Executive Mansion
> Dear Sir: Washington, February 3, 1864.
> Please see Hon. Wm. R. Morrison, and oblige him about the pass-ports for Mr. Merrick if you consistently can. Yours truly A. Lincoln [*ibid.*, VII, 167].

Another one said:

> Will the Secretary of State please see me and hear the bearer Mr. Ulrich & and oblige him if he conveniently can? He is a young man raised in the place of my residence, and of a respectable family, and he is myself. A. Lincoln
> Jan. 30, 1865 [*ibid.*, 247].

Calling on Seward, as head of the cabinet, Lincoln was even polite in asking the secretary of state to assemble the cabinet:

Please invite all members of the Cabinet to be [present] at the meeting today. Yours truly. A. Lincoln [*ibid.*, 330].

Lincoln's use of the enthymeme to Seward is generally quite short with very little material to support the premises or conclusion, if any are missing:

> This gentleman, though plain spoken, in pursuit of an office, is highly recommended as a worthy gentleman.
> Aug. 23, 1862 A. Lincoln [*ibid.*, V, 391].

In this enthymeme, Lincoln states the premise that *the man is in pursuit of an office,* followed by the second premise that *the man is highly recommended,* and then the missing conclusion that the *man should be given a job.* Lincoln adds some supporting material in the form of "though plain spoken" and the qualifying phrase "as a worthy gentleman." Lincoln could have added that he wanted to secure a position for the man, but he deems that not necessary since he believes that his letter already makes that point.

Besides these various short notes written to Secretary of State Seward, President Lincoln rarely used deliberative rhetoric to outline a particular order or mission for Seward. The orders that Lincoln makes are put into simple commands like "please oblige" and the like, phrased in short sentences and not in long arguments. In contrast to this approach, the following order deals with a very important mission about meeting Confederate representatives to discuss the possibility of peace. Notice how specific and formal the language is, indicating exactly what Lincoln wanted and his not being willing to take anything less than that outlined in the memorandum. While there had been earlier overtures from the Rebel government that had come to naught, here also Lincoln suggests he was not willing to negotiate anything less than the terms he lists for the secretary, including such things as recognition of the Confederate States of America as a legitimate country after the close of hostilities, and demand for freedom for the slaves as outlined in the Emancipation Proclamation:

> Hon. William H. Seward   Executive Mansion
> Secretary of State   Washington, January 31, 1865
> You will proceed to Fortress-Monroe, Virginia, there to meet, and informally confer with Messrs. Stephens, Hunter, and Campbell, on the basis of my letter to F.P. Blair, Esq., on Jan. 18. 1865, a copy of which you have.
> You will make known to them that three things are indispensable, to wit:
> 1. The restoration of the national authority throughout all the States.

9. Letters to His Cabinet

2. No receding, by the Executive of the United States on the Slavery question, from the position assumed thereon, in the late Annual Message to Congress, and in the preceding documents
3. No cessation of hostilities short of an end of the war, and the disbanding of all forces hostile to the government.

You will inform them that all propositions of theirs not inconsistent with the above, will be considered and passed upon in a spirit of sincere liberty. You will hear all they may choose to say, and report it to me.

You will not assume to definitely consummate anything. Yours &c Abraham Lincoln [*ibid.*, VII, 250–251]

Looking at the document itself, the reader is quickly drawn to the emphasis on future action. Lincoln for example, uses future tense markers like *will* in sentences like, "You *will* proceed to Fortress-Monroe, Virginia, there to meet and informally confer with...." He closes with a third future tense marker: "You *will* not assume to definitely consummate anything." The action Lincoln is proposing and that which Seward is to follow are clearly future actions, as in deliberative discourse.

Next, the document exhibits a great deal of formal language in the document itself. Rather than a short note to Secretary Seward, giving him a command that does not need a long explanation, Lincoln uses formal language and structure in what might be called legalese: phrases such as "to wit" and formal structures emphasizing parallelism: "you will." Lincoln, too, organizes the document formally, using numbers to organize the points he wants Seward to remember. In addition, Lincoln uses a great deal of parallelism, by using a series of sentences with five sentences that begin with "you will" and two sentences that begin with a definitive "no." Finally, he signs the entire document with his whole name: "Abraham Lincoln," rather than the usual "A. Lincoln." The Emancipation Proclamation, another formal document, is also signed "Abraham Lincoln."

The document is also a kind of rhetorical argument in which Lincoln acknowledges the premise that attempts at peace are good as long as the opposition accepts that certain tenets (the "recognition of National authority," "no receding ... on the Slavery question," "[no] cessation of hostilities short of the end of the war," and "the disbanding of all forces") cannot be dismissed. The formal layout and language reinforce the seriousness of the letter: what the Confederates would have to accept in order to *begin* negotiations. To say it another way: If the Confederates accept the premises, then negotiations are possible; if not, then no negotiations were possible. And as a closing, Lincoln reminded Seward, "You will not assume to definitely consummate anything." Presumably, the president and/or the Congress would have to approve any agreement that Seward could effect. As president, Lincoln closes the letter to Seward by spelling out just what he wanted done at this important meeting with Confederate diplomats. Lincoln was also careful not to acknowledge that he considered these men to be legitimate members of a recognized government.

Taken as a whole, the biographies of Lincoln or Seward imply that Lincoln and Secretary Seward saw each other very frequently. During these face-to-face meetings, Lincoln could very easily state what he wanted Seward to know or to do without the need for a formal memorandum or letter. But in this case Lincoln's careful instructions helped to reinforce the importance of these negotiations.

In letters, Lincoln also addressed Secretary of War Edwin Stanton, appointed January 20, 1862, who set about repairing relations with Congress by streamlining a department that had previously been under the auspices of Simon Cameron, whom Lincoln had removed from office. A native of Steubenville, Ohio, Stanton, who served briefly as attorney general under President James Buchanan, found the War Department in disarray and often at odds with the legislative branch. James McPherson in his history of the times observes that, "In Stanton and [Quartermaster General] Montgomery Meigs, aided by the entrepreneurial talent of northern businessmen, the Union developed superior managerial talent to mobilize and organize the North's greater resources for victory in the modern industrialized conflict that the Civil War became" (1988, 857). Another historian, Phillip Shaw Paludan, in his discussion of the Lincoln presidency echoes those

Secretary of War Edwin Stanton. Stanton often complained about Lincoln's pardons, but Stanton managed a wartime economy well.

9. Letters to His Cabinet

remarks: "Stanton ran the most vital of government departments with a brisk and decisive energy" (1994, 106). Richard Carwardine's *Lincoln: A Life of Purpose and Power* avers, "Stanton brought his own distinctive energy to the War Department" (2003, 200). But John Palmer Usher says that Stanton was "a dyspeptic and because of his temper was irascible and unequable" (2013, 22). Yet Usher acknowledges that Stanton "was a man of immense power" and qualifies his remarks about Stanton's "distemper," saying, "Lincoln appreciated his loyalty, his devotion and his ability" (24).

Lincoln's letters to Stanton, though there are many, fall into roughly four categories, even though the greater part of them are short and direct. In the first category are letters in which Lincoln gives Stanton specific orders. The following letter asks Stanton to appoint someone to a position:

> Hon. Sec. of State   Executive Mansion
> Sir—   Washington, July 29, 1862
> Gen John Cook tells me he has never had an Assistant Quarter Master, and he wants Joseph B. Tully, now First Lieu. In the N.Y. 69th appointed to that position. Unless there be some insurmountable obstacle, let him be appointed.
> Yours Truly
> A. Lincoln [Basler, V, 348].

As in his orders to Secretary of State William Seward, Lincoln is polite in asking for Stanton to make an appointment "[unless] there be some insurmountable obstacle." This "politeness" adds to Lincoln's ethos as a man of authority who is giving an order a "gentlemanly" way.

Another letter of appointment with an interesting twist: Stanton's objection and Lincoln's not going back on his word:

> Hon. Sec. of War   Executive Mansion
> My dear Sir—   Washington, May 9, 1863
> I wish you would make out the appointment of Lilley at once. He has my word in writing, and I can not afford to break it. I appreciate your opposition to him, but you can better afford to let him be disappointed, than I can afford to break my word with him.
> Yours as ever A. Lincoln [*ibid.*, VII, 208]

The letter is quite interesting. The letter seems to say that Stanton can more afford living up to the promise Lincoln had made to Lilley than Lincoln. If Stanton didn't take the blame and assign it to Lincoln, the president's ethos would be severely damaged. In asking Stanton to "take the fall," the letter shows a side of Lincoln not often revealed. Basler's notes to this letter details the story of Lilley, who is "characterized by the most cowardly and brutal treatment ... [apparently including] in one or two instances of criminal indecency [and his] gross insult of the wife of the only loyal man in South Carolina" (*ibid.*, VII, 208). Lilley surely was a truly unsavory character whom Lincoln felt obligated to appoint to a quartermaster's position, rather than to go back on his word.

The next letter is an order written to Stanton about a military matter:

Hon. Sec. of War   Executive Mansion
Dear Sir Washington,   June 18, 1864
   Hon. L. Anderson and Judge [Rufus K.] Williams are here, first, that assessments, for some time urging suspended in West Ky. again put in operation; and secondly, that Gen. E. A. Paine be assigned to command them. Do both these things for them unless you know some reason to the contrary. I personally know Gen. Paine to be a good man, having a West Point education; but I do not know much as to his military ability. Yours truly A. Lincoln [*ibid.*, VI, 400].

Again, Lincoln is very polite in giving Stanton an order. In this letter, he uses a qualifying phrase, "unless you know some reason to the contrary." A little bit different, yet in the same vein as his earlier letter, Lincoln offers to withdraw the order, if there are reasons. In addition, Lincoln's use of the power of his own ethos by saying, "I personally know Gen. Paine," more obvious in his endorsement. Lincoln also organizes the letter with transitional markers "first" and "secondly" to make sure that Stanton understands that there are two parts to the order. Lincoln also strengthens the entire letter by building the ethos of Gen. Paine with the phrase, "Gen. Paine to be a good man, having a West Point education," curiously though, but he qualifies his remarks about Paine: "but I do not know much as to his military ability." In doing so he seems not let his and Paine's appeal to ethos override Stanton's own authority to dismiss the order, if he chooses.

The next letter to Stanton is also an order:

February 25, 1864
   I am told there are one hundred colored men in Alexandra, Va. Who wish to go to Massachusetts; with their own consent and the consent of Gov. Pierpont, let them go.
   A. Lincoln [*ibid.*, VII, 204].

In the above letter, the governor asks to outfit a unit for Massachusetts, and Lincoln gives his consent to the governor's wishes. As outlined in the Emancipation Proclamation, the letter recognizes the commitment that Lincoln had made to use colored troops in the war. The order also reinforces the role of the president, using his ethos, to issue such an order to Stanton.

9. Letters to His Cabinet

Lincoln's letters to Stanton in the next category are interesting for their form. In these letters Lincoln uses a number of hypothetical syllogisms, using "if clauses." Essentially, they take the form of the following form: *If A is true, then B is also true*. In the use of logical form, they seem to illustrate Lincoln's use of the logic that he employed in the letters to Carl Schurz, discussed earlier.

> If there be a vacancy such as mentioned within [an earlier document], and it not be in the regular Army, let it be filled as herein requested. A. Lincoln May 19, 1862 [*ibid.*, V, 224].

The hypothetical syllogism he used contains not only an "if clause" but also a particular qualification: "and not be in the regular Army" a condition necessary for this syllogism to be complete.

In the next example, Lincoln states the syllogism and provides evidence afterwards:

> If the [evidence] within showing Col. Ballier's case is correct, I think he should be restored.
> It shows that he was sick in hospital when discharged from service, and without knowledge of his discharge from service he made premature efforts to return to duty [*ibid.*, VI, 86].

In still another example, Lincoln mentions the ethos of a person he knows, and he strengthens the power of the syllogism with the assertion of his own ethos:

> If consistent with the service, I would like for my friend, Major Fell, to be obliged as within requested. A. Lincoln
> Feb. 20, 1863 [*ibid.*, VI, 113].

Once again, Lincoln is arguing for a particular action and if that action is true as asserted in the "if clause," then the action he is arguing for should necessarily happen. Sometimes he qualifies certain elements of the syllogism to add strength to the syllogism, but the use of such a structure displays Lincoln's thinking in what is effective and clear form.

In this final example, Lincoln again makes use of the hypothetical:

> The writer of the within,—Charles King—is President of Columbia College, N.Y.—son of *the* Rufus King of revolutionary memory, and I, believe, father of our Gen. Rufus King. If his request within, can be consistently granted, I shall be glad.
> March 25, 1863, A. Lincoln [*ibid.*, 149].

In this "if clause," Lincoln seems to a bit political by qualifying his requested action based on the supposition that Rufus King is the son of

The Rhetoric of Lincoln's Letters

the Rufus King. Then, such action that Rufus King requested would be a popular decision if indeed he is indeed the son of *the* Rufus King. Many do not see Lincoln as the politician he appeared to be.

Besides hypothetical syllogisms and other structures, Lincoln once in a great while made use of, for want of a better term, an "inductive example." The "inductive example" uses a series of particular instances or reasons and then closes by reaching a conclusion drawn from the particulars. Sometimes the list of particulars is relatively long, with the writer using complicated syntactical structures, or at other times the list of particulars is short. The following inductive example is typical of Lincoln. Notice, too, his appeal to emotion, something the Greeks called "pathos":

> Hon. Sec. of War   Executive Mansion
> Dear Sir: Washington,   September 15, 1863
> The bearer of this, Mrs. Craddock, tells me she has a nephew—Edwin Selvage—who was in the rebel service, made a prisoner, and is now at Fort-Delaware; that he has two brothers in the Union Army, is yet under twenty one years of age; and wishes to take the oath of allegiance and be discharged. Upon reasonable proof of all of this, let him take the oath and be discharged.
> Yours Truly A. Lincoln [*ibid.*, 452].

First, the letter mentions that an aunt is appealing for release of her nephew. Second, the nephew used to be a rebel, and third, he is a prisoner of war at Fort-Delaware. Fourth, he has two brothers in the Union army. Fifth, that he is only twenty-one years of age. Sixth, he is willing to take the oath of the allegiance. Seventh, followed by a reprieve from Lincoln, he would then be discharged.

Then Lincoln uses a hypothetical syllogism that says that if "[u]pon reasonable proof of all of this" and he takes the oath, he would then "be discharged." Initially, the argument seems to be quite simple, but close examination of Lincoln's letter is quite complicated. The use of pity, that is, the fact that a lady is making the request, may have influenced Lincoln's final decision. So, too, is that he is an under-twenty-one-year-old "boy" who unlike his brothers in the Union army joined the rebel army, but who apparently now sees the error of his ways and is quite willing to take the oath—all appeals both to pity and reason that apparently Lincoln heard from the aunt and are quite convincing factors in Lincoln's mind, especially the fact that he is but a boy who is willing to take the oath of allegiance. But Lincoln is not through. The veracity of all of these factors must be true before Lincoln can grant the request.

In another instance, the enthymemes that Lincoln uses in his letters to Stanton, like his enthymemes to Seward, are fairly short. Here is one example:

> In a long verbal conversation with me, Judge Fisher assured, as within, of his confident belief that Dr. Worrell is partially insane. I suppose that on this ground, he should be discharged.
> Feb. 12, 1865 　　　　　　　　　　　　A. Lincoln [*ibid.*, VIII, 293].

In this enthymeme, Lincoln advances the premise that *Dr. Worrell is partially insane.* The next part of the enthymeme is not a premise but the conclusion: *I suppose that on this ground, he should be discharged.* In this case, the enthymeme leaves out the obvious premise that people who are insane do not make good soldiers. Along the way, Lincoln uses what he accepts as expert testimony of Judge Fisher, who assures him that Worrell is *partially insane*, and thus accepts the premise that insane individuals do not make good soldiers. As in all enthymemes when part of it is left out, the writer runs the risk of not being clear, but the writer runs the risk of that not being the case in gaining the reward of not including unnecessary information.

This examination of Lincoln's letters to Stanton, his secretary of war, reveals that Lincoln does use short notes to give Stanton orders and make appointments, but further examination shows that Lincoln also employs syllogisms, enthymemes, and "inductive examples" to write what are ultimately rhetorical arguments in his letters to Stanton. Lincoln was, then, not afraid to write to his cabinet in verbal structures in sophisticated forms.

Lincoln's appointee to be attorney general was Edward Bates, a Missourian, who like Simon Cameron, William Seward, and Salmon Chase, was a contender for the presidency with Lincoln at the 1860 Republican Convention. John Paul Usher, an insider in the Lincoln White House, wrote that Bates was "a man of ostentatious manners, easily approached by all who wished to see him and highly respected by all" (2013, 25) Usher added that Bates "rendered important service to the Government" but "when he was driven to it, he was firm and unmovable" (25). In contrast, writing soon after the Civil War, A.K. McClure's *Abraham Lincoln and Men of War-Times* maintained that Bates was "old and conservative" (1996, 60). The *Abraham Lincoln Encyclopedia* says that Bates and Lincoln, on occasions, disagreed about matters such as whether or not West Virginia should be admitted as a state, and Lincoln's proclivity toward pardoning almost all who came to his attention (Neely, Jr., 1982, 21). But Bates was never harsh in his disagreements with Lincoln. When Lincoln wrote to him, the president often spoke to the fellow lawyer in "legalese," probably because Lincoln felt that such language was appropriate for their communication, both being by profession members of the bar. The letters are then quite deliberative in content, but Lincoln used a variety of other rhetorical strategies with his attorney general, whose reputation was that he was quite well-reasoned in arriving at his decisions. Bates proved to be, in the end, a loyal supporter of Lincoln. In a short time, Bates, unlike Salmon Chase, for example, gave up on undermining President Lincoln's conduct as a leader of the country. For the most part, Lincoln's letters to him, like those to other cabinet members, revolve around his business as the attorney general. Yet there are other types of rhetorical strategies, like writing to Bates in legalese, that appear in Lincoln's letters. Here is a typical order:

> Hon. E. Bates   Executive Mansion
> My dear Sir: March 11, 1861
>   This introduces Hon. I.N. Morris, with whom I wish you would converse in relation to the Russell fraud. I think it may subserve [serve?] the public interest.
>   Yours truly A. Lincoln [Basler, IV, 281].

Rather than "wasting" the attorney general's time with appointing Lincoln's choice of applicants for government positions, for the most part Lincoln uses his attorney general's time wisely. But Lincoln does ask Bates to appoint people to particular positions, as he does in the following:

> Hon. Atty. General   Executive Mansion
> My dear Sir: March 27, 1861
>   Senator Foote sends me word that the Vermont delegation desires George Howe to be District Attorney; and C.C.P. Baldwin to be Marshal for Vermont. The initials I can not help. I send them as sent to me. Send me the blank appointments.
>   Yours &
>   A. Lincoln [*ibid.*, 299].

Very rarely this time, Lincoln employs hypothetical syllogism, making use of "if clauses":

>   Executive Mansion
> My Dear Sir   Washington, December 14, 1863
>   If upon examination of this case you find that the facts are in accordance with the statement of the petition and that Dr. Ratliffe took the oath of allegiance at the invitation of our military authorities & has since has been inviolate, let

9. Letters to His Cabinet

Attorney General Edward Bates. Lincoln's letters to him reflected a mutual knowledge of legal language.

him be pardoned for any reasonable practice previous to such recantation, and freed from the penalties now hanging over him.

                                                                       Your Obt. Servant

Attorney General will please have a pardon made out for Robert B. Nay, mentioned within.

A. Lincoln   Feb. 13, 1863 [*ibid.*, VI, 103].

The form is simple and to the point, offering no evidence for granting the pardon, simply asking Bates to fill out the paper work.

The next letter shows at least one instance where Lincoln enhances his own ethos by asking for help from Bates on a legal matter. While Lincoln probably had the expertise for the legal matter, he asks Bates to research the matter and give his opinion, certainly a proper decision for a busy man like Lincoln, but showing his respect for Bates by asking the attorney general to do the research. In that way, Lincoln enhances his own ego as a man who is willing to ask someone else to perform a duty:

> Hon. Attorney General   Executive Mansion
> My dear Sir   Washington, Feb. 6, 1862
>   As you see, Gen. McClellan, approves the finding of the Court Martial in the case of which the accompanying is a Copy of the Record. Please give me your opinion.
>   Yours truly A. Lincoln [*ibid.*, 129].

Lincoln could have taken the information from General McClellan and decided on his own, but instead he seeks Bates' opinion, a gentle gesture indicating how Lincoln maintained the confidence and devotion of most of his cabinet. The honorific "Hon. Attorney General" indicates that Lincoln is capable of using an appropriate and respectful designation to a cabinet member, instead of something like, "Look at this."

Secretary of the Treasury Salmon Chase. Lincoln's letter asking for his resignation shows classic restraint.

Secretary of the Treasury Solomon Chase was, as A.K. McClure observes, "the most irritating fly in the Lincoln ointment from the inauguration of the new administration in 1861 until the 29th of June, 1864, when his resignation was finally accepted" (1996, 132). Fairly strong words, but even Lincoln would agree with such an evaluation of Chase, as he expressed in his acceptance of Chase's third letter of resignation:

9. Letters to His Cabinet

Hon. Salmon P. Chase Executive Mansion
My Dear Sir. Washington, June 30, 1864
Your resignation of the office of Secretary of the Treasury, sent me yesterday, is accepted.
Of all I have said in commendation of your ability and fidelity, I have nothing to unsay; and yet you and I have reached a point of mutual embarrassment in our official relation which seems can not be overcome, or longer sustained, consistently with the public service. Your Obt. Servant, A. Lincoln [*ibid.*, VII, 419].

Always confident that he could change Lincoln's thinking about political issues by periodically resigning his cabinet post, Chase never gave up on his dream of succeeding Lincoln in the presidency. Chase and Lincoln's relationship was solid, "after Chase had performed the important duty of finding enough money to finance a major war," as Geoffrey Perret terms it (2004, 19). After all, Chase had introduced a national bank and paper money, and gently guided the financial forces of the Lincoln presidency. But Paludan observes that in spite of all the good work he had done, he "somehow never felt at peace with the world around him," often "spreading rumors about the men whom Lincoln respected" (1994, 40–41). A.K. McClure concludes that Chase "never forgave Lincoln for the crime of having been preferred for President over him" (1996, 132). Even after his welcomed resignation, Chase continued to worry Lincoln with his "intrigues," scheming just how he could be Lincoln's successor, but telling Lincoln that his ultimate goal was the Supreme Court (1961, Hendrick, 540).

As a person in his cabinet whom Lincoln learned to loathe, Chase received a small number of letters from the president. Perhaps Lincoln left Chase to his good work, but we can also speculate that the president avoided Chase because of Chase's questionable conduct. Almost always, then, Lincoln's letters to Chase concern the business at hand:

Hon. Secretary of Treasury Executive Mansion
Dear Sir April 10, 1861
Mr. Wood thinks that possibly he can save you something in the matter of engraving Treasury Notes. Please give him an interview, & see what there is of it.
Yours truly A. Lincoln [Basler, IV, 326].

The note is short and direct and uses few words to construct a simple enthymeme in which the major premise reads something like, *Mr. Woods can save us money on engraving treasury notes.* The missing element in the enthymeme is that saving money is good, followed by the conclusion: *Please give him an interview, & see what there is to it.*

Another example of these "all business" Lincoln wrote to Chase was written later in the Lincoln Administration:

> Hon. Sec. of Treasury, Please see Mr. Erskine who wishes a brief interview in relation to U.S. bonds. A. Lincoln
> August 29, 1863 [*ibid.*, 371].

The note is "all business," but is addressed to Chase in respectful designation, but lacks a direct statement of Lincoln's wishes.

Lincoln uses a hypothetical syllogism with "if clauses" and added evidence in a note to Chase:

> Executive Mansion,   May 16, 1861
> My dear Sir: I have not at all considered the qualifications of the applicant for appraiserships [*sic*] at New York. Mr. David Webb seems to understand that he has no opposition for one of the places. If this is so, or, in any event, if you wish to appoint him, send me the commission. A. Lincoln [Basler, IV, 371].

"If" clauses—"if this is so" and "if you wish to appoint him"—appear; however, one clause contains evidence that if true, makes the hypothesis true: "Mr. Webb seems to understand he has no opposition," while Lincoln adds another hypothesis "if you wish to appoint him." The effect of the "if" clauses is to essentially leave the decision about Mr. Webb's qualification up to Chase, a way of building an ethos in Lincoln that Chase could possibly interpret as Lincoln's confidence in him.

In this example, Lincoln asks Chase to provide him with some information:

>   Executive Mansion
> Hon. Secretary of Treasury: January 11, 1864
> My dear Sir: I am receiving letter and dispatches indicating an expectation that Mr. Barney is to leave the Custom House, at New York. Have you anything on the subject? Yours very truly,
> A. Lincoln [*ibid.*, VII, 120].

Again, the inquiry is about business and only the business about the Custom House, but this note is asking a question that Lincoln thinks that Chase will know the answer to. Apparently answering this question is important to Lincoln. Lincoln apparently assumes that Chase will know the information Lincoln is seeking.

Lincoln's correspondence with Chase is quite limited, each letter usually having just a few words. Whether that is because Lincoln has lost

9. Letters to His Cabinet

patience with the secretary of the treasury, or because of the nature of his position within the cabinet is not entirely clear, but Lincoln wrote to Chase fewer times than he did to other cabinet members.

In summary, Lincoln wrote a large number of letters to cabinet members in his attempt to conduct the work of his presidency. These same letters display a number of rhetorical strategies. Lincoln uses inductive examples and enthymemes to make clear what his wishes were. He also uses a number of hypothetical syllogisms or what might be called more complex structures to get his point across to the cabinet members. All of the cabinet member were educated writers, and they were an audience that could respond to Lincoln in letters appropriate for the content and audience. Lincoln's use of more complex rhetorical structures suggests that Lincoln was not locked into only using simple syntactic structures. In other words, he was willing to try to write letters in organizational syntactic patterns similar to those he read in the prose of other writers, including, in this case, writers such as his own cabinet members. By using more complicated prose, Lincoln was willing to try to improve his writing by studying and using the writing of other writers and attempting to write in a similar way—what rhetoricians call "imitation."

But Lincoln had not only to write to cabinet members in clear prose; he also had to write to them so that they would accept what he had written, and believe his arguments. In other words, as he often said, he had to "make friends" with them if he wished to get them to do what he asked. If he came across to them as too distant and aloof, and didn't remember that they had been rivals for the presidency, Lincoln was not likely to be a successful communicator. He indeed had not only to consider their wounded pride at not being president, but also to convince them of what work had to be done in order to be a successful presidential administration and to save the Union from its time of great peril. To say it another way, he needed them to help him keep the country together during its most critical period. Deftly, he addressed each cabinet member with a great degree of respect so that he could project the ethos that he knew was appropriate for their cabinet position. To be an effective communicator, Lincoln wanted to show them that he valued them and their important work, without being a sycophant. When he wrote letters and notes to each, for example, he used titles like "Honorary" or the abbreviated form, "Hon.," followed by their respective offices, such as secretary of state. Each letter or note then contained a line that read: "Hon. Secretary of State."

He then avoided what to him in this situation would be the too-familiar designations such as "William," "Edwin," or "Salmon." Invariably when he asked one of them to do something, he also used a respectful "please."

With this "tipping of the hat" to lubricate "good feelings" in what could have been a contentious environment, Lincoln sought to create a working environment of respect and, to a certain degree, harmony within the cabinet. After all, he had used a type of respectful prose that created an appropriate rhetorical stance. Although Lincoln had not studied the fundamentals of psychology, sociology, or business administration, he keenly understood how to motivate men in ways that convinced them that he respected them and the work they were doing for him and the country during these most trying times.

Conclusions

This study of Abraham Lincoln's letters has yielded a number of conclusions.

Abraham Lincoln was a prolific writer, with well over five thousand letters already attributed to him, and others sure to follow. Writing that many letters certainly gave Lincoln an extended practice in writing.

Modeling his letters on those he received, in the end, Lincoln became an experienced letter writer. As a youngster Lincoln wrote letters for his illiterate neighbors and friends, and continued the practice of writing letters for his entire life. At the same time, he also learned that letter writing was a valued skill for writing for his neighbors and himself. He became aware, then, that letter writing was the social norm, the habitus, for people to communicate at a distance, and the letter was a valued form of communication. As a result, Lincoln wrote letters to a number of different kinds of audiences, gaining the necessary practice in the epistolary form. Letter writing, then, was seminal to his learning to write, employing the theories of "taste" he gleaned from the most popular nineteenth century rhetorician in the United States at the time, Hugh Blair.

Lincoln was probably unaware that the letter forms for various kinds of letters, the letter to a friend or the letter of consolation, for example, followed formats from ancient Greek and Roman sources. Granted, he was fairly widely read for his day, but the chances are that the Greek and Roman writers were probably not ones he had read and studied. Nevertheless, those letters had a long-established tradition in the writing of his contemporaries, and he was quick to follow that tradition. Lincoln made use of imitation as a way to learn to write, a large part of his growth as a writer being derived from studying the letters he received.

Lincoln composed many types of letters: friendship letters, endorsements

Conclusions

for positions, and letters to his clients, fellow lawyers, and cabinet members. He even had a hand at letters of romance to people such as Mary Owens, and to Mary Todd Lincoln as a husband and father. In addition, he often communicated his feelings to the country in "public letters," seeing those as fundamental to communicating to the citizenry. As a letter writer, Lincoln often displayed an appropriate understanding what ethos was and how to project it in writing. Most notably, the letters to his cabinet display this careful attention to "making friends" with his audiences. In his letters, Lincoln did on occasion try more complex rhetorical structures when he felt they were necessary for the communication of his main idea in a clear fashion.

While this study of his letters is a beginning look at this body of his writing, more study of Lincoln the letter writer would help others understand how his prose in his most famous pieces derived from extended study of what he thought were successful pieces from other writers, and how he in turn employed what he had learned from other letter writers in his own letters.

This study may also open up the discussion of Lincoln as a seminal figure in the history of American stylists. Studying the writing of his contemporaries would aid in understanding of how Lincoln's writing in the main represents a departure from these traditions.

Studying Lincoln's letter writing may also aid students in understanding of how Lincoln often took complex ideas and communicated them in simple prose. Lincoln faced some of the most complicated problems in our country's history. How and why did he choose to communicate them in the manner he did? Much can be learned from observing Lincoln the letter writer as he learned valuable writing skills from the letters he received and imitated in his own writing, as the sheer volume of letters he composed provided him with valuable experience in writing.

Lincoln aged considerably over the course of the war.

Bibliography

Abbott, Henry Livermore. 1991. *Fallen Leaves: The Civil War Letters of Henry Livermore Abbott*. Ed. Robert Garth Scott. Kent, OH: Kent University Press.
Altman, Janet Gurkin. 1982. *Epistolarity: Approaches to a Form*. Columbus: Ohio State University Press.
Anderson, Howard, Phillip Daghlian, and Irvin Ehrenpreis, eds. 1966. *The Familiar Letter in Eighteenth Century*. Lawrence: University Press of Kansas.
Angle, Paul. 1981. "Lincoln's Power with Words." *Papers of the Abraham Lincoln Society* 3: 9–27.
Anonymous. 2001. "Principles of Letter Writing." In *The Rhetorical Tradition*, eds. Patricia Bizzell, and Bruce Herzberg, pp. 492–502. 2nd ed. Boston: Bedford/St. Martin.
Aristotle. 1932. *Rhetoric*. Trans. and ed. Lane Cooper. Englewood Cliffs, NJ: Prentice-Hall.
Arnold, Isaac N. 1885. *The Life of Abraham Lincoln*. Chicago: Jansen, McClurg.
Bacon, Francis. 1937. "Of Studies." In *Essays, Advancement of Learning, New Atlantis, and Other Pieces*, ed. Richard Foster Jones, pp. 145–45. New York: Odyssey.
Baker, Jean H. 1987. *Mary Todd Lincoln*. New York: W.W. Norton.
Barton, William E. 1925. The Life of Abraham Lincoln. Indianapolis: Bobbs Merrill.
Barzun, Jacques. 1971. *On Writing, Editing, and Publishing*. Chicago: University of Chicago Press.
———. 1975. *Simple and Direct: A Rhetoric for Writers*. New York: Harper and Row.
Basler, Roy P. 1939. "Abraham Lincoln's Rhetoric." *American Literature* 11 (May): 167–182.
———, ed. 1946. *Abraham Lincoln: His Speeches and Writings*. Cleveland, OH: DaCapo.
———, ed. 1953–55. *The Collected Works of Abraham Lincoln*. 9 vols. New Brunswick, NJ: Rutgers University Press.
———. 1974. *The Collected Works of Abraham Lincoln, Supplement 1832–1845*. Westport, CT: Greenwood.
———. 1990. *The Collected Works of Abraham Lincoln, Supplement 1848–1865*. Westport, CT: Greenwood.
Bates, David Homer. 1995. *Lincoln in the Telegraph Office*. Lincoln: University of Nebraska Press.
Benjamin, James. 1996. "Deliberative Oratory." In *Encyclopedia of Rhetoric and Composition*, ed. Theresa Enos, pp. 171–172. New York: Garland.
Berlin, James A. 1984. *Writing Instruction in Nineteenth-Century American Colleges*. Carbondale: Southern Illinois University Press.
Black, Edwin. 1992. *Rhetorical Questions*. Chicago: University of Chicago Press.
Blackstone, William. 1979. *Commentaries on the Laws of England*. Ed. Stanley Katz. 4 vols. Chicago: University of Chicago Press.

Bibliography

Blair, Hugh. 2005. *Lectures on Rhetoric and Belles Lettres*. Edited and introduced by Linda Ferria-Buckley and S. Michael Halloran. Carbondale: Southern Illinois University Press.
Bloch, Mark. 1961. *Feudal Society*. Trans. L.A. Manyon. Vol. 2. Chicago: University of Chicago Press.
Boden, Margaret A. 1991. *The Creative Mind: Myth and Mechanisms*. New York: Basic.
Bourdieu, Pierre. 1990. *The Logic of Practice*. Stanford: Stanford University Press.
_____. 1991. *Language and Symbolic Power*. Ed. John B. Thompson. Trans. Gino Raymond and Matthew Adamson. Cambridge: Harvard University Press.
Bridgman, Richard. 1966. *The Colloquial Style in America*. New York: Oxford University Press.
Briggs, John Channing. 2005. *Lincoln's Speeches Reconsidered*. Baltimore: Johns Hopkins University Press.
Burlingame, Michael, ed. 2000. *Inside the White House: Memoirs and Reports of Lincoln's Secretary*. Lincoln: University of Nebraska Press.
_____. 2008. *Lincoln: A Life*. 2 vols. Baltimore: Johns Hopkins Press.
Bushman, Donald E. 1996. "Example." In *Encyclopedia of Rhetoric and Composition*, ed. Theresa Enos, p. 147. New York: Garland.
Carwardine, Richard. 2003. *Lincoln: A Life of Purpose and Power*. New York: Vintage.
Cashin, Joan. 2002. "Deserters, Civilians, and Draft Resistance in the North." In *The War Was You and Me*, ed. Joan Cashin, pp. 262–265. Princeton, NJ: Princeton University Press.
Chesterfield, Philip Dormer Stanhope. 1857. *Chesterfield's Art of Letter Writing Simplified*. New York: Dick and Fitzgerald.
Cicero. 1938. *Cicero Philippics*. Trans. Walter C.A. Ker. Cambridge, MA: Harvard University Press.
Cmiel, Kenneth. 1990. *Democratic Eloquence: The Fight over Popular Speech in Nineteenth-Century America*. New York: William Morrow.
Colavito, Joesph. 1996. "Pathos." In *Encyclopedia of Rhetoric and Composition*, ed. Theresa Enos, pp. 492–494. New York: Garland.
Cooke, Increase, 1819. Ed. *Eloquent Extracts*. New Haven, CT: Sydney Press.
Corbett, Edward, and Robert Connors. 1999. *Style and Statement*. New York: Oxford University Press.
Corbett, Edward P.J. 1971. *Classical Rhetoric for the Modern Student*. 2nd ed. New York: Oxford University Press.
Decker, William Merrill. 1998. *Epistolarity Practices: Letter Writing in America before Telecommunications*. Chapel Hill: University of North Carolina Press.
Demetrius. 2006. *On Style*. Trans. W. Rhys Roberts. Retrieved 24 October 2012 from www.attalus.org/info/demetrius html.
Demosthenes. 1970. *Demosthenes*. Vol. 1. Trans. J.H. Vince. Cambridge, MA: Harvard University Press.
Dolliver, James I. 1956. "Story of the Postal Service." *Congressional Digest* 35.1: 164–166.
Donald, David Herbert. 1996. *Lincoln*. New York: Simon & Shuster.
_____. 2003. *We Are Lincoln's Men*. New York: Simon & Schuster.
Dorris, J.T. 1998. "President Lincoln's Clemency." *Journal of the Illinois State Historical Society* 20.4: 547–568.
Duffy, Bernard K. 1996. "Richard Weaver." In *Encyclopedia of Rhetoric and Composition*, ed. Theresa Enos, pp. 757–759. New York: Garland.
Eggleston, George Cary. 1959. *A Rebel's Recollection*. Bloomington: Indiana University Press.
Emerson, Jason. 2006. "America's Most Famous Letter." *American Heritage*, February/March, 41–47.
_____. 2007. *The Madness of Mary Lincoln*. Carbondale: Southern Illinois University Press.

Enos, Theresa, ed. 1996. *Encyclopedia of Rhetoric and Composition*. New York: Garland.
Fahnestock, Jeanne. 1996. "Arrangement." In *Encyclopedia of Rhetoric and Composition*, ed. Theresa Enos, pp. 32–36. New York: Garland.
Flower, Linda, and John Ackerman. 1994. *Writers at Work: Casebook for Teachers and Students: Nine Scenarios for Discussion and Practice*. New York: Harcourt Brace.
Fuller, Wayne E. 1972. *The American Mail: Enlarger of the Common Life*. Chicago: University of Chicago Press.
Fulwiler, Toby. 1990. "Looking and Listening for My Voice." *College Composition and Communication* 41.2 (May): 214–20.
Gage, John T. 1996. "Enthymeme." In *Encyclopedia of Rhetoric and Composition*, ed. Theresa Enos, pp. 223–235. New York: Garland.
Garrison, Webb B. 1993. *The Lincoln No One Knows*. Nashville, TN: Rutledge Hill.
Goodwin, Doris Kearns. 2006. *Team of Rivals: The Political Genius of Abraham Lincoln*. New York: Simon & Schuster.
Halloran, S. Michael. 1990. "From Rhetoric to Composition: The Teaching of Writing in America to 1900." In *A Short History of Writing Instruction: From Ancient Greece to Twentieth-Century America*, ed. James J. Murphy, pp. 151–82. Davis, CA: Hermagoras.
Harman, Charles E. 2002. *Critical Commentaries on Blackstone*. Brookings, OR: Old Court.
Harrison, Lowell. 2009. *Civil War in Kentucky*. Lexington: University Press of Kentucky.
Hendrick, Burton J. 1961. *Lincoln's War Cabinet*. Garden City, New York: Doubleday.
Hendrix, Diane L. 1996. "Rhetorical Question." In *Encyclopedia of Rhetoric and Composition*, ed. Theresa Enos, pp. 608–609. New York: Garland.
Herndon, William. 1930. *Life of Lincoln*. New York: A. and C. Boni.
Herndon, William H., and Jesse W. Weik. 1983. *Herndon's Life of Lincoln*. New York: De Capo.
Hewitt, Elizabeth. 2004. *Correspondence in American Literature 1770–1865*. New York: Cambridge University Press.
Holzer, Harold. 1995. "I Should Not Say Any Foolish Things." *Civil War Times Illustrated* 34:5 (November–December): 22, 106–15.
———. 2000. *Lincoln the Writer*. Honesdale, PA: Boyds Mill.
———. 2004. *Lincoln at Cooper Union: The Speech That Made Abraham Lincoln President*. New York: Simon & Schuster.
Horner, Harlan Hoyt. 1952–53. "Lincoln Scolds a General." *Wisconsin Magazine of History* 36.2 (Winter): 90–96, 143–146.
Houser, M.L. 1951. *Lincoln's Education and Other Essays*. New York: Bookman.
Hubalek, Linda K. 1996. *Thimble of Soil: A Woman's Quest for Land*. Lindsborg, KS: Butterfield.
Hubbard, Charles, ed. 2003. *Lincoln Reshapes the Presidency*. Macon, GA: Mercer University Press.
Jacobs, Debra L. 1996. "Voice." In *Encyclopedia of Rhetoric and Composition*, ed. Theresa Enos, pp. 748–52. New York: Garland.
Jasinski, James. 2001. "Public Letter." In *Sourcebook on Rhetoric*, pp. 470–473. Thousand Oaks, CA: Sage.
Johnson, Nan. 1991. *Nineteenth Century Rhetoric in North America*. Carbondale: Southern Illinois University Press.
Johnson, Thomas, ed. 1964. *The Letters of Emily Dickinson*. Vol. 1. Cambridge, MA: Harvard University Press.
Joseph, Sister Miriam, and Marguerite McGlinn. 2002. *The Trivium: The Liberal Arts of Logic, Grammar, and Rhetoric*. Philadelphia: Paul Dry.
Kaplan, Fred. 2008. *Lincoln: The Biography of a Writer*. New York: HarperCollins.

Bibliography

Kasson, John F. 1990. *Rudeness and Civility: Manners in Nineteenth-Century Urban America*. New York: Hill and Wang.

Katz, Stanley. 1979. "Introduction to Book I," Blackstone, William. In *Commentaries on the Laws of England*, ed. Stanley Katz, pp. iii–xii. Chicago: University of Chicago Press.

Kentucky Adjutant General's Office. 1866. *Report of the Adjutant General of the State of Kentucky: Civil War*. 2 vols. Frankfort, KY: John H. Harvey. Rpt. Utica, KY: McDowell, 1984.

Kinneavy, James L. 1996. "*Kairos:* A Neglected Concept in Classical Rhetoric." In *Composition in Four Keys*, ed. Mark Wiley et al., pp. 211–224. Mountain View, CA: Mayfield.

Kirkham, Samuel. 1829. *English Grammar in Familiar Lectures*. New York: Robert B. Collins.

Klingaman, William C. 2001. *Abraham Lincoln and the Road to Emancipation, 1861–65*. New York: Viking.

Lamon, Ward Hill. 1872. *A Life of Abraham Lincoln*. Boston: James S. Osgood.

Lang, H. Jack. 1965. *Lincoln's Fireside Reading*. Cleveland: World.

Lanham, Richard. 1991. *A Handlist of Rhetorical Terms*. Berkley: University of California Press.

Lonn, Ella. 1928. *Desertion During the Civil War*. Gloucester, MA: Peter Smith.

Lystra, Karen. 1989. *Searching the Heart: Women, Men, and Romantic Love in Nineteenth-Century America*. New York: Oxford University Press.

Marrou, H.I. 1956. *A History of Education in Antiquity*. Trans. George Lamb. New York: Sheed and Ward.

Martinez, David. 2008. "Remembering the Thirty Eight: Abraham Lincoln, the Dakota, and the U.S. War on Barbarism." *Wicazo Sa Review* 28.1 (Fall): 5–29.

Matrau. Henry. 1993. *Letters Home of Henry Matrau of the Iron Brigade*. Ed. Marcia Reid-Green. Lincoln: University of Nebraska Press.

McClure, A.K. 1996. *Abraham Lincoln and Men of War-Times*. 4th ed. Lincoln: University Press of Nebraska.

McLure, John R. 1970. *Hoosier Farmboy in Lincoln's Army*. Ed. Nancy Niblack Baxter. n.p.: Guild Press of Indiana.

McMurtry, Gerald. 1999. *The Lincoln Migration from Kentucky to Indiana 1816*. Utica, KY: McDowell. Rpt. from *Indiana Magazine of History* 33:4 (Dec. 1937): 385–421.

McPherson, James. 1988. *Battle Cry of Freedom*. New York: Oxford University Press.

_____. 1991. *Abraham Lincoln and the Second American Revolution*. New York: Oxford University Press.

_____. 2008. *Tried by War*. New York: Penguin.

Miller, Perry. 1954. *The New England Mind: The Seventeenth Century*. Cambridge: Harvard University Press.

Miller, William Lee. 2002. *Lincoln's Virtues: An Ethical Biography*. New York: Alfred A. Knopf.

Morgan, Aron. 1996. "Medieval Rhetoric." In *Encyclopedia of Rhetoric and Composition*, ed. Theresa Enos, pp. 429–444. New York: Garland.

Murfin, Ross C., and Supryia M. Ray. 1997. *The Bedford Glossary of Critical and Literary Terms*. Boston: Bedford.

Murphy, James. 1971. *Three Medieval Rhetorical Arts*. Berkley: University of California Press.

_____. 2001. *Rhetoric in the Middle Ages: A History of Rhetorical Theory from Saint Augustine to the Renaissance*. Tempe: Arizona Center for Medieval and Renaissance Studies.

Murray, Lindley, 1799. English Reader. New York, NY: Isaac Collins.

Myers, Marshall. 1990. "Lincoln, the Law, and a Lady." *Back Home in Kentucky*, January/February, 30–31.

———. 1999. "The Influence of the Purpose of a Business Document on Its Syntax and Rhetorical Schemes." *Technical Writing and Communication* 29.4: 401–408.
———. 2012. "Abraham Lincoln and the Other Mary from Kentucky." In *Great Civil War Stories of Kentucky*, pp. 37–43. Morley, MO: Acclaim.
Myers, Marshall, and Chris Propes. 2004. "I Don't Fear Nothing in the Shape of Man." *Register of the Kentucky Historical Society* 101.4: 457–478.
Neely, Mark. 1982. *The Abraham Lincoln Encyclopedia*. New York: Da Capo.
———. 1993. *The Last Best Hope of Earth: Abraham Lincoln and the Promise of America*. Cambridge: Harvard University Press.
Nicolay, Helen. 2006. *Personal Traits of Abraham Lincoln*. Mechanicsburg, PA: Stackpole.
North, Ingoldsby. 1867. *Love Letters: How to Write Them and When to Use Them*. New York: Dick and Fitzgerald.
O'Rourke, Sean Patrick. 1996. "Progymnasmata." In *Encyclopedia of Rhetoric and Composition*, ed. Theresa Enos, 562–563. New York: Garland.
Paludan, Phillip Shaw. 1994. *The Presidency of Abraham Lincoln*. Lawrence: University of Kansas Press.
Perret, Geoffrey. 2004. *Lincoln's War*. New York: Random House.
Phelan, James. 1996. "Rhetoric and Fiction." In *Encyclopedia of Rhetoric and Composition*, ed. Theresa Enos, pp. 609–612. New York: Garland.
Poster, Carol, and Linda Mitchell. 2007. *Letter-Writing Manuals and Instruction from Antiquity to the Present*. Columbia: University of South Carolina Press.
Radford, Bruce. 1986. *The Converse of the Pen: Acts of Intimacy in the Eighteenth Century Familiar Letter*. Chicago: University of Chicago Press.
Randall, Ruth Painter. 1953. *Mary Lincoln: A Portrait of a Marriage*. New York: Dell.
Randall, Willard Sterne. 1997. *George Washington: A Life*. New York: Henry Holt.
Redford, Bruce. 1986. *The Converse of the Pen: Acts of Intimacy in the Eighteenth Century Familiar Letter*. Chicago: University of Chicago Press.
Robinson, Luther Emerson. 1923. *Abraham Lincoln as a Man of Letters*. New York: G.P. Putnam's Sons.
Roland, Charles P. 1991. *An American Iliad*. Lexington: University Press of Kentucky.
Ruckman, P.S., Jr., and David Kincaid. 1999. "Inside Lincoln's Clemency Decision Making." *Presidential Studies Quarterly* 29.1: 84–99.
Sandburg, Carl. 1993. *Abraham Lincoln: The Prairie Years and the War Years*. New York: Gallahad.
Schultz, Lucille M. 1999. *The Young Composers*. Carbondale: Southern Illinois University Press.
Scott, James Calvert. 1998. "Dear ???: Understanding British Forms of Address." *Business Communication Quarterly* 61.3: 50–59.
Sheehan-Dean, A. 2015. "Desertion (Confederate) During the Civil War." *Encyclopedia Virginia*. Virginia Foundation for the Foundation for the Humanities, 4 April 2012. Retrieved from http://www.encyclopediavirginia.org/desertion_confederate_during.
Slater, Joseph, ed. 1964. *The Correspondence of Emerson and Carlyle*. New York: Columbia University Press.
Sloane, Thomas, ed. 2001. *Encyclopedia of Rhetoric*. New York: Oxford University Press.
Smith, Richard Norton. 1993. *Patriarch*. Boston: Houghton Mifflin.
Stiller, Glenn E. 1998. *Analyzing Everyday Texts: Discourse, Rhetoric, and Social Perspectives*. Thousand Oaks: Sage.
Stowers, Stanley K. 1986. *Letter Writing in Greco-Roman Antiquity*. Philadelphia: Westminster.
Swartz, Tom. 2006. E-mail to author. 5 May 2012.
Swisher, Carl Brent. 1943. *American Constitutional Development*. Boston: Houghton Mifflin.

Tackach, James. 2002. *Lincoln's Moral Vision: The Second Inaugural Address.* Jackson: University of Mississippi.
Thompson, Roger. 2002. "Ralph Waldo Emerson and *American Kairos*." In *Rhetoric and Kairos*, eds. Phillip Sipiora, and James S. Baumlin, pp. 187–198. Albany: State University of New York Press.
Townsend, William H. 1955. *Lincoln and the Bluegrass: Slavery and Civil War in Kentucky.* Lexington: University Press of Kentucky.
Tripp, C.A. 2002. *The Intimate World of Abraham Lincoln.* New York: Thunder's Mouth.
Tufte, Virginia. 2006. *Artful Sentences: Syntax as Style.* Chesire, CT: Graphics.
Twain, Mark. 1965. *Adventures of Huckleberry Finn.* New York: Holt, Rinehart and Winston.
United States War Department. 1880–1901. *War of the Rebellion: A Compilation of the Official Records of the Union and Confederate Armies.* 70 vols. Washington, D.C.: Government Printing Office.
Usher, John Palmer. 2013. *Lincoln's Cabinet.* New Delhi, India: Isha.
Watson, Lillian. 1948. *The Bantam Book of Correct Letter Writing.* Revised ed. New York: Bantam.
White, Ronald, Jr. 2002. *Lincoln's Greatest Speech: The Second Inaugural Address.* New York: Simon & Schuster.
White, Ronald. 2004. *The Eloquent President: A Portrait of Lincoln Through His Words.* New York: Random House.
Williams, David Cratis. 1996. "Consubstantiality." In *Encyclopedia of Rhetoric and Composition*, ed. Theresa Enos, p. 40. New York: Garland.
Williams, Joseph. 2007. *Style: Lessons in Clarity and Grace.* 9th ed. New York: Person.
Williams, T. Harry. 1952. *Lincoln and His Generals.* New York: Gramercy.
Wills, Garry. 1992. *Lincoln at Gettysburg: The Words That Remade America.* New York: Simon & Schuster.
Wilson, Douglas. 1998. *Honor's Voice: The Transformation of Abraham Lincoln.* New York: Alfred Knopf.
_____. 2006. *Lincoln's Sword: The Presidency and the Power of Words.* New York: Alfred A. Knopf.
Wilson, Douglas, and Rodney Davis, eds. 1998. *Herndon's Informants.* Urbana: University of Illinois Press.
Wilson, Edmund. 1962. *Patriotic Gore.* New York: Oxford University Press.
Wilson, Rufus Rockwell. 1932. *What Lincoln Read.* Washington, D.C.: Pioneer.
Winkle, Kenneth J. 2001. *The Young Eagle.* Dallas: Taylor Trade.
Winkler, Donald. 2004. *Lincoln's Ladies.* Nashville, TN: Cumberland House.
Woldman, Albert A. 1936. *Lawyer Lincoln.* New York: Carroll & Graf.
Woods, Brett F. 2013. *Abraham Lincoln: Letters to His Generals.* New York: Algora.

Index

Able, Mary 158, 165
Abraham Lincoln Association 17
Ackerman, John 26
Adams, John 180
Adventures of Huckleberry Finn 76
The Advertiser 1, 2
Aesop's Fables 57–58, 60
Affordable Care Act 183
Alberic 18
Altman, Janet: *Epistolarity: Approaches to a Form* 19
Anderson, Howard: *The Familiar Letter in the Eighteenth Century* 18
Angle, Paul 64
Antietam 126
argumentum ad hominem 47
Army and Navy Journal 42
Aristotle 9, 28, 75, 144, 182
Arnold, Isaac 60
ars dictiminis 25, 32
assertion 76

Bacon, Francis 63, 143
Baker, Jean 175, 177
Bakhtin, Mikhail 24
balance of probabilities 62
Barton, William E. 36
Barzun, Jacques: *Simple and Direct* 51, 36, 67
Basler, Roy: "Abraham Lincoln's Rhetoric" 13; *Collected Works of Abraham Lincoln* 13, 16–17, 20, 60, 62, 65
Bates, Edward 131, 193–194, 195–196
Bates, Homer 63–64, 69, 193
bdelygma 46
Bedford Glossary of Literary Terms 45
benevolentia 32–34
Benjamin, James 75
Berlin, James: *Writing Instruction in Nineteenth Century American Colleges* 22, 61–62

Bible 21, 28, 32, 34, 35, 38, 60
Bixby letter 14, 36–42, 43–45
Black, Edwin 53
Blackstone's Commentaries 111
Blair, Hugh: *Lectures on Rhetoric and Belle Lettres* 27, 52, 61–62, 69, 84, 110
Blair, Montgomery 23
Blake, William 137
Bloch, Mark: *Feudal Society* 25
Boden, Margaret 62
bounty jumping 127
Bourdieu, Pierre: *The Logic of Practice* 29–30, 37, 42
Bowers, Jacob 138
Bowling, Norma vi
Bridgman, Richard: *Colloquial Style in America* 54–55
Briggs, John: *Lincoln's Greatest Speeches Reconsidered* 11, 45
Brooks, Noah 64–65
Browning, Mrs. Orville 27, 73–74, 164–165
Buell, Don Carlos 87, 101–102, 109, 116
Bullard, Lauriston 36
Burke, Kenneth 24
Burlingame, Michael 64
Burnam, John 137
Burnside, Ambrose 87, 105, 118
Burr, Aaron 181

Carwardine, Richard 19
Cashin, Joan 126
Chase, Salmon 181, 196–198
Chesterfield's Letter-Writer 26, 28–29, 31, 34–36, 69–70, 148–151, 193
Cicero 46–49
Clay, Henry 83, 168
Cmiel, Kenneth: *Democratic Eloquence* 51, 60–61
Colavito, Joseph 74, 133–134
"colored soldiers" 122–124

209

Index

commonplace 38, 40
Conklin, James 119
Connor, Robert 91
Cooke, Increase: *Elegant Extracts* 61
Cooper Union Speech 179
Corbett, Edward P.J. 22, 91

Davis, Jefferson 52
Decker, William Merrill: *Epistolary Practices* 19–21, 144
"Declaration of Amnesty and Reconstruction" 132
deliberative rhetoric 75, 182–183
Demetrius: *On Style* 28, 40, 46–49, 69–70
Demosthenes, 47
desertion 126, 128–130
Dickinson, Emily 32
Dilworth's Spelling Book 59
Dolliiver, James 21
Donald, David Herbert 3, 21, 46, 52, 58–59, 119, 152, 179, 184
dreams 173–174

Eckert, Capt. Thomas 65
Edwards, Matilda 174
eighteenth century 14
Ellsworth, Ephraim 36, 41, 44
Ellsworth, Phoebe 36, 41, 44
Emancipation Proclamation 67, 120–124, 186–187, 190
Emerson, Jason 36
Emerson, Ralph Waldo 33, 43
Encyclopedia of Rhetoric 46
Encyclopedia of Rhetoric and Composition 46, 57, 65
enthymeme 183, 186, 192–193, 199
epideictic rhetoric 9
ethos 28, 40, 69, 75, 78, 81, 120, 132–136, 141–142, 144
example 183

family business 173
first inaugural address 52, 67
Fitzgerald, Thomas: *On Grace in Writing* 85
Flower, Linda 26
Frémont, John 102, 104, 181
Fuller, Wayne: *The American Mail* 23
Fulwiler, Toby 65

Garrison, Webb 52
general pardon 127
Gettysburg Address 55, 83, 179
Goodwin, Doris Kearns: *Team of Rivals* 23
Grant, U.S. 87, 107–108, 118

Greco-Roman sources 14, 20, 34, 52, 70, 110, 201
Greeley, Horace 82, 112
Grimshaw, William 60
Grisby, Nate 55

habitus 29–30
Hain, Sally vi
Halleck, Henry 116
Halloran, Michael: *Short History of Writing Instruction* 61
Hamilton, Alexander 180–181
Hamlin, Hannibal 67
Hanks, Dennis 60
Herndon, William 27, 56, 65, 84
Hewitt, Elizabeth: *Correspondence in American Literature: 1700–1865* 19
Hodges, Albert 82
Holt, Joseph 141
Holzer, Harold: *Lincoln at Cooper Union* 10–11, 62–63, 85; *Lincoln the Writer* 10–11, 36, 62–63
Hooker, Joseph 15, 50, 87, 104–105, 109, 118
Horner, Harlan 116
Houser, M.L.: *Lincoln's Education and Other Essays* 22, 58–59
Huckleberry Finn 2, 46
Hunter, Dr. Gil vi
hypothetical syllogism 191–192, 194–195

imitation 199
Indians and pardons 138–139

Jamieson, Alexander: *A Grammar of Rhetoric and Polite Literature* 62
Jasinski, James: *Sourcebook on Rhetoric* 46
Jefferson, Thomas 180–181
jeremiad 10
Johnson, Nan: *Nineteenth Century in North America* 75, 84–85
Johnston, John 15, 48–49

kairos 11, 42–43
Kaplan, Fred: *The Biography of a Writer* 1, 5
Kasson, John: *Rudeness and Civility* 29
Keller, Dr. James vi
Kentucky 128–130, 137
Kincaid, David 129
Kinneavy, James 11, 42
Kirkham, Samuel: *English Grammar* 59
Klingaman, William C.: *Abraham Lincoln and the Road to Emancipation* 10, 65–67
Knox, Henry 180

Index

lack of federal service 128
Lang, Jack: *Lincoln's Fireside Reading* 21, 56, 58
Lanham, Richard: *A Handlist of Rhetorical Terms* 46–47
letters of endorsement 81
letters of introduction and recommendation 81
letters to lawyers 78–80
Lincoln, Abraham: attractiveness to women 155–156; backwardness with women 152–153
Lincoln, Eddy 174
Lincoln, Mary Todd 27, 50, 167–171, 174–179, 202
Lincoln, Robert Todd 27, 66, 105–107, 109, 173–174
Lincoln-Rutledge romance 153–154, 156
literary examples 67, 84
logos 133–134, 136, 139, 141–142
Lonn, Ella: *Desertion in the Civil War* 126
love letter manuals 146
Lystra, Karen 146–147

Mark Antony 46
Marrou, H.I.: *A History of Education in Antiquity* 57
Marshall, Humphrey 129
Martin, William 139–140
McClellan, George 1, 87–101, 109, 114, 116
McClure, A.K.: *Men of War-Times* 193, 196
McDowell, Irving 87, 93
McMurtry, Gerald 57
McPherson, James: *Abraham Lincoln and the Second American Revolution* 51–52, 121; *Tried by War* 86
Meade, George 23–24, 87, 131
Meeker, Caroline 153, 169
Middle Ages 14, 18, 25
Miller, Perry 55
Miller, William Lee 32, 57
models, Greek and Roman 7, 14, 19–20
Morgan, Aron 18
Muller, Mary vi
Murphy, James: *Rhetoric in the Middle Ages* 40; *Three Medieval Arts* 24
Murray, Lindley: *The English Reader* 60–61, 65, 85
Myers, Marshall 44, 152–153

Neeley, Mark: *Lincoln Encyclopedia* 36, 51, 130, 193
Newman, Samuel: *A Practical System of Rhetoric* 62
Nicolay, Helen 119

North, Ingoldsby: *Love Letters: How to Write Them and When to Use Them* 150–151

O'Rouke, Sean Patrick 34, 57, 74
Owens, Mary 27, 50, 72–73, 156–159, 160–166, 169, 178, 202

palilogia 47
Pate, Arretta 153
Pate, Samuel 153
pathos 74, 116–117, 133–136, 140–142, 192
Perret, Geoffrey: *Lincoln's War* 86
Philip of Macedon 46
philippic 2, 45–47; *Pilgrim's Progress* 60
plain style 52–55
Plato 75
Principles of Letter Writing 25
printing 57
progymnasmata 34, 57–58, 74
public letter 2, 82, 119, 202

Radcliff, Dr. Charles 140
Randolph, Edmund 180
Redford, Bruce: *The Converse of the Pen* 18–19, 24
Reese, Joanne vi
revision 63
Rhetoric Review vi
rhetorical question 121–122
rhetorician 6
Robinson, Luther: *Abraham Lincoln as a Man of Letters* 36
Robinson Crusoe 60
Roland, Charles: *American Iliad* 51
Ruckman, P.S. 129
Rutledge, Ann 22, 153–154

salutation 27–28
Sandburg, Carl 20, 58–59
Schultz, Lucille 61
Schurz, Carl 109–110, 112–118
Scott, James 25–26
Scott, William: *Lessons in Elocution* 60, 85
second inaugural address 1, 49, 55, 83, 179
Sellers, Dr. John vi, 17–18
sentimental style 52–54
Seward, William 52, 181, 184–189
Sheehan-Dean, A. 126
Sherman, William T. 106–107, 130
Shinkle, Susy vi
Sibley, H.H. 138
Sinbad the Sailor 60
Speed, Joshua 27, 71–72
Stanton, Edwin 181, 188–191, 193

211

Index

Stillar, Glen: *Analyzing Everyday Texts* 30, 37, 42
Stoddard, William 64–66-67
Stowers, Stanley K.: *Letter Writing in Greco-Roman Antiquity* 18, 34–35, 70–71, 77
Sutton, Robert 136–137

Tackach, James: *Lincoln's Moral Vision* 1, 10
taste and style 61
telegraph office 7
Thompson, Roger 42–43
Thrasher, Eli, 153
Toles, William 138
Townsend, William: *Lincoln and the Bluegrass* 60
The Transcript 42
types of discourse 182
types of letters 70, 201–202
types of pardons 132
typical endings 82–83

University of Michigan Corpus 39; Digital Library Production Service 17
Usher, John Palmer 189

voice 65

Weaver, Richard 24
Webster's 1828 *Dictionary* 39
Weems, Parson: *Life of Washington* 60
Whig Convention in Philadelphia 176
Whipple, Henry 139
White, Ronald: *The Eloquent President* 11–12, 112; *Lincoln's Greatest Speeches* 1, 10–11, 55, 64, 66
Williams, David 24
Williams, Harry T.: *Lincoln's Generals* 86
Williams, Joseph: *Style* 120
Wills, Gary: *Lincoln at Gettysburg* 1, 5, 9, 51, 63–64
Wilson, Douglas: *Lincoln's Sword* 1, 11–13, 22, 58–59, 109, 145, 152
Wilson, Edmund 51
Wilson, Rufus Rockwell 60
Winkle, Kenneth 54–56
Witherspoon, John: *Lectures on Eloquence* 62
Woldman, Albert: *Lawyer Lincoln* 78, 111
Woods, Brett: *Abraham Lincoln: Letters to His Generals* 86, 90

www.ingramcontent.com/pod-product-compliance
Ingram Content Group UK Ltd.
Pitfield, Milton Keynes, MK11 3LW, UK
UKHW041959140426
5217IPUK00015B/873